MEXICO

MICHAEL D. COE
JAVIER URCID
REX KOONTZ

MEXICO

FROM THE OLMECS
TO THE AZTECS

**8TH EDITION,
REVISED AND EXPANDED**

200+ ILLUSTRATIONS, 186 IN COLOR

 Thames & Hudson

Contents

On the cover: Detail of a painted wall at Cacaxtla, Tlaxcala. Illustration by Elbis Domínguez, 2008

Frontispiece: Wooden funerary mask encrusted with turquoise mosaic and shell. Mixtec or Aztec. © British Museum

Mexico © 2019 Thames & Hudson Ltd, London

Text by Michael D. Coe, Rex Koontz, and Javier Urcid

First published in 1984 in the United States of America by Thames & Hudson Inc., 500 Fifth Avenue, New York, New York 10110

www.thamesandhudsonusa.com

This eighth edition 2019

Library of Congress Control Number 2019938669

ISBN 978-0-500-293737

Printed and bound in China, Lion Productions Ltd

Preface

The subject matter of this book is the story of the pre-Spanish indigenous cultures of Mexico, who with their neighbors the Maya formed some of the more complex societies north of the Andes. The term "Mexico" will here refer to all the land in that Republic that lies between the western border of the Maya civilization and the northern frontier where Mexican farmers once met the nomadic groups of the desert. This is roughly the area covered by the old Viceroyalty of New Spain in early colonial times.

We have incorporated in this new edition of *Mexico* many of the most recent findings, from a number of disciplines. The long-standing puzzle of the origin of maize farming has at last been solved. Several spectacular new discoveries throw more light on the Olmec culture, Mexico's earliest complex society. At the great city of Teotihuacan, recent investigations in the earliest monumental pyramid indicate the antiquity of certain sacrificial practices and the symbolism of the pyramid. The Huastec region of the northeastern Gulf of Mexico is covered in greater detail than in previous editions. And further discoveries in the sacred precinct of the Aztec capital Tenochtitlan have allowed us to refine our understanding of the history and symbolism of this hallowed area.

The latest revised edition of *The Maya* can be read with this book, as the Maya civilization of the Yucatan Peninsula and Central America was so complex that to do it justice would be impossible within the confines of the present volume. Although part of Maya territory was within the boundaries of the present-day Estados Unidos de México, the Maya would, with a few notable exceptions, appear to have remained within their own borders throughout the centuries; accordingly, other indigenous cultures of the Republic can be considered quite independently.

"Mexico" and "Aztec" seem almost synonymous, but we cover the Aztecs here in only one chapter as we now know that in the total span of human occupation of that country, the Aztecs were late arrivals, their empire but a final and brilliant flicker before the light of their civilization was radically transformed. Nevertheless, thanks to the accounts of Spanish friars and conquistadores, and to indigenous and creole (Mexican-born) historians, we have more information on this civilization than on any other indigenous culture in the Americas. Each generation of scholars brings new insights and understandings to the study of the Aztecs, and we have tried to incorporate some of the latest into this volume.

It is all too easy to treat the pre-Spanish cultures of Mexico and Central America as "dead," yet in spite of the cataclysm of the Conquest and the ensuing epidemics that decimated the indigenous populations, these groups have endured through the Spanish colonial period and into the present; in fact, much of the flavor of modern Mexico derives, both consciously and unconsciously, from its ancient heritage. Accordingly, we have included an Epilogue that takes these populations through the Conquest up to our own time.

A matter that must be touched upon is the pronunciation of the very formidable-looking words and names of ancient Mexico. Most of these are in Nahuatl, the national tongue of the Aztec state, and were transcribed in Roman letters by the early Spanish friars in terms of the language spoken in central Spain in the sixteenth century. As a result, vowels and most consonants are generally pronounced as they would be in Spanish, with these exceptions:

x has the sound of the English *sh*, as it once had in Spanish (witness the derivation of "sherry" from the Spanish *Xerez*).

tl—this cluster is a voiceless surd consonant, much like the Welsh *ll*.

hu followed by a vowel is pronounced like English *w*.

In Nahuatl, word stress always falls on the penultimate (next-to-last) syllable. We have therefore omitted all accents in such words and names. Various corruptions have, however, crept into Nahuatl from Spanish, including occasional stress placed on the final syllable (for example, in many books, Teotihuacán is found in place of the more correct Teotihuácan).

We have used the correct Nahuatl form Moteuczoma ("One Who Frowns Like a Lord") for the third and seventh Aztec kings, although Motecuhzoma or Moteuhczoma are also permissible. The familiar "Montezuma" is hopelessly wrong and merely reflects the inability of most Spaniards to pronounce Nahuatl names.

In recent decades, there have been important advances in the accurate correlation of dates derived from radiocarbon determinations with those of the Christian calendar (or "sidereal years"). Dendrochronological studies of the bristlecone pine now affirm that prior to the Christian era, radiocarbon dates are significantly younger than "true" years. For example, according to radiocarbon determinations, the rise of social complexity at San Lorenzo begins around 1200 BCE, but the new calibration curve would more accurately place this some 300 years earlier. In this edition, all ages based upon the radiocarbon method have been so calibrated, as they have in *The Maya*.

Many scholars have aided us in the preparation of this and earlier editions, if only through their published work. For the present edition, we would especially like to thank the anonymous reviewers who provided us with insightful observations. We also thank the staff of Thames & Hudson for their help in enabling us to present often complex archaeological research to the general reader.

Mexico: From the Olmecs to the Aztecs is also available in North America as a PDF e-book, and images from inside the book will also be accessible on the Archaeology Global Gallery for the benefit of students and instructors: www.thamesandhudsonusa.com/books/college. Readers outside North America should please email education@thameshudson.co.uk for further information.

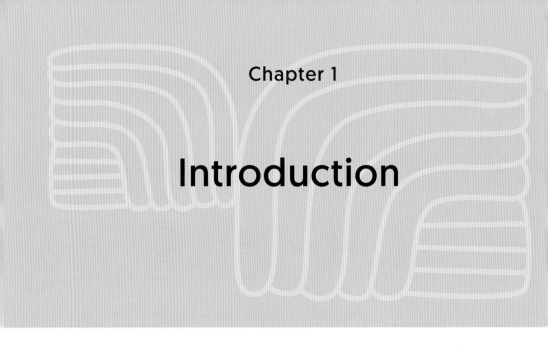

Chapter 1

Introduction

The ancient cultures of Mexico along with the Maya civilization comprise the larger entity known to archaeologists as "Mesoamerica," a name first proposed by the anthropologist Paul Kirchhoff and including much of the great isthmian, or constriction of land, that separates the masses of North and South America (**figure 1**). Above all, the population of Mesoamerica were farmers, and had been somewhat isolated for thousands of years from the cultivating societies of the American Southwest and Southeast by the desert wastes of northern Mexico, through which only semi-nomadic, hunting aborigines ranged in pre-Spanish times. Beyond the southeastern borders of Mesoamerica lay the smaller, non-centralized chiefdom societies of lower Central America, distinguished by a high production of fine ceramics and quantities of jade or gold ornaments, lavishly heaped in the tombs of their great chieftains.

Further south yet, in Ecuador, Peru, and Bolivia, was the Andean area, most noted for its final glory, the immense Inca empire, but having native civilizations as far back in time as the tenth century BCE, and substantial temple constructions even earlier than that. The Andean area and Mesoamerica were the twin peaks of Native American cultural development, from which much else in the Western Hemisphere seems both peripheral and sometimes derived; yet this picture may be oversimplified, because research in the Pacific lowlands of Ecuador, the Caribbean coast of Colombia, and the upper reaches of the Amazon has shown that the important criteria of settled life—agriculture, pottery, and villages—may have developed in those areas also.

Setting them apart from the rest of the hemisphere, the diverse cultures of Mesoamerica shared a number of features, most of which were generally confined to their area. The most distinctive of these is a complicated calendar based upon the permutation of a 260-day sacred cycle with the solar year of 365 days. Other shared features in Mesoamerica are hieroglyphic writing (the Andean area never developed a phonetic script); bark-paper or deer-skin manuscripts that fold like screens ("screenfolds"); maps; an extensive knowledge and use of astronomy;

a team game resembling basketball played in a special court with a solid rubber ball; expansive, well-organized markets and favored "ports of trade"; chocolate beans as money and as the source of a drink; wars for the purpose of securing sacrificial victims; private penance by drawing blood from the ears, tongue, or penis; and a pantheon of remarkable complexity.

The cultures of Mesoamerica followed a number of other customs that are widespread among Native Americans, such as ceremonial tobacco smoking, but their typical foodways—the societal customs relating to food production and consumption—appear to be unique. The basis of the diet was the foursome of maize, beans, squash, and chile peppers. Maize was, and still is, prepared by boiling it with lime, then grinding the swollen kernels with a hand stone (known as a *mano*, the Spanish word for "hand") on a trough- or saddle-shaped quern (*metate*, from the Nahuatl *metlatl*). The resulting dough is either toasted as flat cakes known in Spanish as *tortillas*, or else steamed or boiled as *tamales*. Always and everywhere in Mesoamerica, the hearth comprises three stones, and being the conceptual center of the world, is construed as sacred. An enduring legacy of ancient Mesoamerica is its unique complex of food (maize, chocolate, beans, and chile being only a few), each discovered and carefully cultivated or domesticated many thousands of years ago. It is difficult now to imagine what global cuisines were like before the foods of Mexico and Peru were introduced to the wider world.

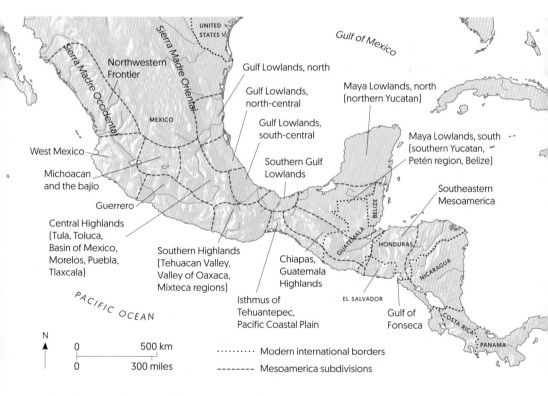

1 Map of major regional subdivisions of Mesoamerica.

The Geographic Setting

On the map, Mexico resembles a great funnel, or rather, a cornucopia, with its widest part toward the north and its smallest end twisting to the south and east, meeting there the sudden expansion of the Maya area. There are few regions in the world with such a diverse geography as we find within this area; Mexico is not one but many landscapes. All the climatic extremes of our globe are found, from arctic cold near the summits of the highest volcanoes to the steam-bath atmosphere of the coastal jungles. Merely to pass from one valley to another is to enter a markedly different ecological zone.

This variation would be of interest only to the tourist agencies if one neglected to consider the effect of these contrasts upon the human occupation of Mexico. A topsy-turvy landscape of this sort means a corresponding diversity of natural and cultivated products from region to region—above all, different crops with different harvest times. It means that no one region is now, or was in the past, truly self-sufficient. From the most remote antiquity, there has been an organic interdependence of each zone with the others, of each culture or nation with all the rest. As a result, no matter how heterogeneous their languages or civilizations, the people of Mexico exchanged products and ideas that bound them together and aided the development of sociopolitical complexity in the region.

2 Central highlands of Mexico, with Popocatepetl volcano in the distance.

3 *Chinampas* in the vicinity of Xochimilco, Basin of Mexico.

Most of this funnel-shaped country lies above 3,000 ft (900 m), with really very little flat land. The Mexican highlands, our major concern in this book, are shaped by the mountain chains that swing down from the north, by the uplands between them, and by numerous volcanoes that have raised their peaks in fairly recent geological times (**figure 2**). The western chain, the Sierra Madre Occidental, is the loftiest and broadest of these, being an extension of the Rocky Mountains. It and the Sierra Madre Oriental, which is situated to the east, enclose between their pine-clad ranges an immense inland plateau that is covered by mesquite-studded grasslands and occasionally even approaches true desert. Effectively outside the limits of Mesoamerican farming, the Mexican plateau was the homeland of partially or wholly nomadic foragers. As we move south, the two Sierras gradually approach each other until the interior wastelands terminate some 300 miles (480 km) north of the Basin of Mexico.

The Basin of Mexico, the center of the Aztec empire, is one of a number of natural basins in the midst of the Volcanic Cordillera, an extensive region of intense volcanism and frequent earthquakes. A mile and a half high, with an area of 3,000 sq. miles (7,800 sq. km), much of the Basin was once covered by a shallow lake of roughly figure-eight shape, now almost disappeared through ill-advised drainage and the general desiccation of central Mexico in post-Conquest times. Since the Basin of Mexico has no natural outlet, changing rainfall patterns have produced severe fluctuations in the extent of the lake. As will be seen in Chapter 10, the Aztec table was amply supplied by foods raised on its swampy margins in the *chinampas*: rectangular raised fields bordered by water-filled ditches (**figure 3**). Surrounded by hills on all sides, the Basin is dominated on the southeast by the snowy summits of the volcanoes Popocatepetl ("Smoking Mountain") and Iztaccihuatl ("The White Lady").

Other important sections of the highlands are the Sierra Madre del Sur, the escarpment of which fronts the Pacific shoreline in southern Mexico, and the mountainous uplands of Oaxaca; both of these fuse to form a highland mass heavily dissected into an abundance of valleys and ranges. Separated from this rugged topography by the Isthmus of Tehuantepec, the southeastern highlands form a continuous series of ranges from Chiapas down through Maya territory into lower Central America.

Although snow falls in some places at infrequent intervals, the Mexican highlands are temperate; before denudation by humans, they were clothed in pines and oaks, with true boreal forests in the higher ranges. As elsewhere in Mexico, there are two strongly marked seasons: a winter dry period when rain seldom, if ever, falls, and a summer wet spell. The total rainfall is less than half that of the lowlands, so conditions are occasionally arid and somewhat precarious for the farmer, in spite of the general richness of the soil. This is especially true of the boundary zone between the agricultural lands and the northern deserts.

The lowlands are confined to relatively narrow strips along the coasts, of which the most important is the plain fronting the Gulf of Mexico. Of alluvial origin, this band of flat land extends unbroken from Louisiana and Texas down through the Mexican states of Tamaulipas, Veracruz, and Tabasco to the Yucatan Peninsula, and played a critical role in the origins of settled life and the growth of civilization in Mexico.

A bridge between the Gulf Coast plain and the narrower and less humid Pacific Coast plain is provided by the Isthmus of Tehuantepec, a constriction in the waist of Mesoamerica, with a gentle topography of low hills and sluggish rivers.

Lowland temperatures are generally torrid throughout the year, except when winter northers come down the Gulf Coast, bringing with them cold rains and drizzle. So heavy is the summer precipitation that in many places the soils are red in color and poor in mineral content as a result of drastic leaching. When these rains cause flooding of rivers, however, the soils can be highly productive since they are annually replenished with silt along the natural river levees. The winter dry season is generally well defined, even in the tropics, where many trees lose their leaves at this time of year. But where there is an unusually great amount of rain (along with winter northers), one encounters the evergreen canopies and lush growth of the fully developed rainforest. Dotting the lowlands are patches of savannah grassland, sometimes quite extensive, and of little use to the pre-Columbian Mexican farmer, who was at that time plowless and his work unmechanized.

In response to the opportunities presented by these surroundings, contrasting modes of land cultivation have been developed over the millennia. Highland farmers are quite efficient about their land, since only a moderate period of fallowing is necessary for the fields. On the other hand, many lowland cultivators, faced with immense forests, the low potential of the soil, weed competition, and winter desiccation, have evolved a shifting form of horticulture, which they share with other cultures of the world. This system entails the cutting and burning of the forest from the plot to be sown; a very extensive territory is required for the support of each family, since exhausted and weed-infested fields have to be left fallow for as long as ten years. Such a mode of food-getting could never have supported a substantial population, and we have every evidence to suggest a light occupation of much of the lowland zone throughout its history.

Nonetheless, it is easy to exaggerate the limitations of the lowlands; there are not one but many lowland environments, and a diversity of human responses to them. For instance, one could point to the use of fertile river levees by ancient and modern farmers of the southern Gulf Coast plain, which led to increased population density.

Tragically reduced in today's Mexico, game abounded in ancient times. The most important food animals were the white-tailed deer and the collared peccary, found everywhere. Confined to the lowlands were the tapir, the howler monkey, and the spider monkey, all of which are still eaten by the indigenous inhabitants. The lowlands also harbored the now rare jaguar, the largest of the spotted cats and the source of much-desired skins for the nobles of pre-Spanish Mexican civilizations; it must have been an object of primal terror to the early dwellers of the coastal plains. Waterfowl, especially ducks, teemed on the lakes and marshes of the uplands, and wild turkeys in the more isolated reaches of the country. Feathers from such tropical birds as the blue cotinga, the roseate spoonbill, the hummingbird, and above all, the quetzal, with iridescent blue-green plumage, provided rainbow-like splendor for headdresses and other details of costume.

The most sizable highland lakes, such as Lake Pátzcuaro in Michoacan and the great lake of the Basin of Mexico, teemed with small fish, while the lowland rivers and the coasts provided such an abundance of fish, for example snook and snappers, and turtles that these food resources were more important to ancient cultures than game mammals.

There were no wild species in the Americas suitable for domestication as draught animals. Human hunters exterminated the native American horse at the end of the Ice Age, probably; the South American llama is amenable only as a pack animal; and modern efforts to tame the North American bison have shown that beast to be completely intractable. As a consequence, none of the indigenous groups prior to the European arrival had wheeled vehicles. Ancient Mexico did without any form of overland transportation other than the backs of men, although the principle of the wheel was known and applied to small, clay animal figurines (see **figure 133,** p. 162). The only warm-blooded animals kept in domestication were the dog and the turkey, both valuable for their meat. Hives of tiny, stingless bees (*Melipona beichii*) were reported by the Spanish to be very popular at the time of European arrival; they were exploited for honey by tropical lowlanders.

Languages and Cultures

An amazing number of languages were spoken in native Mexico. The situation would be even more confusing if it had not been for the efforts on the part of linguists to group them into families, of which some fourteen have been defined within Mesoamerica (**figure 4**).

Of these, the largest and most important to the later pre-Hispanic history of Mexico is Uto-Aztecan, comprising dozens of languages distributed from the northwestern United States as far south as Panama. Since the greatest diversity within this family is found in northwestern Mexico, this region has been suggested as the probable heartland of the Uto-Aztecan cultures. By all odds the major language group within Uto-Aztecan is Nahua, the most significant member of which is Nahuatl, the language of the Aztecs and the *lingua franca* of their empire, still spoken by hundreds of thousands of farmers in the central Mexican highlands and in the state of Guerrero. Since the Conquest, Nahuatl has greatly enriched Mexican Spanish with loan words, and has also contributed such words as ocelot, coyote, tomato, chocolate, tamale, and copal to the English language.

Tarascan or Purépecha, the tongue of a sizable, independent kingdom at the time of the Aztecs that was centered on Lake Pátzcuaro in the western part of the Volcanic Cordillera, is entirely unrelated to any other language in the world. Otomí-Pame was spoken by groups who followed a semi-nomadic way of life to the north of the Basin of Mexico, on the fringe of Mesoamerica. Totonac is spoken on the middle Gulf Coast, significantly in the region of the old Tajín civilization. Mixtec and Zapotec are the dominant languages of the state of Oaxaca in southern Mexico, and Zapotec written records go back to at least 500 BCE. The Mixe-Zoquean language family is distributed from the Isthmus of Tehuantepec to the Grijalva Depression, and as discussed in Chapter 5, may have been the language of the ancient Olmecs. Huave was and is spoken by fishermen (now principally turned to cattlemen) on the Pacific Coast of the Isthmus. To the east is the large group of Mayan languages; this family has an enigmatic outlier, Huastec, in the area of the Gulf Coast north of the Totonac that is called, naturally enough, the Huasteca. The location of Huastec remains a puzzle for Mesoamericanists. Evidence from the branch of linguistic research known as glottochronology, or lexicostatistics, suggests that it might have separated from the main group of Mayan languages about 900 BCE, but what this means for the development of Mesoamerican cultures has yet to be ascertained.

It would be a fruitless task to try to reconstruct Mexican history merely on the basis of these distributions. Nevertheless, it is evident that the expansion of Uto-Aztecan through much of Mexico must have been drastic; the isolated islands of Nahua speech as far south as lower Central America, Nahua placenames, and the presence of Nahua words in many other languages, testify to substantial movement of groups. In this case, we know of Nahua conquests and migrations having taken place long before the imperialism of the Nahuatl-speaking Aztecs, events recorded in the traditional histories of these groups. The role that they have played on the stage of the history of the Western hemisphere has certainly been in the grand style.

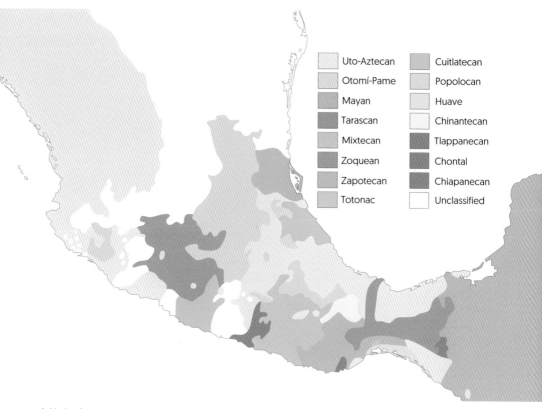

4 Native language groups in Mesoamerica at the time of the Spanish Conquest.

Legend:

Uto-Aztecan	Cuitlatecan
Otomí-Pame	Popolocan
Mayan	Huave
Tarascan	Chinantecan
Mixtecan	Tlappanecan
Zoquean	Chontal
Zapotecan	Chiapanecan
Totonac	Unclassified

Other populations have most likely been more sedentary. But, contradictory as it may seem, while there is fairly good knowledge of the geographic position of most language groups in Mexico at the time of the Conquest, archaeologists are often loath to apply linguistic names to past civilizations unless they are sure beyond any doubt of the identification, as in the case of the Zapotecs and the Maya, whose writings we have, or the Aztecs. Stones and pottery fragments do not tell us who made them, so we must be content with the noncommittal names that archaeologists have given us for past cultures.

Periods

The Aztecs encountered by the Spanish conquistadores and missionaries knew that they had not been the first occupants of the land of Mexico. Time and time again they told their interlocutors that they had been preceded by a marvelous people called the Toltecs, the "People from Tollan." And beyond that epoch lay a mystical land known as Tamoanchan, a paradise inhabited by the gods and ancestors of humans. Further, the Aztec thinkers said that the world had been created and destroyed four times, and that we are now living in the fifth age or "Sun." The Aztecs knew of the great, ruined city of Teotihuacan, to the northeast of their island capital, and said that the gods had met there to create our present era and the Sun that was to give it life and substance.

It was not until the first decades of the twentieth century that archaeology began to render the outlines of the historical sequence of Mexico and its civilizations. The first stratigraphic excavation carried out in the Basin of Mexico demonstrated not only that Teotihuacan was substantially earlier than Aztec, but that the Teotihuacan culture was underlain by the remains of earlier, pottery-using people. How early were these pre-Aztec cultures? There was no real way to know, and most archaeologists were reluctant to think of these ceramic cultures as pre-dating the Christian era. They looked enviously at the American Southwest, where dendrochronology, or tree-ring dating, gave an absolute, year-to-year chronology for the ancient adobe pueblos, and for the Maya area, where a similarly detailed time scale had resulted from the correlation of the Maya and Christian calendars.

All this was changed by the advent of radiocarbon dating in the mid-twentieth century. Some of those early cultures turned out to date to the beginning of the first millennium BCE; and Teotihuacan proved to be a contemporary of the earlier part of the Maya Classic (250–900 CE) period, and had nothing to do with the Toltecs, as some had thought. The Toltecs, in fact, appeared on the scene as the Classic came to an end (see p. 174), and as the Aztec ethnohistories had affirmed.

There is general agreement among scholars about the periods or stages of socio-cultural change in pre-Conquest Mexico, even though many details remain unclear. The first occupation is here called Early Hunters (identical to the Paleo-Indian period of some specialists), and extends from the time of the earliest migrants into the area—a topic still under debate—until about 7000 BCE. During this era, people lived in tiny, nomadic bands, following a way of life centered on the collection of wild plant foods and on the hunting of now extinct big game. During the subsequent Archaic (or "Incipient Agricultural") period, ancestral Meso-americans began to domesticate those food plants—above all, maize—upon which all subsequent civilizations in this hemisphere rested. With the introduction of pottery and village life at about 1800 BCE, the Formative period opens, lasting until around 150 CE. Radiocarbon dating and field archaeology have shown that Olmec and other ancient civilizations flourished in this epoch. The Classic period, which follows on its heels, marks a new level of complexity in Mesoamerican civilization, with the rise and decline of such mighty states as Teotihuacan and Monte Albán. The Epiclassic witnessed the demise of Teotihuacan, while such smaller, innovative cities as Xochicalco and El Tajín replaced the Classic powers in the Mesoamerican world. During these latter two periods the lowland Maya civilization to the east experienced its zenith, with cities, several of which had important ties to Mexican cultures, dotting the jungle. Many Maya and Mexican cities were abandoned or fast-fading by 900 CE, to be replaced by the city-states of the Post-Classic, beginning with the expansionist state of the Toltecs and culminating with the hegemonic interests of the Aztecs.

First encountered by the Spaniards in 1519, Aztec civilization was vibrant until it was radically transformed by the intruders in 1521, bringing at least 15,000 years of Native American history to a dramatic turn.

Chapter 2

Early Hunters

The date for when humans first entered the Western hemisphere is a hotly debated topic. Even the how is controversial. The last major stage of the Pleistocene, or Ice Age, is known as the Wisconsin in North America. It began around 50,000 years ago and continued, with many fluctuations, until 10,000 years ago. Because their water was taken up into ice, the oceans of the world were 200 ft (60 m) lower during the advances of the late Wisconsin than they stand at present, sufficiently exposing a platform to form a land bridge at least 1,000 miles (1,600 km) wide between Siberia and the western coast of Alaska, called the Bering Land Bridge. Although an enormous sheet of ice then covered much of North America as far south as the Great Lakes of today, the Bering Land Bridge was ice-free, as was western Alaska and the Yukon Valley. Many of the earliest migrant hunters into the Americas would then have crossed from Asia through a tundra-covered, cold region, covered with thin and patchy snows in winter, and inhabited by herds of woolly mammoth, horse, bison, and other ungulates.

Archaeologists have divided broadly into two camps over the date and mode of entry of these earliest Americans. One camp firmly believes in a "short chronology": that the first movements into this hemisphere from Asia could have taken place only when there was a land bridge in place (Beringia would have been drowned by rising sea levels beginning about 10,000 years ago), and that this occurred no earlier than 14,000 to 16,000 years ago. The other school holds to a "long chronology," pointing to far older—if often disputed—radiocarbon dates than this for early human remains in the hemisphere. The argument regarding the land bridge put forward by the "short chronology" school holds weight only if boat travel was unknown in the world during the late Pleistocene. Yet early humans had reached Australia, which was never connected to the Asiatic mainland by a land bridge, by 50,000 years ago, surely by boat. This raises the possibility of perhaps equally early migrations into

5 Sites of the Early Hunters and Archaic periods.

North America via the Pacific coast of Beringia and southern Alaska, although there is yet slight evidence for them, as key sites must lie in deep waters (**figure 5**).

The First Americans

Who were these first Americans? All of the early skeletons that are presently known from the Early Hunters stage in North America (including Mexico) are of the anatomically modern human species (*Homo sapiens*); no remains of *Homo erectus*, *Homo neanderthalensis*, or any other archaic form of our genus have ever been found in this hemisphere. Since no indisputably Last Interglacial artifacts have ever come to light in North or South America, we may surmise that humans entered Alaska via Beringia at the earliest during the Wisconsin, both by land and by sea.

In recent years, key evidence for the very earliest inhabitants of the American continent has unexpectedly appeared in Mexico in the Tulum area of Yucatan's

Caribbean coast. The eastern part of the Yucatan Peninsula is underlain by a massive system of limestone caves; these had been dry, until they were drowned by a rising water table occurring at the end of the Pleistocene. In some of these caves, skilled archaeological divers have discovered eight human skeletons. One, from the Hoyo Negro cave, had been an undernourished teenage girl who met her death tumbling into a 190 ft (58 m) pit, probably in search of water. A radiocarbon test on her tooth enamel yielded a date of 10,900 BCE. Mitochondrial DNA extracted from one of her molar teeth links her genetically with the present-day Native Americans in both North and South America. Such discoveries as these, of such early remains in southerly regions, suggest that the picture of peopling the Americas was a complex one.

The Western hemisphere must have been both a land of opportunities and challenges for the first hunting people. Extensive herds of such large grazing animals as mammoths, mastodons, camels, horses, and giant bison roamed through both subcontinents. In such ideal conditions, population expansion and spread were probably fairly rapid. Radiocarbon dating has demonstrated that people were hunting sloth, horse, and guanaco (a member of the camel family, similar in appearance to the llama) at the Straits of Magellan by at least 10,000 BCE. In southern Chile, an archaeological project directed by Tom Dillehay at the site of Monte Verde has produced evidence of a far older occupation at 12,500 BCE. This was a small settlement of about twelve huts made of wood posts possibly supporting hide covers. Their stone toolkit was limited to crude stone flakes, and they were primarily subsisting on seashore life (including seaweed), yet they hunted such substantial animals as gomphotheres—distant and somewhat smaller relatives of mammoths and mastodons, long thought to have died out before the arrival of humans in the Americas. More recently, an even earlier occupation has been found at Monte Verde, dated to 16,500 BCE.

Tools of the First Hunters

To understand the significance of finds of late Pleistocene date that have been made in Mexico, it is necessary to consider them in the light of the Early Hunters stage for North America as a whole, especially for the United States, where research on this problem has been most intensive. The opinion of many (but not all) archaeologists is that the earliest known remains are those of a culture of hunters and gatherers in which the majority of tools were very simple, percussion-chipped, pebble artifacts. Coarse choppers, chopping tools, scrapers, and knives are found at a number of campsites and open stations (unsheltered sites where people rested while roaming the landscape) in the western United States under conditions of seemingly great antiquity; since this inventory is exactly that of the late Pleistocene population of east Asia, it is believed to represent the non-perishable part of the tool-kit of the first immigrants.

6 Clovis point, about 3.9 in. (10 cm) long, from Fin del Mundo, Sonora.

By approximately 11,500 BCE an immense technological change had taken place, with the invention of complex percussion- and pressure-flaked stone points of the type known as Clovis (**figure 6**). These have a broad channel or flute extending up from the base on one or both sides, formed by the removal of long, narrow flakes. The technique was risky: it has been estimated that ancient Clovis flintknappers unintentionally broke about 15 to 20 percent while fluting; but it was worth the risk, as modern tests on replicas have proved that fluting points provided shock absorption and prevented breakage on impact when in use.

In recent years, archaeologists of Mexico's National Institute of Anthropology and History (INAH) have made significant discoveries at "Fin del Mundo" (World's End), an Early Hunters site in Sonora, about 120 miles (200 km) south of the Arizona border. A number of fine Clovis spear points and other stone tools have been found associated with the bones of gomphotheres. These bulky animals had been killed and butchered in what was then a swamp. Reliably dated to 11,390 BCE, Fin del Mundo may be the oldest Clovis horizon site presently known in North America.

Clovis points are found over much of North America, from Alaska down to Panama; some magnificent examples come from mammoth "kill" sites in Arizona near the Mexican border. In the American Midwest and West, at about 10,300 BCE, a modification in fluting produced the well-known Folsom point. Examples of this type follow Clovis, and are often associated with extinct bison "kills." All these points, because of their size and weight, are considered to be the tips of darts that were hurled with the aid of a thrower (or *atlatl*, to use the Nahuatl term). Experiments carried out by Dennis Stanford of the Smithsonian Institution have shown the high efficiency of this tool over the hand-held spear: the *atlatl*-hurled dart has fifteen times the speed and 200 times the impact. It comes as no surprise that the *atlatl* stayed in favor until the Spanish Conquest, and is known to have still been in use well into the first quarter of the twentieth century. The bow and arrow was a late arrival in Mexico and was not adopted at all in many areas.

Concurrently with Folsom, in the Great Plains as far south as Texas appeared a number of related industries all characterized by bifacially chipped lanceolate points (points shaped similarly to a lance head) (Angostura, Scottsbluff, etc.); in actuality, this lanceolate point "horizon" covers much of Latin America as well. The origin of the techniques and concepts involved in the production of bifacially chipped spear points in this hemisphere is not known.

All the tool inventories were the equipment of groups who were without agriculture and who lived mainly by the chase and the gathering of wild plant foods. From what we know about societies with a similar way of life who were documented ethnographically in the first half of the twentieth century, such as the Australian Aborigines, concentrations of population greater than the small band (which typically consists of around twenty people) were impossible. The biologist and ecologist Edward Deevey once estimated that on this level of development, corresponding roughly to the Upper Palaeolithic of Europe, 25 sq. miles (65 sq. km) of territory are required for the support of one person. In all the Americas prior to 7000 BCE there may never have been more than half a million persons at any one moment in time, with about 30,000 of these in Mexico—a crude guess, to be sure, but not unreasonable.

Landscapes of the Early Hunters

Late Pleistocene Mexico presented a landscape considerably different from that which we see now. Rain poured then on places it hardly touches today, and many semi-deserts must have been seas of grass in those remote times. The great lake in the Basin of Mexico, where the most significant finds of the Early Hunters stage have been made, was a great deal broader and deeper, as testified by old strand lines on the surrounding hills.

Freshwater sediments over 250 ft (75 m) thick underlie Mexico City and all areas of the now dry beds of the great lake in the Basin of Mexico. Geological work has established a stratigraphy for the upper part of these deposits that corresponds to a climate sequence beginning at the later part of the Pleistocene. Crucial to the problem of the ancient occupation in the Basin is the Becerra Formation, layers of geological deposits that contain a wealth of archaeological evidence. The formation is divided into an Upper and a Lower; the Lower probably pertains to the early or middle Wisconsin Stage from about 115,000 years ago, while the Upper Becerra Formation can be assigned with some confidence to the late Wisconsin (11,000–8000 BCE), on the basis of a single radiocarbon date and the kind of artifacts associated with this stratum. The archaeological evidence within these deposits allows us to trace some of the earliest examples of hunting in Mexico.

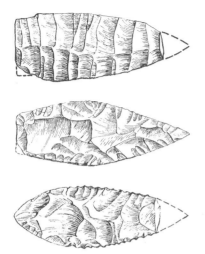

7a–c Chipped-stone tools found in association with mammoths at the two kill sites at Santa Isabel Iztapan. The three types of lanceolate points are present: a) Flint Scottsbluff point; b) Angostura point; c) Flint Lerma point.

8 The second fossil mammoth from Santa Isabel Iztapan, Basin of Mexico. The hind leg that had become caught in mud can be seen in the foreground. Early Hunters period.

The Upper Becerra is a fine, green muck, and has lenses of ash deposited by the volcanoes that were in frequent eruption when it formed. Over this is a layer of brown, sandy sediments that were deposited at a time when the great lake was shrinking. Presumably this layer represents the first part of the warmer period, known as the Hypsithermal Interval, following the end of the Ice Age. A turn to really dry conditions and desiccation of the lake bed is indicated by a layer of caliche, or calcium carbonate, marking the climax of the Hypsithermal. From the caliche layer to the surface are several further layers that probably date from the late Hypsithermal to modern times and that contain abundant potsherds.

In 1952, on the northeast edge of the old lake flats near Santa Isabel Iztapan, Mexican archaeologists—following up a chance find by workers opening a drainage ditch—excavated the skeleton of an imperial mammoth (*Mammuthus imperator*). This lay entirely within the green muck of the Upper Becerra Formation, and was therefore dated to the late Wisconsin, between 11,000 and 8000 BCE. The animal had been butchered in situ, a fact that could be deduced from the disarticulated position of the bones alone. Most importantly, six human artifacts were indisputably associated with the skeleton. These included a flint projectile point of the type known as Scottsbluff, one of the most widely distributed artifacts of the lanceolate point horizon on the Great Plains of the United States (**figure 7a**). The other artifacts were utilized in cutting up the mammoth, and comprised a scraper, knife, and fine prismatic blade, all of obsidian, and an endscraper and retouched blade of flint.

In 1954, the construction of another ditch by the Santa Isabel Iztapan villagers resulted in the lucky find of a second mammoth "kill," again with artifacts that had been lost during the butchering process (**figure 8**). Here a hind leg of the animal had been caught in the Upper Becerra muck, probably as it was fleeing its human pursuers. During the butchering process, the head and tusks had been dragged back across the body, and some bones showed deep cuts made by stone knives while the meat was being hacked off. Three chipped-stone artifacts found among the bones comprise an Angostura point of a dark igneous material, a Lerma point of flint, and a chert, bifacially worked knife. The Angostura points can be ascribed to the lanceolate point horizon on the Great Plains, which was known to be later than the Clovis horizon (**figure 7b**). Lerma points have an even wider spread in the late Wisconsin Glacial, being found in Texas and northeastern Mexico (where they appear as early as 8000 BCE), and are one of the most common types of point ascribed to the Early Hunters stage in South America as far south as Argentina (**figure 7c**). We have no radiocarbon dates on the Santa Isabel Iztapan finds, but charcoal from a hearth next to a skeleton of yet another slaughtered mammoth in the same formation has been dated to 9200 BCE by this process.

Hunting in the Basin of Mexico

The Becerra Formation has therefore offered us valuable insight into not only when but also how hunting took place in the Basin of Mexico. We can surmise something of the life and environment of these hunters some 11,000 years ago, although it must be remembered that we lack all knowledge of their campsites and have the chance evidence only of their hunting prowess. The climate was cooler and more humid than that of today; in fact, the now barren outskirts of the Basin were covered with pine forests. In the distance, the young cones of the active volcanoes poured out smoke, ash, and lava, perhaps disturbing the tempo of life in the Basin from time to time, but not seriously disrupting it. The imperial mammoth seems to have favored the swampy margins of the wide, shallow lake. These beasts must have been relatively easy game to organized groups of hunters, who, armed with darts hurled from *atlatls* and equipped with stone knives and other butchering tools, drove the heavy beasts into shallower water where they became hopelessly mired in the treacherous lake bottom. There each mammoth was isolated and dispatched, although probably not without danger since the risk of impalement by the formidable tusks of the surrounded animal must have been considerable—to kill any elephant with darts would require bravery.

A broader picture of Ice Age life in Mexico comes from the Tehuacan Valley in Puebla, where an ambitious project directed by Richard MacNeish disclosed a late

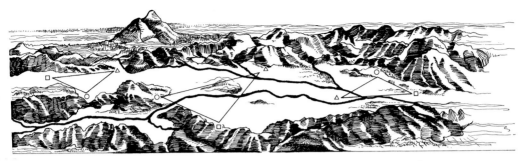

9 Probable community patterns, Ajuereado phase in the Tehuacan Valley. Groups moved from wet-season camps (circles), to fall camps (squares), to dry-season camps (triangles).

Pleistocene occupation called the Ajuereado phase. Radiocarbon dates suggest that it ended before 8000 BCE, but it must have been in part coeval with the Iztapan kills found in the Becerra Formation.

The evidence shows that the climate in the Tehuacan Valley was cooler and drier than that now prevailing, with open steppe covering the valley floor. In this setting grazed subsequently extinct horses and pronghorn antelope, which were hunted with darts fitted with Lerma points. The inhabitants also sought smaller game, for example jackrabbits, gophers, and rats. The tool technology was totally based upon chipped stone; in addition to projectile points, there were knives, choppers, sidescrapers (for dressing hides), and blades. Ground stone tools, which could have been used to prepare vegetable foods, are absent, although some wild plants, such as prickly-pear cactus and *Setaria* grass, were surely collected.

The inhabitants of Tehuacan during Ajuereado times were probably grouped into about three nomadic families or microbands of four to eight people each, and the evidence of cave-floor occupations shows that camps were changed three or four times a season, since there never was enough food in any one ecological niche to support settled life, a state of affairs that also prevailed throughout the succeeding Archaic stage (**figure 9**).

It would be a dangerous misconception to consider this period, viewed as a whole, as the time when people hunted only such huge Pleistocene animals as mammoth, horse, and so forth. As a matter of fact, in actual habitation sites of this date in Texas and elsewhere in the United States, the vast majority of animal bones and remains come from relatively small animals, as humble as rodents, snakes, snails, and mussels. The people living at these sites gathered and ate everything that was edible, and probably had to survive some very lean seasons (as the undernourished girl in the Hoyo Negro cave, p. 19, suggests). Since most of the sites that we have are substantial and conspicuous "kills," we have been deluded into thinking that we are dealing with some sort of ancient "big-game hunters" who disdained smaller animals or plant foods. It is true that big herbivores were slaughtered, but from this we must not assume that the late Pleistocene was a time of plenty. In a similar manner to the modern Mbuti of the African rainforest, who also hunt elephants, success in the chase probably meant a short feast marked by voracious gluttony, with long intervals in which people ate whatever they could lay their hands on.

Chapter 3

The Archaic Period

Six thousand years of almost uninterrupted high temperatures—as much as 2°C (3.6°F) above present averages in some places—commenced around 7000 BCE. The pleasant term "Climatic Optimum" has been invented for this Hypsithermal period in western Europe, for there the inhabitants of the lands facing the Atlantic enjoyed significantly wetter and warmer weather, perhaps the most balmy ever seen in those regions. Such favorable conditions hardly obtained elsewhere in the world, and in much of North America this long interval was primarily one of desiccation. In contrast to the oak forests of humid Europe, vast areas of North America were transformed into desert wastes.

Odd though it may seem, people continued to live throughout even the most desiccated zones of North America during the Hypsithermal. Species after species of large game perished not long after its onset, or even before it; while climate change has often been advanced as a cause of this ecological disaster, several scholars argue that this was a case of Pleistocene overkill by the Native Americans. Among the animals that disappeared at this time were the mastodon, mammoth, gomphothere, horse (not to reappear until the coming of the Spaniards), camel, giant bison, ground sloth, and dire wolf. But people survived. New tools, especially food-grinding implements, new hunting methods, other sources of food, perhaps different forms of shelter—all these enabled people to adapt to radically altered conditions of life.

The new stage of cultural adaptation attained by the inhabitants of the Americas is called the Archaic, and it is the full equivalent of the Mesolithic stage in the western part of Europe and the Middle East. Denied the more varied hunting economy of their late Pleistocene predecessors, small bands of Native Americans concentrated on more efficient methods of killing smaller game, on fishing and gathering mollusks, and, to an ever-increasing extent, on the collection of specific plant foods. The Archaic is the period in which we find first evidence for cultivation of plants and the beginnings of plant and animal domestication in Mexico:

a crucial moment in the history of Mesoamerica, as it was the cultivation of maize, beans, and squash that made possible all the subsequent cultures of Mexico, and, to a certain degree, those of Peru as well.

The Desert Culture in North America

In the dry semi-deserts of the Great Basin and southwestern United States, as well as north to Oregon and south to Texas and Mexico, these Archaic hunters and collectors inhabited caves and open sites near the ever-dwindling lakes or by seepages of water. The region that concerns us here, Mexico, must have been quite hot and dry, as indicated by known shrinking of the great lake of the Basin of Mexico and by the overwhelming appearance of dry-pollen indicators in the cores at this time. The pattern that enabled humans to eke out a livelihood in this challenging environment has been named the Desert Culture, which persisted into the nineteenth century BCE among the nomadic groups of the Great Basin. Its salient features include a sparse population; caves and rockshelters favored for settlements; a subsistence pattern based on the seasonal exploitation of such food resources as rabbits, wild-plant seeds, and insects; preparation of plant foods by grinding them on a flat milling stone with a cobble *mano*; abundant basketry, matting, and sandals (known as early as 7000 BCE in caves in Oregon); darts tipped with relatively small, percussion-chipped points and hurled by means of the *atlatl* (dart thrower); a wide variety of scrapers, choppers, scraper planes, and so forth; and the dog, present for the first time in North America, but probably brought by humans during the initial colonization of the continent.

The discovery of an Archaic period of Desert Culture type in highland Mexico has unexpectedly thrown light on one of the great problems in archaeology: where, when, and how the major food plants were domesticated. The domestication of maize, beans, and squash was one of the most important foundations to all that followed in Mexico. This chapter describes the effort of archaeologists to bridge the gap between the ancient hunters and the first indications of cultivation and full-blown village life.

The Origins of Mexican Cultivated Plants

There is no simple definition of the term "domestication." There is a difference between the domestication of such an animal as the dog or pig, which can and often does revert to the "wild" state, and such a creature as the Egyptian chicken, the reproduction of which entirely depends upon the presence of human populations, for it has lost the ability to incubate its own eggs. We are clearly dealing here with a broad spectrum, in which the degree of domestication may vary widely;

one might therefore adopt the definition proposed many years ago by the Russian geneticist Nikolai Vavilov, and say that domestication is co-evolution, directed by the interference of humans. Essentially, this implies that human beings have in some way tampered with the reproduction of a certain species—a process that may be systematic or totally unwitting.

As in animals, in its most extreme form, plant domestication ends up with species that cannot reproduce by themselves, and which are therefore without wild populations. In the case of cereals and other plants that reproduce by means of seeds, this implies that artificial selection has resulted in species that lack the ability to disperse their seeds. It is no accident that all the important food plants of the world belong in this category of entirely captive populations, since the reduction of the ability to self-reproduce has resulted in greatly increased food values in the plants concerned.

The Importance of Maize

The Aztecs believed that their hero-god Quetzalcoatl, who created humanity with his own blood, turned himself into an ant in order to be able to steal a single grain of maize that the ants had hidden inside a mountain; this he gave to humans so that they might be nourished. Maize was and is the very basis of settled life in Mexico and, indeed, throughout the civilizations of the Americas in Pre-Columbian times.

Maize (*Zea mays*) is a grass—in fact, a giant grass. Where and when was it first domesticated? For much of the second half of the twentieth century, a fierce controversy, of such rancor and virulence that one journalist described it as the "Corn Wars," raged about the origin of this all-important plant. On the one hand were the advocates of the "Tripartite Hypothesis," advanced by botanist Paul C. Mangelsdorf and his colleagues; they were convinced by decades of experimental research that a wild relative of maize called teosinte must have crossed with an extinct wild ancestor of true maize in order to have produced an annual teosinte, which then evolved into the maize that we know today. Subsequently, this newly domesticated plant had crossed with *Zea tripsacum*, another closely related wild grass, giving it added resistance against pests and improving yields.

The first to counter Mangelsdorf's hypothesis was an eminent geneticist, George W. Beadle, who argued that any theory based on an extinct or unknown ancestor was unsatisfactory. Beadle contended that the simplest explanation was also the best: that maize arose solely from the process of human selection of teosinte plants, and teosinte is therefore the only ancestor of maize. Beadle has posthumously won the "Corn Wars," for recent studies of the molecular biology of maize and its putative ancestors point directly to teosinte as the sole progenitor. Genetic studies undertaken at the University of Wisconsin have traced the origin of all maize to a particular strain of teosinte found today in the Balsas River drainage, in the southern Mexican state of Guerrero.

How old is domesticated maize? We have gained a broad picture of plant domestication in Pre-Columbian societies from cutting-edge research in the tropical Americas by Dolores Piperno, of the Smithsonian Institution, and her colleagues. As she and others have shown, while macroscopic plant remains are poorly preserved in most sites in the tropics (except for dry caves), microfossils of these plants— including maize—often are well preserved. Pollen can be recovered from layers of sediment in lake bottoms, but unfortunately, pollen grains of teosinte and maize are impossible to tell apart. More useful is the microscopic analysis of phytoliths (silica crystals in plant cells that vary between species) and starch cells, which are often preserved on stone grinding tools used in food processing.

Crucial evidence has been found by the Piperno team in the rockshelter of Xihuatoxtla, in the Balsas basin. The combination of stratigraphy, radiocarbon dating, and microscopic analysis of phytoliths and starch grains make it virtually certain that maize was first transformed from wild teosinte to a domesticate early in the seventh millennium BCE, and spread from Guerrero to most of Mesoamerica and then south to the rest of the American tropics. Archaeologists Mary Pohl and Kevin Pope have found large maize phytoliths (probable domesticates) dated to 4800 BCE at San Andrés on the Gulf Coast of Tabasco. There are no known wild species of *Zea* native to coastal Tabasco, which means these plants were introduced to the region, almost certainly by humans. At the same level, the archaeologists found evidence of large-scale forest clearance of the type associated with maize cultivation in this area. If this Tabasco material is true maize cultivation, then it is the earliest record of such activity that we have.

In the highlands, the earliest firmly dated maize cob was found in Guilá Naquitz cave in Oaxaca and dated to 4300 BCE. Cobs from caves in Tehuacan, Puebla, found

10 Maize from the Tehuacan Valley. The earliest in date (far left) is about 1 in. (3 cm) high. The cobs originate from 3500 BCE and after.

by Richard S. MacNeish and long thought through radiocarbon dating of associated materials to date to around 5000 BCE, have been subjected to direct dating of the cobs themselves and found to originate from 3500 BCE and after (**figure 10**). This Tehuacan sequence is crucial for the domestication of maize in particular and the Archaic period in general, for it is mainly through the work of MacNeish and his colleagues that we obtained our first systematic picture of this period (see "The Tehuacan Valley and Early Domestication," p. 32).

There is still much to learn about the evolution of domesticated maize, but the most important general fact remains: many thousands of years BCE, the human inhabitants of Mesoamerica brought a wild form of maize under their control through a slow process of selection. This was indeed the most crucial process along the road leading to the great Pre-Columbian civilizations.

Other Cultigens

Although maize was certainly the most important plant for the people of ancient Mesoamerica, it was not the first to be domesticated. Archaeologist Bruce D. Smith has found evidence of domesticated squash (*Cucurbita pepo*) as early as 8000 BCE, which would make it easily the earliest reliably dated Mesoamerican domesticate. The seeds and other plant remains used to date the domestication were found in Guilá Naquitz cave in Oaxaca, and it has been suggested that the type of squash found there is a distant relative of today's pumpkin. Around this same time, Archaic foragers were probably utilizing the bottle gourd (*Lagenaria siceraria*), which is a relative of the early squash. While the squash seeds provided a source of protein that was easy to store and to transport, the bottle gourd provided a portable container for drinking water, so important to these early nomadic bands.

While maize is at the center of the Mesoamerican food complex, other vegetable foods, especially chile peppers, always accompany it. Native Americans consumed a remarkable array of plant foods, from various kinds of beans to squashes to chile peppers to fruits. In fact, it is difficult to imagine what Western cuisines were like before the European presence in Mexico and Peru.

The common bean, known in many varieties today, is the most popular in Mexican diets and presumably has been so since very early periods. Its nutritional importance stems from the fact that its proteins complement those of maize. On the basis of a distribution of wild forms, Nikolai Vavilov suggested a primary domestication in Mexico or Guatemala.

Of the squashes, there are three major species in Mexico: pumpkin, warty or crookneck squash, and walnut squash. The forms of all three are virtually legion, as any visitor to a Mexican food market can readily testify. The origins of all of these, whether from wild ancestors or through hybridization, are very little understood, although a very early domesticate has been identified, and the sequence of their appearance in Mexico is now established. The same might be said of chile peppers, today the major ingredient in "hot" foods the world over, but of Mexican and Peruvian origin; the major problem with this particular seasoning (also an important source of vitamins to indigenous populations) is the difficulty of distinguishing between wild and domesticated seeds.

The history of the bottle gourd, usable only as a container because the meat is inedible, is now known through ancient DNA analysis of archaeological specimens. This plant is definitively not original to the Americas, with an initial center of domestication in Africa, from which it reached East Asia. Early and entirely unfounded speculation had suggested that the bottle gourd might have been carried to the Americas by African voyagers, but the molecular evidence makes it certain that the *Lagenaria siceraria* of the Western hemisphere arrived from Asia, presumably across the Bering Strait. According to AMS radiocarbon dating of the earliest domesticates from five caves in Mexico, the earliest evidence of *Lagenaria siceraria* in Oaxaca dates to 7970 BCE, and it has been found to be present in Tehuacan by 5250 BCE and in Tamaulipas by 4490 BCE. The bottle gourd is, together with squash, therefore the most ancient cultigen of the Western hemisphere.

Archaeological evidence for the origins of many other cultigens is rare to non-existent, in part due to the perishable nature of root crops. Nevertheless, manioc pollen appears at about 4600 BCE at the San Andrés site in Tabasco, and it remains an important food plant in lowland Mesoamerica today. Also important are the decorative plants of Mexico, such as the dahlia, marigold, and zinnia; the marigold, for instance, has a significant part to play in the long roster of Mexican medicinal plants. (See p. 259 for a table showing the principal domestic plants of pre-Spanish Mesoamerica.) There are also many economically important trees that are protected rather than actually domesticated, such as the breadnut tree, the sacred ceiba (symbolic of the Tree of Life), mahogany, and the sapodilla tree, which produce valuable fruit, wood, and chicle latex for chewing gum.

Caves and Rockshelters of Northeastern Mexico

The search for the origins of agriculture and settled life in Mexico follows the influential research of Richard S. MacNeish from the 1950s. Most later researchers build on his work while debating his conclusions. MacNeish's research first led him to the almost rainless, semi-desert environment of Tamaulipas, the northeasternmost Mexican state. While during a few centuries before the arrival of Europeans Tamaulipas was a frontier zone of Mesoamerica, the groups encountered by the Spaniards in this region were, with few exceptions, hunters and collectors. MacNeish was drawn to this region because the aridity of Tamaulipas has meant ideal conditions of preservation in cave and rockshelter sites, of which a good many were discovered. In the course of his excavations, he uncovered the first evidence for an entirely new chapter in our knowledge of the ancient history of Mexico: the Archaic or "Incipient Agricultural" period, lasting from about 7000 BCE to after 2000 BCE.

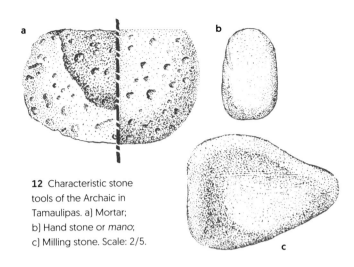

11 Ovoid biface of obsidian, which would have been used as a generalized cutting tool, Archaic period of Tamaulipas. Scale: over 2/5.

12 Characteristic stone tools of the Archaic in Tamaulipas. a) Mortar; b) Hand stone or *mano*; c) Milling stone. Scale: 2/5.

The Archaic Tamaulipas tool inventory is fairly typical of the Desert Culture throughout western and southern North America (**figure 11**). In chipped stone, there were scrapers, choppers, pebble hammerstones, and disk scrapers, most of which were probably used in the preparation of vegetable foods; projectile points, used in the hunting of deer, were fixed with resin to shafts of long darts, to be hurled with the *atlatl*. Plant products were also processed with such ground stone tools as mortars, pestles, *manos*, and expedient milling stones (**figure 12**). MacNeish concluded that the economy depended primarily upon hunting, collecting, and the grinding of wild seeds. As part of this complex, there were nets and turned and coiled baskets, while cordage was made from the fiber of such wild plants as yucca and agave. People slept on twilled mats; these, known in the Nahuatl language as *petates*, are still standard sleeping gear for many people throughout Mexico.

Plant materials and dried feces, or "coprolites," were remarkably well preserved and abundant in these rockshelters, the latter providing direct evidence of what people ate. The diet was heavy in vegetable foods, some of which came from domesticated plants. The earliest found were bottle gourds, dating to 6500 BCE.

Other plants occur in the Tamaulipas sequence at somewhat later dates, including pumpkin, scarlet runner beans, chile peppers, common beans, and squashes, in that order. There was no wild maize in MacNeish's excavations, but cobs of a tiny-eared pop corn with many pod-corn characteristics appear between 3000 and 2200 BCE. This suggested to MacNeish that he should be looking further south for the origins of maize.

Santa Marta Rockshelter

In the arid Chiapas highlands is the Santa Marta rockshelter, near the town of Ocozocoautla on the Pan-American Highway. The rockshelter was tested by MacNeish and Fredrick Peterson in 1959 and revealed five successive Archaic occupations, directly overlain by later pottery-bearing deposits belonging to the later Early Formative Horizon (see Chapter 4). Radiocarbon dates for the Archaic levels indicate a span from at least 6700 BCE through an extremely dry period (after 5000 BCE). The complex of tool and point types duplicates that of Tamaulipas, and includes dart points, gouges, scraper planes, pebble *manos*, and boulder querns. Four burials were found together at the Santa Marta rockshelter, three of them flexed in fetal posture and one extended above, all the dead having been covered as a group with some *metates*. Burials of this sort occur in Desert Culture contexts as far north as Wyoming.

Maize pollen makes its appearance only in the later Early Formative Horizon that included the pottery deposits. Both pollens and other maize plant parts were completely absent from the Archaic, pre-pottery levels.

The Tehuacan Valley and Early Domestication

In 1960, MacNeish turned his attention to the Tehuacan Valley in southeastern Puebla, some 130 miles (200 km) southeast of Mexico City (**figure 13**). Lying in the rain shadow of the Sierra Madre range that protects it on the east, the valley is an arid cactus- and thorn-scrub-covered desert, not unlike southern Arizona. MacNeish's preliminary reconnaissance of the bone-dry caves and rockshelters that border the valley led to a four-season project that uncovered layer upon layer of occupation, each constituting a phase of occupation from 7000 to 1500 BCE. Through these phases, it is possible to see the adoption of plant cultivation, and from 5000 BCE, tiny cobs of very early domesticated maize (**figure 14**).

As we have seen, the Ajuereado phase, an Early Hunters occupation of the valley, ended around 7000 BCE. During the succeeding phases, called the El Riego (c. 7000–5000 BCE), two significant changes came about. The first is that the climate turned warmer, perhaps resulting in the disappearance of "big game." Although the role of humans in the extinction of Pleistocene megafauna is hotly debated, there is no direct evidence in Mesoamerica in support of such anthropogenic impact. The second significant change is that by the end of the phase, the Tehuacan people had begun interfering with the reproduction of certain plants: surely domesticated were the avocado, chile peppers, amaranth (this remained a grain of secondary importance in the highlands right through the Spanish Conquest), and walnut squash. As in Tamaulipas, the preponderance of vegetable food, both wild and domesticated, in the diet is reflected by numerous mortars and pestles, and by milling stones and pebble *manos*; sizable plano-convex scrapers and choppers were probably used for pulping various plant materials. Chipped projectile points for *atlatl* are present, used in hunting deer and other relatively small game.

There are some surprising features in El Riego. Two bolls of domestic cotton were recovered, apparently the world's first. Some quite elaborate burials from the phase were found in caves, the bodies being wrapped in blankets and nets. Some of the cranial remains appear to have been manipulated once the flesh had decayed, including the removal of desiccated tissue that left cutmarks and a brief

13 View of the Tehuacan Valley, looking out from Coxcatlan Cave.

14 Cob of early domesticated maize from the Coxcatlan phase, Tehuacan Valley.

exposure to a low-intensity fire, which led to the smoking and black coloration of the ectocranial surface.

While population size had increased, the El Riego-phase people remained seasonally nomadic. During the dry season, camps were occupied by microbands who lived mainly by hunting. In the spring, these moved into the slopes of the valley, collecting seeds, and in the summer "wet season" they were able to pick fruit. Perhaps when there was more rain than usual, they were able to coalesce into macrobands. In the fall, with a diminution of food supplies, they moved back to their winter abodes.

One of the major local changes in subsistence is to be seen in the phase of occupation following the El Riego: the Coxcatlan phase (c. 5000–3400 BCE). The economy and settlement pattern in the Tehuacan Valley remained much the same, but to the list of domesticates were added the bottle gourd, common bean, black sapote, and warty squash. The evidence is now quite clear that these and other plants were domesticated in different places and at different times. Maize makes its first appearance in the Tehuacan sequence at this time, and was probably planted, as were existing cultigens, when microbands came together in the spring. Some of the minuscule cobs so closely approached Mangelsdorf's reconstructed ancestral maize that he was confident they were wild. In particular, they exhibited the extended glumes, the tiny kernel size, and the bearing of the male tassel on the ear of the hypothetical progenitor, as well as showing no variation among themselves—a wild characteristic. But, as proponents of the teosinte theory have pointed out, they look disconcertingly similar to teosinte.

The next phase of the Tehuacan sequence, called the Abejas phase (c. 3400–2300 BCE) saw a distinct shift in settlement pattern, with small hamlets of five to ten pithouses down on the valley floor. Domestic plants newly added to the cuisine were tepary beans, perhaps the pumpkin, and hybrid maize showing introgression ("capture" of genes by backcrossing) with teosinte. While a study by Eric Callen of Abejas coprolites reveals that 70 percent of the diet was still based on wild plants and animals, the increasing cultivation of crops for storage in specially made caches and pits was associated with longer and longer stays in band encampments. The result was the possibility of staying in one place all year; sedentism was gradually replacing nomadism.

As discussed in the next chapter, Early Formative pottery centers on the neckless jar or *tecomate*, and the flat-bottomed bowl with outslanting sides. It is probably significant that in the Abejas phase these same shapes are seen in beautifully made ground stone vessels, perhaps prototypes for later ceramics.

In fact, during the final Archaic phase in the valley, the poorly known Purrón (c. 2300–1500 BCE), roughly fashioned, gravel-tempered pottery makes its appearance—late in the sequence, but certainly by 1650 BCE. The so-called "Pox pottery," found by Charles and Ellen Brush in middens on the coast of Guerrero, is close in appearance to the Purrón ceramics and has similarly early radiocarbon dates. In the hot, fertile Soconusco coast of southeastern Chiapas, on the border between Mexico and the Maya area, the people of the Barra culture were already making highly crafted ceramics that are at least in part contemporary with Purrón, and may be the source from which most of the pottery traditions of the Mesoamerican Formative stem. Nonetheless, it is quite unlikely that pottery—that material index of fully sedentary life—was independently developed in Mesoamerica, for agricultural villages with well-crafted ceramics have a far greater antiquity along the Caribbean and Pacific Coasts of northern South America, and many archaeologists believe that the idea of firing clay to make vessels spread from there to Mexico.

Other Archaic Sites

The multiple phases of occupation in the Tehuacan Valley have allowed such archaeologists as MacNeish to follow the early stages of domestication, the first signs of sedentism, and the first ceramics. In the Valley of Oaxaca, Kent Flannery and his associates have uncovered a long preceramic sequence paralleling that of Tehuacan in some respects, but adding new and sometimes contradictory data.

Most of Flannery's sites are caves, such as Guilá Naquitz cited above, but the open-air site of Gheo-Shih is particularly interesting as it shows evidence of such activity features as a possible dance-floor (or ball court) area, some 65 ft (20 m) long and 23 ft (7 m) wide, bordered with stones. As for food plants, there are pollen grains of the genus *Zea* in 7400 to 6700 BCE levels, which apparently represent wild maize. Rinds of bottle gourds and seeds and peduncles (stalks) of pumpkins are also this early, and so predate their appearance in Tehuacan.

The role of coastal lowlands, plagued by poor archaeological preservation, is relatively unknown, although current research is certainly enlarging the part it will play in future accounts of the Archaic. It is probable that maize is a seed crop of highland origin, but lowland root crops, such as manioc, leave little, if any, archaeological evidence. A single manioc pollen grain was found in Tabasco, associated with maize cultivation, and dated to 4600 BCE, but pollen evidence cannot identify species, leaving the question of domestication open. Jeffrey Wilkerson found an extensive Archaic village at Santa Luisa, on the coast of northern Veracruz, and while there are good data on hunting, gathering, and fishing, the absence of *manos* and *metates* need not necessarily mean an absence of cultivation, since manioc preparation does not require these. Similarly, pre-pottery levels in shell middens at Puerto Marquez and Islona de Chantuto on the Pacific Coast may well be manifestations of an otherwise unknown "incipient agricultural" way of life.

One of the most important Archaic discoveries has been at Tlapacoya, once an isolated island in the southern part of the Basin of Mexico; circular houses resembling those of the Abejas phase at Tehuacan have been uncovered, along with a roughly shaped female figurine of pottery, dating to around 2300 BCE, the oldest discovered in Mesoamerica and apparently the beginning of a tradition that was to flourish in the Formative period (**figure 15**).

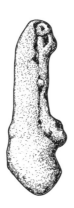

15 Front, side, and back views of baked-clay cylinder with human features from the Archaic settlement of Zohapilco, south shore of Lake Chalco, Basin of Mexico. Dating to around 2300 BCE, this is the earliest known figurine in Mesoamerica. Ht 1.8 in. (4.5 cm).

The Origins of Settled Life

The consequences of food production were, in the long run, of the greatest importance to the following developments in Mexico, but it was not a sudden change. The idea that the invention and adoption of food production led to a "revolution" in the advancement of humankind was elaborated by V. Gordon Childe and has influenced the way almost all who deal with this point in human history think. At the time that Childe wrote (between 1925 and 1956), almost nothing was known of the transition between hunting and gathering and the food-producing way of life, either in the Eastern or Western hemispheres. The mere absence of the evidence made the shift seem almost more sudden than subsequent work has shown it actually to have been. Now, for both Peru and Mexico, we have evidence of a very slow process toward fully settled life: the alleged "revolution" was seemingly more in the nature of a leisurely evolution. But this evolution was significant. Deevey has demonstrated that the density of population of early agriculturalists was twenty-five times greater than the figure for early foragers—the domestication of plants and animals resulted eventually in a quantum increase in the world's population, no matter how long the process took.

In Mexico, and probably in Mesoamerica in general, the development of plant cultivation during the Archaic period took place in a context that is almost indistinguishable from that of the Desert Culture, known so well in the Great Basin region of the American West. Back in this remote time, the ancestors of the mighty Aztecs and other civilizations of Mexico probably closely resembled the resourceful foragers of Nevada and California who relied mainly on tubers. Semi-nomadic bands were forced into a seasonal cycle of hunting and collecting by the relatively rainless environment. As the hot Hypsithermal wore on, however, their efficiency at collecting plant foods began to outweigh their hunting prowess, with an increasing amount of settling down; seasonal camps took on the appearance of tiny villages. As the result of systematic exploitation and selection of certain kinds of plants, especially of such wild grasses as teosinte, vegetable foods and their energy were tamed and captured. According to present evidence, the process began with the bottle gourd, which may have been an accidental introduction, and squash, followed by beans and chile peppers. Maize was most likely domesticated before 5000 BCE, although at that time it hardly resembled the giant hybrid plants of modern Iowa cornfields. Other domesticated food plants are much later and a few, for example the peanut, were probably disseminated to Mexico from South America in post-Archaic times.

By the time of the first village-farming cultures, at the onset of the Formative period, many of the features of settled life were already present: all the important domesticates, the milling stones and *manos* on which maize was prepared, baskets, nets, cordage, mats, and apparently even wattle-and-daub houses. With the elaboration of pottery, and with the increased productivity of maize at this great transition, the stage was set for a way of life that has remained unaltered to this day in some rural parts of Mexico.

Chapter 4

The Formative Period: Early Villagers

In the late nineteenth century, there was no idea at all of the historical sequence in pre-Spanish Mexico. Of course, everyone knew perfectly well that the Aztecs were quite late, and that they had spoken of an earlier people called the Toltecs. There was also a vague feeling that the great ruins of Teotihuacan were somehow the products of an even earlier people—but that was about all. Imagine the delight, then, of Mexican antiquarians when there began to appear in their collections little hand-made clay figurines, of a vivid and amusing style totally removed from that of the mold-made products of later civilizations in the Basin of Mexico. Most astonishing was their obvious antiquity, for some had been recovered from deposits underlying the Pedregal (the lava covering much of the southwestern part of the Basin). Scholars, prone to labels, immediately named the culture that had produced the figurines, and the very abundant pottery associated with it, "Archaic."

It was not very long before the "Archaic," or something like it, was turning up all over Mexico and Central America, wherever, in fact, the archaeological spade went deep enough. Similar materials were found even in South America: in Peru, along the waterways of the Amazon basin, and on the Caribbean coast of Venezuela. On the basis of this distribution, Herbert Spinden in 1917 proposed that there was an "Archaic" foundation underlying all the civilizations of the Western Hemisphere; a unitary culture that had originated with the supposed first domestication of maize in the Basin of Mexico and had spread with that plant everywhere, bearing along the little figurines as a hallmark. Quite naturally, this idea—based on incomplete evidence—met with very determined opposition, especially by those whose subsequent delvings into "Archaic" remains had shown them the considerable diversity within this allegedly monolithic culture.

Today, the old "Archaic" is known as the Formative (or Preclassic) period. The Formative period is when farming based on maize, beans, and squash really became widespread, in the sense that villages and hamlets had sprung up everywhere in Mexico. As such, the Formative period is quite comparable to the Neolithic of Africa,

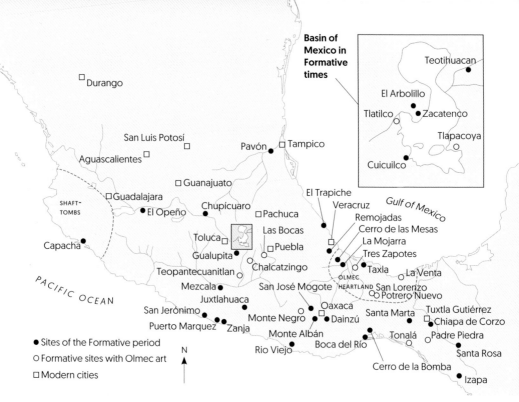

16 Sites of the Formative. The inset shows the distribution of Formative centers in the Basin of Mexico.

the Middle East, and Europe—and almost all of its associated practices, with the exception of animal husbandry, were present: the establishment of villages as compact settlements, pottery, loom weaving, working of stone by grinding as well as chipping, and the modeling of female figurines in clay.

Broadly speaking, the result of a greatly increased supply of food is the capability to feed people, and so the development of larger clusters of settlements. What had happened to bring about this increased food supply? As outlined in the previous chapter, the plants involved had already been domesticated for several millennia prior to the Formative. We may be seeing the result of a rapid increase in the size and number of kernels of the maize ear through systematic selection by observant farmers. A resulting population spiral could have suddenly filled all of central and southern Mexico, and indeed all of Mesoamerica, with land-hungry farmers, and hamlets and camps might have become permanently settled villages in almost a few generations (**figure 16**).

When did all this take place? Somewhat arbitrarily, it must be admitted, we set the earlier limits of the Formative at the first appearance of pottery in abundance, about 1800 BCE, according to radiocarbon dates. The later boundary of this period is more problematic. In the lowland Maya area, the first carved and dated monuments appear in around 250 CE, and this is usually taken as the beginning of the Classic throughout eastern Mesoamerica. In central Mexico, however, the Classic is initiated in around 150 CE, when Teotihuacan reached urban proportions; we shall adopt the latter date as the termination of the Formative. These dates therefore span some nineteen-and-a-half centuries.

Archaeologists generally agree that the Formative period can be divided into three parts: Early, from 1800 to 1000 BCE; Middle, from 1000 to 400 BCE; and Late, from 400 BCE to 150 CE. It is also increasingly apparent, as we shall see, that both village cultures and more complex social formations can be detected in all three subperiods. The emerging picture is far more intricate than could have been imagined fifty or even thirty years ago.

The Early Formative in Chiapas

The Early Formative period (c. 1800–1000 BCE) marks the first appearance of pottery, and the transition to more expansive village settlements. Some of the best information on this period in Mexico comes from the Olmec area (see Chapter 5), but important information is also found in Oaxaca (see p. 40) and Chiapas. We encountered the latter in Chapter 3, in the Santa Marta cave that included archaeological remains of pottery as well as the pollen of maize and other plants, set above preceding Archaic stratigraphic layers.

In the Soconusco region, the broad, Pacific coastal plain of southeastern Chiapas neighboring Guatemala, the oldest Formative cultures of all have been revealed by archaeological work, beginning with the Barra culture, and continuing through the complex and elaborate Ocós culture (these have been treated separately in *The Maya*). We now know that the Early Formative occupation of Chiapa de Corzo (**figure 17**) is an extension of developments by the probably Mixe-Zoquean-speaking inhabitants of Soconusco.

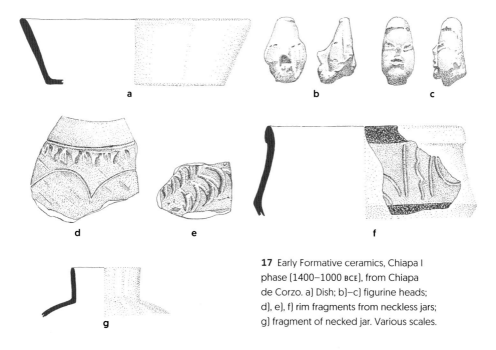

17 Early Formative ceramics, Chiapa I phase (1400–1000 BCE), from Chiapa de Corzo. a) Dish; b)–c) figurine heads; d), e), f) rim fragments from neckless jars; g) fragment of necked jar. Various scales.

Knowledge of the Early Formative in Chiapas began in the 1950s with the interest of the New World Archaeological Foundation (NWAF) in Chiapa de Corzo. Excavations conducted at that site, lying in the center of the dry Grijalva Depression of Chiapas, have disclosed no fewer than eighteen successive occupations from the earliest times to the present. For much of its history, the Grijalva drainage basin seems to have been little more than a buffer region between the Maya to the east and other cultures to the west, south, and north. In the Formative period, however, each of several distinct cultures was linked to other more distant village cultures, chiefdoms, and even states in southeastern Mexico and the Maya area.

Early Formative Villages in Oaxaca

The Central Valleys of Oaxaca are famous for being the homeland of the Zapotec people and the location of the remarkable Monte Albán culture from later periods, but it is also a region with rich evidence of Early Formative villages. The Central Valleys consist of three broad alluvial extensions known as the Etla, Tlacolula, and Zimatlan valleys. It was once thought that prior to 500 BCE, the portion where these valleys converge had a lake, and that therefore no earlier cultural remains would ever be found. This has been totally disproved by the large-scale University of Michigan archaeological-ecological project, directed by Kent Flannery, which has shown that there was always a river system here, and never a lacustrine habitat. The Flannery group has uncovered a cultural sequence extending all the way from the earliest preceramic Archaic right through to what is known as the Danibaan phase (550–300 BCE).

Survey and excavations carried out by the Michigan archaeologists have identified seventeen permanent settlements from 1400 to 1150 BCE, known as the Tierras Largas phase, but almost all of these are little more than hamlets of ten or fewer households. The most substantial settlement in the Valley of Oaxaca at that time was San José Mogote, located in the Etla arm of the valley, which at that time ranked as a small village of about 150 persons, sharing a small, lime-plastered public building. The villagers grew maize and cultivated avocados, collected wild plant foods, and hunted deer, cottontail rabbits, and other game.

By 1150 to 850 BCE, known as the San José phase, San José Mogote had grown into a village of 80 to 120 households covering about 50 acres (20 hectares), with an estimated population of 400 to 600 persons. Carbonized seeds recovered by the flotation method show that a number of crops were raised, probably on the high alluvium: maize, chile peppers, squashes, and possibly the avocado (although this may have been traded in from the lowlands). Our old friend teosinte grew in corn-fields and crossed with local maize, either by accident or design.

San José Mogote included bell-shaped pits, which here, as elsewhere in Formative Mesoamerica, are associated with household clusters. Food storage was probably the main function of such pits; many could have held a metric ton of maize, and if capped with a flat rock, might have inhibited insect growth through lack of oxygen. As they "soured" or otherwise lost their usefulness for preservation of grain, they were employed for other purposes, such as the storage of household items and implements, for refuse disposal, or even as burial places.

The only domestic animals eaten were dogs—the principal source of meat for much of Formative Mesoamerica—and turkeys, which were understandably rare because that familiar bird consumes considerable quantities of corn and is therefore expensive to raise. Wild animals in the San José Mogote diet were cottontail rabbits, deer, and peccary, which were hunted on the mountain slopes, an area that also produced acorns and black walnuts.

Houses were rectangular and about 20 ft (6 m) long, with slightly sunken floors of clay covered with river sand. The sides were of vertical canes held between wooden posts, and were daubed with mud, then white-washed; roofs were thatched. Sleeping arrangements were typically Mesoamerican: the people slept on mats rolled out on the floor. Within houses, clear signs of labor division are apparent; concentrations of bone needles, deer-bone cornhuskers, and spindle whorls made from potsherds were separated from areas of chipped-stone debris, stone burins, and drills used in the manufacture of shell and mica ornaments.

Not all households were alike in status. Some houses, for instance, specialized in the manufacture of small, flat mirrors made of magnetite, an iron ore that takes a high polish. The concentration of magnetite mirrors—an item rich in symbolic prestige because it was connected, as we shall see, with the burgeoning and contemporary Olmec civilization of the Gulf Coast—was unequal across the village. There was a marked degree of social differentiation in the goods accompanying burials; high-status individuals tended to have such burial offerings as mirrors, cut shell, jade labrets and earspools, and above all, gray or white pottery vessels with Olmec-style designs. This was no egalitarian society, and bore a marked Olmec imprint, a state of affairs that we shall find repeated for Tlatilco, in the Basin of Mexico.

The Site of Tlatilco

Evidence from excavations in the Basin of Mexico makes clear that some settlements had taken precedence over others in both social rank and in economic advantage. Here, the key site for the Early Formative is Tlatilco, which came to light in 1936 during excavations carried out by brickworkers—not, alas, by archaeologists—digging for clay. Today, the site is transformed into an extensive industrial zone of factories and warehouses, surrounded by dense, low-income urbanism. In actuality, only a tiny fraction of Tlatilco was ever cleared under scientific conditions.

Settled by about 1300 BCE, Tlatilco was a very sizable village (or small town) sprawling over about 160 acres (65 hectares). Located to the west of the great lake on a small stream, it was not very far removed from the lakeshore, where fishing and the snaring of birds could be pursued. The Tlatilco refuse includes the bones of

18 Sub-floor burials with offerings of pottery
bottles, bowls, dishes, and figurines at Tlatilco,
Early Formative period, 1500–1200 BCE.

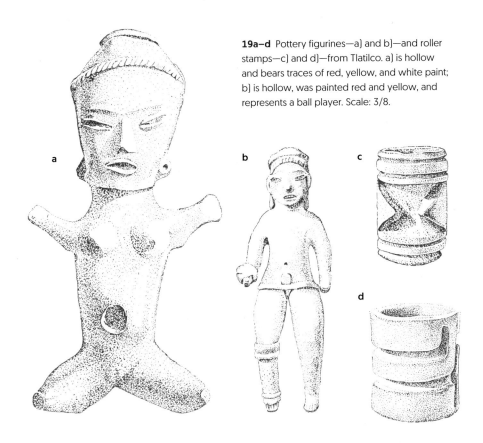

19a–d Pottery figurines—a) and b)—and roller stamps—c) and d)—from Tlatilco. a) is hollow and bears traces of red, yellow, and white paint; b) is hollow, was painted red and yellow, and represents a ball player. Scale: 3/8.

deer and waterfowl, while represented in the potter's art are armadillos, opossum, wild turkeys, bears, frogs, rabbits, fish, ducks, and turtles. Conspicuously present in those parts of the site actually excavated by archaeologists were the outlines of underground, bell-shaped pits. They were filled with dark earth, charcoal, ashes, figurine and pottery fragments, animal bones, and lumps of burned clay from the walls of pole-and-thatch houses; as in Oaxaca, they must have served originally for the storage of grain belonging to various households.

No fewer than 340 burials were uncovered by archaeologists at Tlatilco, but there must have been many hundreds more—perhaps a thousand—destroyed by brickworkers. All these were extended skeletons accompanied by the most lavish offerings, especially by figurines, which only rarely appear as burial furniture in Formative-period Mexico (**figure 18**).

There are two sorts of figurines: one that is sizable and hollow, and painted red (**figures 19a, 19b**), and the other small, solid, and of exceptionally delicate and accomplished workmanship. The latter usually represent females with little more to wear than paint applied in patterns—probably using the clay roller stamps that have been found in the excavations (**figures 19c, 19d**)—although some are attired in what would seem to be grass skirts. Here we encounter males as well, clothed in breechclouts. What an extraordinary glimpse of the life of these Formative-period people is provided in their figurines! We see women affectionately carrying children

20, 21 Pottery figurines of a ballplayer (LEFT) and a two-faced female. Tlatilco, Basin of Mexico. Early Formative period. Hts 2.7 in. and 3.7 in. (6.7 cm and 9.5 cm) respectively.

or dogs; dancers, some with rattles around the legs; acrobats and contortionists; and couples on couches. Many figurines show players wearing the hand and knee protection that was required in the ritual sport of the ball courts, which becomes so prominent in later periods (**figure 20**).

A distinctly innovative streak appears in the art of the inhabitants of Tlatilco, possessed by a psychological bent that delighted in conceptual representations. To illustrate this point, one might mention such figures as two-headed persons, or heads with three eyes, two noses, and two mouths (**figure 21**); hunchbacks; scary and sometimes-masked individuals who may be shamans; and many other singular conditions. Many actual clay masks have been found, of the most puzzling appearance; a few of these are split vertically into two distinct faces, one of which might be a skull, for instance, and the other a gesturing face with protruding tongue. It should be noted here that dualism—the unity of such basically opposed principles as life and death—constitutes the very foundation of the later religions of Mexico, no matter how great their complexity. Here we see the origin of the concept.

The pottery of Tlatilco bears a vague relation to the later peasant wares of El Arbolillo and Zacatenco, but there the resemblance ends (**figure 22**). Within the bounds of the Formative-period tradition of plastic decoration and the restrained use of color, the potters of this village made ceramics that are among the most aesthetically satisfying ever produced in ancient Mexico. Forms include bowls, neckless jars, long-necked bottles, little spouted trays (possibly for libations), bowls and jars with three tall feet, and, most peculiarly, jars with spouts that resemble stirrups.

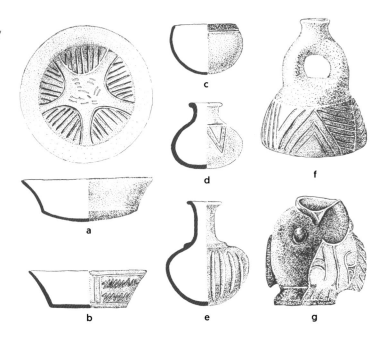

22 Representative pottery vessels from Tlatilco, Early Formative period. a) Polished brown bowl with "sunburst" striations on the interior; b) rocker-stamped dish; c) red-rimmed bowl; d)–e) necked jars; f) black stirrup-spout jar; g) black effigy in the shape of a fish, polished in zones. Scale: 1/5.

One or two colors of slip, such as red and white, are sometimes applied; colors and all kinds of roughening of the surface are confined to definite areas of the vessel by broad, grooved outlines. Particularly favored were contrasting zones of matt and polished surfaces, as well as zoned rocker-stamping. Such designs as stylized caiman paws were carried out by cutting away part of the surface; the deep areas were often filled with bright-red pigment after firing.

There was great excitement in archaeological circles when the Tlatilco complex came to light, for something resembling it was already known elsewhere— thousands of miles to the south, in Peru. There also, in the very earliest civilization of the South American continent, the Chavín culture (c. 900–200 BCE), were found such peculiar pottery shapes as stirrup spouts and long-necked bottles, associated with such singular techniques as rocker stamping and red-filled excising, as well as roller seals, figurines of Mexican appearance, and split-face dualism. A chance resemblance or not?

Early editions of this book leaned heavily toward the idea that such resemblances were the result of Mexican intrusion on the north coast of Peru, but this now seems unlikely. There is an overwhelming body of evidence that points to an independent evolution of ceremonial architecture, art, and therefore civilization in Peru. If there were intercontinental interaction at such an early time, it might well have been cultural spread to both areas from the lowland Pacific coastal area of Ecuador, where such indications of settled life as substantial villages, ceramics, and maize agriculture extend back beyond 3000 BCE. Two finds in western Mexico suggest that such was the case. At the heavily looted site of Capacha, in Colima, Isabel Kelly unearthed grave goods that are almost certainly coeval with Tlatilco; these emphasize pottery bottles and stirrup spouts, forms that point to an

Ecuadorian origin. An elaborate tomb in El Opeño, in Michoacan, has very similar ceramics with a radiocarbon date of about 1300 BCE.

On the other hand, it is certain that domesticated maize was transmitted to Peru from the north, and only a few South American specialists are opposed to the idea that Early Formative iconography—focused upon the awesome images of the jaguar, caiman, and harpy eagle—was shared through diffusion between the two areas. It must be admitted, however, that the conclusive evidence bearing on this most important problem of long-range interaction in the hemisphere has yet to be gathered.

There is another curious element in the burial offerings of Tlatilco, namely, the presence in a minority of burials of a distinct art style known to have originated at the same time in the swampy jungles of the Gulf Coast. This style, called "Olmec," was produced by the first complex culture of Mesoamerica, and its iconography, which often represents a crying baby, is unmistakably apparent in some of the figurines and pottery. It is highly probable that these objects were actually made by potters at the vast site of San Lorenzo in Veracruz, and exported to Tlatilco. It is clear that the Tlatilco people had greater wealth and social complexity than their contemporaries in the Basin of Mexico. The great expert on the pre-Spanish art of Mexico, Miguel Covarrubias, reasoned that this was the result of an influx of Olmec aristocrats from the eastern lowlands. This may possibly have been so, but it is equally likely that these villagers were a favorably placed people under heavy influence from "missionaries" spreading the Olmec tradition, or a nascent elite emulating a foreign prestigious ideology, without a necessary movement of populations. But more about the Olmecs in the next chapter.

Established Villages of the Middle Formative

Let us turn now from the Early Formative to the somewhat incomplete information that is at hand for the villages in the Basin of Mexico during the Middle Formative (c. 1000–400 BCE). A word of caution, however: because of our first knowledge of these sites, the impression has been given that the Basin had more ancient Formative beginnings than elsewhere. On the contrary, the Basin probably remained inhabited by small agricultural villages and hamlets until the Classic period, when it became and stayed the center of urban life. Notwithstanding its later social complexity, the Basin was then a prosperous but provincial region, which occasionally received or emulated new items that were developed elsewhere.

Middle Formative villages fringed the placid waters of the great lake of the Basin of Mexico, which was once more fully expanded. Their remains are now swallowed up by the urban sprawl of Mexico City. From the reed-covered marshes, abounding in waterfowl, across the rich, soft soils in the bottomlands of the Basin, to the forested hills populous with deer, this was an environment favorable in the extreme.

The first phase at the site of El Arbolillo seems to mark the initial Middle Formative occupation of the Basin. This small village was established directly on the sands of a beach fronting an arm of the great lake. Protected from the chill winds of winter by the slopes of a nearby hill, the farmers drew sustenance from the products of their fields and from the lake. That the village was occupied for many centuries is indicated by the more than 23 ft (7 m) of accumulated midden deposits cut into by the excavator, consisting of refuse, casts of maize leaves, and burned daub that had fallen from the walls of pole-and-thatch abodes.

Zacatenco, another site similarly placed on the edge of the lake, provides further evidence for the intensity of the village-farming life in the Basin. So much refuse was deposited that the villagers were forced to level it from time to time, forming terraces along which they built their wattle-and-daub houses. They were farmers, but the chase also provided much food for the villagers, as is well documented in the immense quantities of bones from deer and aquatic birds in the refuse. They hunted with small lance points chipped from obsidian, a hard, black volcanic glass worked with ease but requiring much skill. Deer provided not only meat but also hides, which were cleaned of fat with little obsidian scrapers, and bones from which were fashioned awls and bodkins (tools for working baskets and skins). Within each house, the ground maize was soaked on the familiar quern, although for some reason this was absent at El Arbolillo. For cooking and storage, the villagers had a pleasant but undistinguished pottery, usually reddish brown in color and finely burnished. A somewhat elaborate type was produced at El Arbolillo: little three-legged bowls, smoked black, with red paint rubbed into geometric designs incised on the surface.

At these two sites, and elsewhere in the Basin, the midden deposits are stuffed with thousands of fragments of clay figurines, all female, providing a lively view of the costume of the day, or its lack. Although nudity was apparently the rule, these representations have elaborate face and body painting in black, white, and red; the depicted headdresses and coiffures were very elaborate, with wraparound turbans being most common. The technique of manufacture was similar to that with which gingerbread figures are made today, features being indicated by a combination of punching and filleting. Significantly, no recognizable depictions of gods or goddesses have ever been identified in these villages, suggesting the possibility that the only cult was that of the figurines, which may have been objects of household devotion in the same manner as the Roman *lares*, perhaps concerned with the fertility of the crops.

The dead were buried under the floors of houses—the usual fashion in Mesoamerica—but also occasionally together in cemeteries. With knees drawn up against the chest, and wrapped in the mat upon which he or she had slept in life, the deceased was placed in a simple grave dug in the sand, although sometimes this was outlined and covered by stone slabs. A few pots or implements left in the grave, and a jade bead occasionally placed in the mouth, tell something of a belief in an existence after death. Child mortality was high; a good percentage of the skeletons found are of immature individuals.

23 Polychrome tripod jar, Chupícuaro culture, Guanajuato. Late Formative period. Ht 5.5 in. (14 cm).

24 [RIGHT] Pottery figurine of a pregnant woman, Chupícuaro culture, Guanajuato. Late Formative period. Ht about 4.2 in. (10.6 cm).

Late Formative Cultures of the Central Highlands

The isolation of the Basin of Mexico from what was happening in the rest of Mesoamerica became even more pronounced in the period from 400 BCE to 150 CE, known as the Late Formative. The mainstream of social complexity in that period was running through the lowlands of eastern Mexico and up the river valleys into the southern highlands and southeastern part of Mesoamerica, but not into the Basin of Mexico. This isolation holds true for much of the central highland region, except where direct Olmec intrusions had taken place or nascent local elites were emulating the Olmec style to augment their political and economic clout.

Bright colors and an increase in the size and length of vessel feet were the concern of the potter in Late Formative times. The predilection toward the use of two or more colors in ceramic decoration is well illustrated by Chupícuaro, the burial ground of a village that lay above the Lerma River in the state of Guanajuato, about 80 miles (130 km) northwest of the Basin of Mexico. While the Chupícuaro complex is widespread in the region, until scientific excavations it was known, like Tlatilco, only from commercial pot-hunting. The skeletons of 390 individuals were found, almost all of whom had been laid on their backs in simple graves with abundant offerings of pottery, figurines, jade, and various clay objects. Later cultures believed that the owner's dog would help her or his soul to cross a river in order to reach its final resting place, and we find at Chupícuaro that dogs were also interred, many of them with great care. The pottery vessels found in the cemetery are in both shape and decoration quite exuberant. In form one encounters bowls with all sorts of supports: short tripods, very long and attenuated tripods, swollen feet in the shape of breasts, and pedestal bases (**figure 23**). There are a few stirrup-spout

25 View of a portion of the circular temple platform at Cuicuilco, Basin of Mexico. Late Formative period.

jars, the last time this unique type is seen in Mexico, although it continued to enjoy great popularity in Peru until European colonial days. Vessel painting is lively, the slips used most often being red on buff, red and black on buff, or red and brown on buff, in finely proportioned, abstract designs that appear to have been derived from textiles. Little handmade, clay figurines representing women were likewise deposited into the graves; these are shown nude, with slanting eyes and coiffures that were built up from clay strips (**figure 24**).

The most notable innovation in the Late Formative of central Mexico was the appearance of the temple-pyramid. The earliest temples of the highlands were thatch-roof, perishable structures not unlike the houses of the common people, erected within the community on low earthen platforms faced with sun-hardened clay. There are a few slight indications that some such platforms once existed at Tlatilco. By the Late Formative, however, they had become almost universal, as the nuclei of enlarged villages and even towns. Toward the end of the period, clay facings for the platforms were occasionally replaced by retaining walls of undressed stones coated with a thick layer of stucco, and the substructures themselves had become greatly enlarged, sometimes rising in several stages or tiers. Here we have, then, a definite shift from small villages of farmers with household figurine cults only, to hierarchical societies with rulers who could call the populace to build and maintain sizable religious establishments.

The grandiosity of some of these substructures can be seen at Cuicuilco, located to the south of Mexico City near the National University, in an area covered by the Pedregal—a grim landscape of broken, soot-black lava with a sparse flora eking out its existence in rocky crevices. The principal feature of Cuicuilco is a round platform (**figure 25**), 387 ft (118 m) in diameter and rising in four inwardly sloping tiers to a present height of 75 ft (23 m). Two ramps placed on either side of the platform provide access to the summit, which was crowned at one time by a cone-like construction that brought the total height to about 90 ft (27 m). Faced with volcanic rocks, the interior of the surviving structure is filled with sand and rubble, with a total volume of over 2 million cu. ft (60,000 cu. m).

It is little wonder that Cuicuilco was once thought to be of great, deep antiquity, for the main structure, excavated many years ago, is surrounded and partly covered by lava that had flowed down from Xictli volcano, looming on the western horizon above the Basin floor. Competent authorities made estimates for the age of the flow, varying anywhere from 8,500 to 30,000 years. But this was in the pre-radiocarbon era, and long prior to George Vaillant's careful work on the cultural stratigraphy of the Basin.

On the basis of the associated ceramics and figurines, quantities of which are found beneath the Pedregal, Cuicuilco is clearly Late Formative, as confirmed by radiocarbon dates. The doom of Cuicuilco was set some time around 100 CE, an end that must have been dramatic. The young Xictli first sent out dust and ashes that fell in quantity on the site, then the great eruptions themselves began, molten lava pouring out over the southwestern margin of the Basin. All must have fled in panic from the region. Did the inhabitants have any premonitions of the final cataclysm? One might think so, for prominent among the remains of their culture are clay incense burners in the form of Xiuhtecuhtli, who was Fire God and lord of the volcanoes among the ancient Mexicans.

In lieu of extensive excavations underneath the lava, it is difficult to be precise about the size and function of such a regional center as Cuicuilco. On the basis of his unrivaled knowledge of the Basin of Mexico, however, William Sanders ascribed to it a population of 20,000, the chief center of a total Basin population of perhaps 140,000 people. Regardless of the uncertainty about Cuicuilco, it surely presaged the great Teotihuacan civilization of the Classic period (Chapter 6).

Thanks to another volcanic event, there is a spectacularly preserved Late Formative village at Tetimpa, Puebla, on the northeastern flank of the Popocatepetl volcano. Unlike Cuicuilco, which was buried under a lava flow, Tetimpa was encased in ash falls, preserving much of what the villagers left in haste as Popocatepetl erupted around 100 CE. Archaeologists Patricia Plunket and Gabriela Uruñuela discovered the still-furrowed cornfields under the ash, as well as the houses and domestic artifacts of the farmers who tilled these fields. The house compounds consist of two or three small structures, carefully set at right angles to each other around a central patio. An altar was often placed in the center of the patio, with a volcano effigy, simply carved figure, or plain andesite stela on the summit. The buildings themselves consist of wattle-and-daub structures built on a stone platform. Most importantly, the platforms use the *talud-tablero* form, consisting of a sloping wall surmounted by a horizontal panel, which later becomes an architectural marker of the Early Classic metropolis, Teotihuacan (see p. 115).

The Mezcala Puzzle

Although a rich source for portable jade objects in Olmec style, the rather dry basin of the upper Balsas or Mezcala River, in the state of Guerrero, is one of the archaeologically least-known regions in Mexico. During the Middle and Late Formative, and perhaps developing out of an Olmec substratum, appears the style called Mezcala, known largely from carved pieces of andesite and serpentine recovered by illegal excavations. These objects are highly abstract, usually representations of human figures recalling in pose and technique the simpler small productions of Teotihuacan, which they may foreshadow (**figure 26**). As well as these, miniature facades of colonnaded temples are also known (**figure 27**), and a few effigies of such natural objects as conch shells.

The exact dating and cultural context of Mezcala art have long been unknown, since the overwhelming majority of Mezcala objects come from large-scale looting by the local population; in fact, this practice is known to go all the way back to the Aztecs, as many objects in this style were recovered in dedicatory caches found in archaeological investigations of the Great Temple of Tenochtitlan, as we shall see in Chapter 10. This chronological puzzle was at last solved through the field project carried out by Louise Paradis of the University of Montreal; during the 1989–90 digging season, she excavated an in situ cache of Mezcala objects at the site of Ahuinahuac, just north of the Mezcala River, in a context radiocarbon-dated to between 500 and 200 BCE.

26, 27 [LEFT] Standing figures, 300–100 BCE. Stone, ht 8.1 in. (20.5 cm); marble, ht 10.5 in. (26.6 cm); marble, ht 7.3 in. (18.5 cm). [RIGHT] Stone model of a temple. Ht 4.9 in. (12.5 cm). Both Late Formative period.

28 Pottery-house group from Ixtlan del Río, Nayarit. The base has a diameter of 20.8 in. (53 cm). The exact chronological placement of this is unknown, as so often with western-Mexican hand-modeled figures and groups, but it is probably Late Formative. Here, we see four thatch-roof houses on platforms arranged around a circular plaza, in the center of which is a four-tiered, circular platform. Among the fifty figures are musicians playing trumpets and rasps, two couples, water carriers, children, dogs, and five men gathered around a woman.

The Shaft-Tomb Art of Western Mexico and the Teuchitlan Tradition

The marshy highland area of Jalisco was rich for the development of civilization, with significant mineral riches (obsidian, greenstone, and salt) and a fertile agricultural area covering several interlocking lake basins. By 1500 BCE, shaft tombs with offerings can be found at nearby El Opeño in northwest Michoacan. By 300 BCE, this same burial type is associated with a specific circular architecture, in which a central circular altar is ringed by platforms surmounted by residential or temple structures.

Until recently, the widespread looting of archaeological sites in this area left us woefully ignorant of the cultural and historical context of this culture, now called the Teuchitlan tradition. Three decades of work by Phil Weigand and his associates have found monumental circles distributed around the Volcano of Tequila in the state of Jalisco, which forms the heartland of the Teuchitlan tradition. These concentric circles are found illustrated in the tomb offerings, in which the circles form the stage for elaborate feasting ceremonies and other rituals. The actual circles are often associated with monumental ball courts, the latter also illustrated in the related ceramic sculptures, in some of the most lifelike renderings of the athletic ceremony to come out of Mesoamerica. It is also during this period that a remarkably vivid

29 Pottery dog wearing a mask with a human face, from Colima, western Mexico. Late Formative period. Ht 8.5 in. (21.6 cm).

tradition of portraiture develops in the region, often showing rulers and venerated ancestors in seated postures with accoutrements of rank and ritual.

An earlier school of thought held that this shaft-tomb sculpture was little more than a kind of genre art: realistic, anecdotal, and with no more religious meaning than a Dutch interior. This view was vigorously challenged by the ethnologist Peter Furst, who had worked closely with the contemporary Huichol groups of Nayarit, almost certainly the descendants of the people who made the tomb figures. Among the Huichol and their close relatives, the Cora, religious practitioners are always shamans, powerful specialists who effect cures and maintain the well-being of their people by battling against demons and evil shamans. Furst noted that the warriors with clubs from Nayarit and Jalisco tombs are down on one knee, the typical fighting stance of the shaman. He interprets the Nayarit house models not just as two-story village dwellings, but also as chthonic dwellings: above would be the house of the living, and below would be the house of the dead (**figure 28**). Such a belief is consonant not only with Huichol ideas about death and the soul, but also with the religious ideas of such Southwestern groups as the Hopi. It also agrees with the archaeological evidence, for these "houses" may be identified as the funerary structures ringing the monumental circular architecture.

Furst's hypothesis that the symbolism of shaft-tomb art "conforms closely to characteristically shamanistic initiatory, funerary, and death-and-rebirth beliefs and rituals" is entirely sound considering the funerary context of these sculptures. Dogs, as we have seen with Chupícuaro, had a special mortuary significance in ancient Mexico, and one fine Colima example even wears a human mask (**figure 29**)!

At the same time, Mark Miller Graham has argued that many of these figures are rulers, and not exclusively shamanistic practitioners. Graham is certainly right to call our attention to the political meanings of these figures, for they can no longer be conceived as products of a village culture with little political hierarchy.

A monumental shaft tomb was scientifically excavated by Lorenza López Mestas Camberos and Jorge Ramos de la Vega at Huitzilapa, Jalisco, the first of its kind to be so explored (**figure 30**). The shaft cut down 21 ft (7.6 m) through the center of an elite residential complex. At the bottom of the shaft were two chambers, each containing three individuals and a rich array of offerings. Five of the six individuals exhibited a congenital hereditary condition (the fusion of cervical vertebrae), indicating a close biological relationship. One of the members of this lineage group, a forty-five-year-old male, was treated with more deference, however, as witnessed by the presence of more exotics, especially conch shells from both the Caribbean and Pacific Coasts, along with numerous other objects of shell, greenstone, and quartz. Given that this was seemingly the only shaft tomb constructed at Huitzilapa,

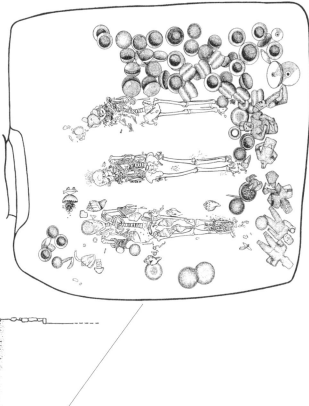

30 Section and plan of the north chamber of a shaft-tomb burial from Huitzilapa, Jalisco. A rich array of grave offerings, including ceramics, shell, and textiles, surround burials from the same elite family. The finery found on the lower skeleton includes cut-shell jewelry and several elaborately decorated conch shells. Anthropomorphic ceramic sculptures, now toppled, once stood guard at the feet of the corpse. Late Formative period.

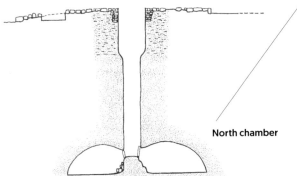

North chamber

31 Pottery figurine of a man striking a turtle-shell with a deer antler, from Nayarit. The face and body have been decorated with polychrome paints. Percussion instruments of this sort are still in use in some rural communities of Mexico. Probably Late Formative period. Ht 15 in. (38 cm).

32 Pottery figurine of a seated person holding a dish, from Jalisco, western Mexico. Probably Late Formative period. Ht 20 in. (50.8 cm).

and that this figure was obviously of higher rank within the community, he was likely a ruler of the site.

All the other individuals, two adult females and three adult males, appear to have died earlier and were prepared and preserved as funerary bundles until the death of the ruler, at which time all six figures were deposited into the shaft tomb.

Outside the heartland, in the states of Jalisco, Colima, and Nayarit, only much smaller shaft tombs and shallow pit burials are found, also with ceramic sculptures and other offerings, suggesting that there was a regional hierarchy centered on the Volcano of Tequila region (**figures 31, 32**). A vast relocation of much of the population to the central area occurred around 200 CE, at the dawn of the Classic period. After this concentration of settlement around the Volcano of Tequila, the shaft tombs become much smaller and simpler, with more emphasis placed on the monumental circular architecture as a sign of power and prestige. By 400 to 700 CE, known as the Teuchitlan I phase, a more complex Classic-period culture is now emerging from the archaeological record, one in which 10 sq. miles (24 sq. km) of ritual and residential precincts covered the central area, alongside over 115 sq. miles (300 sq. km) of intensive agricultural modifications, including extensive terraces and *chinampas*. Between 700 and 900 CE, the Teuchitlan tradition went into decline, signaled by the cessation in the construction of circular building and the introduction, on the edges of the old sacred precincts, of a new architecture based on right-angled buildings. Metallurgy was introduced into western Mexico by 600 CE, and from there to the rest of Mesoamerica. Given the specific technologies used by the west Mexicans, it is almost certain that knowledge of metalworking arose from long-distance contact with much older Central and South American traditions.

Chapter 5

The Formative Period: Early Civilizations

Defining a Civilization

The change in the arts and technology that is implied by the word "civilization" is usually bound up with the idea of urbanism. When we think of cities, we think of such densely occupied metropolises as New York City, Paris, ancient Rome, or Beijing, with street plans often laid out on a grid pattern. Such cities did exist in ancient Mexico—Classic Teotihuacan and Aztec Tenochtitlan come immediately to mind. But elsewhere in pre-Spanish Mesoamerica, especially in the lowlands, urbanism took a very different form: there, substantial populations were spread out in a low-density settlement pattern focused upon one or more temple/administrative complexes, with causeways linking different parts of the city and an intricate network of pathways instead of streets and avenues. This pattern was present among the Olmecs, as we shall see, and became typical of the later Classic Maya as well as the Zapotecs. As a result, the great Maya cities that were once relegated to the status of near-empty "ceremonial centers" are now considered to have been truly urban.

Most of the cultures of Mesoamerica eventually developed systems of writing. As we shall see, Mesoamerican writing has very early origins, appearing in a few areas by the Middle or Late Formative period, and in the case of the Olmecs, possibly in the Early Formative.

"By their works ye shall know them." Archaeologists tend to judge cultures as civilizations by the presence of great public works and unified monumental art styles. Life became organized under the direction of an elite class, usually strengthened by writing and other forms of bureaucratic administration. Early civilizations were qualitatively different from the village cultures that preceded them, and with which in some cases they co-existed. The kind of art produced by these first complex societies reveals the sort of compulsive force that held them together, namely, a state religion in which the political leaders were the intermediaries between gods and humans. The monumental sculpture of these ancient civilizations therefore tends to be loaded with religious symbolism, calculated to strike awe in the breast of the beholder.

Unless the written record is extraordinarily explicit about state functions, which it seldom is in Mesoamerica, it is extremely difficult to detect the first appearance of the state from archaeological evidence alone. A state is characterized not only by a centralized bureaucratic apparatus in the hands of an elite class, but also by the element of coercion: a standing army and usually a policing force. Mesoamerican archaeology provides plentiful data on the emergence of elite, high-status groups, but not very much on warfare or internal control, although both were surely present for over 2,000 years prior to the arrival of the Spaniards. In the absence of inscriptions with explicit administrative records, the argument over whether such cultures as the Olmec had states may never be resolved.

As noted on p. 57, there was considerable variation in the extent of urbanism among the later cultures of Mesoamerica, from those in which an elite center was served by low-density populations, often living in villages scattered through the countryside, to those with substantial cities comparable to those of pre-industrial Europe and China. But all of them had administrative hierarchies, and rulers who could call on the peasantry as corvée labor to build and maintain the temples and palaces, and for food to support the non-farming specialists, whether kings, priests, artisans, or artists. In conjunction with an elaborate ritual calendar, writing sprang up early to ensure the proper operation of this process, and to boast of real or fictitious great events in the life of the elite. Furthermore, markets were held at regular intervals in these centers, in which all sorts of food and manufactures, of hinterland and center, changed hands. This is the fundamental Mesoamerican pattern, established in the Formative, and persisting until Conquest times in many areas.

The Olmecs

The most ancient Mesoamerican civilization is that called "Olmec." For many years, archaeologists had known about small jade sculptures and other objects in a distinct and powerful style that emphasized human infants with snarling, jaguar-like features. Most of these could be traced to the sweltering Gulf Coast plain—the region of southern Veracruz and neighboring Tabasco—just west of the Maya area. American archaeologists Marshall H. Saville and George C. Vaillant recognized the fundamental similarity of all these works, and assigned them to the "Olmeca," the "rubber people" described by Father Sahagún and his Aztec informants as inhabiting jungle country on the Gulf Coast; in this way, the name became established (**figure 33**).

33 Map of the Olmec "heartland."

Actually, nothing is known of the real people who produced Olmec art, neither the name by which they called themselves nor from where they came. Old poems in Nahuatl, recorded after the Conquest, speak of a legendary land called Tamoanchan, on the eastern sea, settled long before the founding of Teotihuacan:

> In a certain era
> which no one can reckon
> which no one can remember,
> where there was a government for a long time.[1]

This tradition is intriguing, for Tamoanchan is not a Nahuatl name but Maya, meaning "In the Land of Rain or Mist." An isolated Mayan language, Huastec, is still spoken in northern Veracruz.

One possibility is that there was an unbroken band of Mayan speech extending along the Gulf Coast all the way from the Maya area proper to the Huasteca, and that the region in which the Olmec civilization was established could, in those distant times, have been Mayan-speaking. This would suggest that the Olmec homeland was the real Tamoanchan, and that the original "Olmecs" spoke an ancient Mayan tongue.

In contradiction to this hypothesis, some compelling evidence has been advanced by the linguists Lyle Campbell and Terence Kaufman strongly suggesting that the Olmecs spoke an ancestral form of Mixe-Zoquean. There are a large number of Mixe-Zoquean loan words in other Mesoamerican languages, including Mayan. Most of these are words associated with high-status activities and ritual typical of early civilization, such as *pom* ("copal incense") and *kakaw* ("chocolate"). Although the dominant language of the Olmec area was until recently a form of Nahua, this is generally believed to be a relatively late arrival; on the other hand, Popoloca, a member of the Mixe-Zoquean family, is still spoken along the eastern slopes of the Tuxtla Mountains, in the very region from which the Olmecs obtained the basalt for their monuments. Since the Olmecs were the great, early, culture-bearing force in Mesoamerica, the case for Mixe-Zoquean is very strong.

There has been much controversy about the dating of the Olmec civilization. Its discoverer, Matthew Stirling, consistently held that it predated the Classic Maya civilization, a position that was vehemently opposed by such Mayanists as Sir Eric Thompson and Sylvanus Morley. Stirling was backed by the great Mexican scholars Alfonso Caso and Miguel Covarrubias, who held for a placement in the Formative period, primarily on the grounds that Olmec traits had appeared in sites of that period in the Basin of Mexico and in the state of Morelos (see p. 46). Time has fully borne out Stirling and the Mexican school. A long series of radiocarbon dates from the important Olmec site of La Venta spans the centuries from 1200 to 400 BCE, placing the major development of this center entirely within the Middle Formative. Another set of dates shows that the site of San Lorenzo is even older, falling within the Early Formative (1800–1000 BCE), making it contemporary with Tlatilco and other highland sites in which strong influence from San Lorenzo can be detected. There are now compelling reasons to assert that all later civilizations in southern Mesoamerica, whether Mexican or Maya, ultimately rest on an Olmec base.

The hallmark of Olmec civilization is the art style (**figure 34**). Its most unique aspect is the iconography on which it is based, through which we glimpse a powerful religion. At the core of the representational system is the emphasis on combining

34 Jade effigy axe, known as the "Kunz" axe. The combination of carving, drilling, and incising seen on this piece is characteristic of the Olmec style. Middle Formative period. When first reported (before the Olmec style was even recognized) the object was attributed to Oaxaca, but without specific provience. Many other Olmec-style objects are also known from Oaxaca. Ht 12.2 in. (31 cm).

human and animal attributes, especially those of such wild felines as jaguars, pumas, and ocelots, but also with the caiman, the harpy eagle, and the shark. In these composites, the human form is usually shown as somewhat infantile throughout life, displaying the puffy features of small, fat babies, with snarling mouths, toothless gums or long, curved fangs, and even claws. The heads are cleft at the top, symbolizing the place where corn emerges. The representations are always sexless, and they are always obese (a trait often associated with eunuchs). In one way or another, the concept of the were-jaguar is at the heart of the Olmec civilization. What was the meaning of such representations?

Covarrubias, an artist-archaeologist with a profound feeling for Mesoamerican art styles, developed a perceptive scheme to show that all the various rain deities of the Classic and Post-Classic cultures could be derived from an Olmec were-jaguar prototype. The subsequent chance find of a sizable greenstone figure near the community of Las Limas, Veracruz, shows that Olmec religion was far more complex (**figure 35**). This figure represents a young personage, holding in his arms a baby, a theme also to be seen on some Olmec stone thrones. Incised on both shoulders and both knees are the profile heads of four other Olmec gods; each of them has distinctive iconographic features, although all four have cleft heads (**figure 36**).

35, 36 Greenstone figure from Las Limas, Veracruz. (LEFT) A young man or adolescent boy holds in his arms an infant who represents the Maize God, while the adolescent's shoulders and knees are incised with the heads of four other deities (see drawings, ABOVE). Olmec culture, Middle Formative period. Ht 21.6 in. (55 cm).

37 Monuments 10 and 52 from San Lorenzo, which represent the deities of rain and maize, respectively.

Following the lead of the Las Limas figure, David Joralemon has been able to show that the Olmecs worshipped a variety of deities, only a few of whom exhibit the features of the jaguar. Representations of these deities showed them combined in a multitude of forms, or rendered from the very iconic to the highly abstract, resulting in images that bewilder the modern beholder. Thanks to iconographic studies carried out by Karl Taube, the were-jaguar infant held by the Las Limas youth has been identified as the Maize God, the most important and ubiquitous Olmec deity. Taube has also demonstrated that Covarrubias's Rain Deity hypothesis was essentially correct, with the caveat that this was only one in a large Olmec family of deities. Within this pantheon, the most important were the god of maize agriculture and the god controlling the rain upon which maize cultivation depended.

Given its singular, highly symbolic and metaphorical content, Olmec art is nevertheless "realistic" and shows a great mastery of form. On the great basalt monuments of the Olmec heartland and in other sculptures, scenes that include what are surely portraits of real persons are present; many of these are bearded. Olmec bas-reliefs are notable in the use of empty space in compositions. The combination of tension in space and the slow rhythm of the lines, which are always curved, produces the overwhelmingly monumental character of the style, no matter how small the object.

The Olmecs were, above all, carvers of stone, from the gigantic Colossal Heads, stelae (tall, flat monuments), and stone thrones of the Veracruz-Tabasco region, to finely carved jade celts, figurines, and pendants (**figure 37**). Typical is a combination of carving, drilling (using a reed or bone and wet sand), and delicate incising. Olmec sculptures are often three-dimensional, to be seen from all sides, not just from the front (**figure 38**). Very small sculptures and figurines of a beautiful blue-green jade and of serpentine were, of course, portable, so we are not always sure of the place of origin of many of these pieces. We now know that the jade was quarried in the Sierra de las Minas in Guatemala, far above the valley of the Motagua River, while the sources of serpentine lay in Oaxaca. Olmec-style objects of small size have been found over much of Mexico (**figure 39**), especially in the state of Guerrero in the

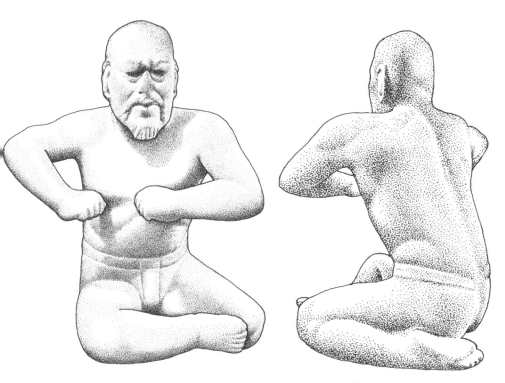

38 (ABOVE) Basalt figure of a bearded man, the so-called "Wrestler." Olmec culture, Early or Middle Formative period, Antonio Plaza, Veracruz. Ht 26 in. (66 cm).

39 Small stone figure of a woman and child, provenience unknown. Olmec style, Middle Formative period. Ht 4.5 in. (11.4 cm).

The Olmecs 63

40 Wooden mask encrusted with jade, supposedly from a cave near Iguala, Guerrero. Olmec style, Middle Formative period. Ht 7.5 in. (19 cm).

western part of the Republic, and some of these could have been carried there by trade or even by Olmec missionaries. Among these are magnificent effigy axes of jade, basalt, or other stone, some of which are so thin and unusable as axes that they must have had a ritual purpose. The gods of rain and maize are on many of these, sometimes inclining towards the feline, sometimes more anthropomorphic, along with other Olmec deities. The Olmec style was also represented in pottery bowls and figurines, and even in wood, as seen in a miraculously preserved mask with jade incrustations from a cave in Guerrero (**figure 40**), and in the offerings at El Manatí (see p. 73).

The crescent-shaped region of southern Veracruz and neighboring Tabasco that fronts the Gulf of Mexico has been justifiably called the Olmec "heartland." Here is where substantial Olmec sites and numerous stone monuments are concentrated, and here is where the core theme of Olmec art—representations of rain and maize deities—appears in its most elaborate form. There is hardly any question that the civilization had its roots and its highest expression in that zone, which is little more than 125 miles long by about 50 miles wide (200 by 80 km). The heartland—or "Olman," as Richard Diehl has dubbed it—is characterized by a very high annual rainfall (about 120 in. or 300 cm) and, before the advent of Europeans, by a very high, tropical forest cover, interspersed with flood-prone savannahs. Much of it is alluvial lowland, formed by the many rivers that meet the nearby waters of the Gulf; during the summer "wet season," these flood much of the low-lying terrain. The so-called "dry season" of the heartland is hardly that, for during the winter, cold, wet windstorms sweep down from the north, keeping the soil moist for year-round cultivation. It was in this seemingly inhospitable, but in actuality nurturing, environment that Mesoamerica's first civilization was produced.

At the western extension of the heartland rise the volcanic Tuxtla Mountains, the only source of the igneous rock with which the Olmecs fashioned enormous sculptures as well as such utilitarian artifacts as *manos* and *metates*.

The San Lorenzo Olmecs

Credit for the discovery of the Olmec civilization goes to Matthew Stirling, who explored and excavated Tres Zapotes, La Venta, and San Lorenzo during the 1930s and 1940s. In 1945, he and his wife Marion were led to the site of San Lorenzo by a report of a "stone eye" looking up from a trail. They realized that this belonged to one of the multi-ton Colossal Heads typical of Olmec culture, and excavated the site through two field seasons, during which they discovered a wealth of sculpture, much of it lying in or near the ravines that surround San Lorenzo. They were, however, able to date neither the sculpture nor the site itself (**figure 41**).

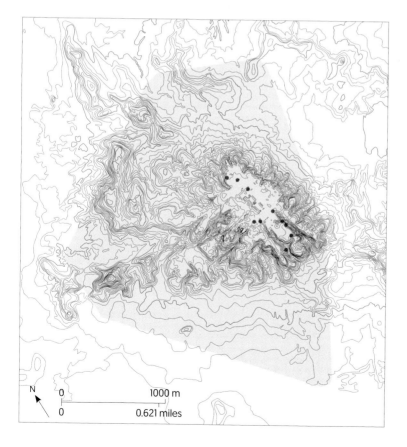

41 Map of San Lorenzo showing the maximum known extent of the settlement (light gray) and the location of Colossal Heads (black dots).

N
0   1000 m
0   0.621 miles

Convinced that San Lorenzo might hold the key to the origin of Olmec civilization, Michael D. Coe and Richard A. Diehl directed a Yale archaeological-ecological project there from 1966 to 1968. Since 1991, extensive investigations of San Lorenzo and its hinterland have been undertaken by a project directed by Ann Cyphers of Mexico's National University (UNAM).

San Lorenzo is the most important of a cluster of three interconnected sites lying near the flat bottomlands of the Coatzacoalcos River, not very far from the center of the heartland. When mapped, it turned out to be a kind of plateau or island rising about 150 ft (45 m) above the surrounding lowlands; about three-quarters of a mile (1.2 km) long in a north–south direction, excavations proved the mesa top to be artificial down to a depth of 23 ft (7 m), with long ridges jutting out on its northwest, west, and south sides. Mirror symmetry is characteristic of San Lorenzo, so that a particular feature on one ridge is mimicked on its counterpart. It is difficult to imagine what the Olmec meant by this gigantic construction of earth, clay, and other materials brought up on the backs of the peasantry, but it is possible that they intended this to be a huge animal effigy, possibly a bird flying east, but never completed because of the destruction of the site.

San Lorenzo had first been settled about 1800 BCE, perhaps by Mixe-Zoqueans from Soconusco, but by 1500 BCE had become thoroughly Olmec. For the next 500 years San Lorenzo was several times larger than any other settlement in Mesoamerica; there was in fact nothing quite like it before or during its apogee. As archaeologists John Clark and Mary Pye have observed, "San Lorenzo had no equals, only peers."

Stunning proof of this assertion was recently obtained by an UNAM site-testing program directed by Virginia Arieta and Ann Cyphers. Slightly more than

42 Artist's hypothetical reconstruction of transport of stone monuments from a source in the Tuxtla Mountains to such Olmec centers as San Lorenzo and La Venta, using balsa rafts.

2,600 cores were used to perforate the entire artificial summit, some of the terraced sides flanking the mesa top, and the periphery. It was found that the summit was where the elite lived, in houses with floors painted with red hematite, while the less prestigious and more humble bulk of the population occupied the terraces below and some of the periphery, in houses with plain floors of gravel. From this program, they have discovered that San Lorenzo, during its apogee between 1200 and 1000 BCE, covered an area of 690 hectares (1,700 acres or 2.7 sq. miles), with an estimated population averaging about 10,000 inhabitants.

San Lorenzo, therefore, was Mesoamerica's first urban civilization, and probably the very first one in all of the Americas. To keep this in perspective, at this time the lowland-dwelling Maya to the east of the Olmec heartland were pursuing a foraging way of life.

Some of the most magnificent and awe-inspiring sculptures ever discovered in Mexico were fashioned using stone technology; petrographic analysis showed them to be basalt that had been quarried from boulders on the volcanic Cerro Cintepec, in the Tuxtla Mountains, a straight-line distance of 50 miles (80 km) from San Lorenzo.

It has been suggested that the finished sculptures were dragged down to navigable streams and loaded on great balsa rafts, then floated first down to the coast of the Gulf of Mexico, then up the Coatzacoalcos River; from there, they would have had to be dragged, possibly with rollers, up ramps onto the San Lorenzo plateau (**figure 42**). Another hypothesis posits that boulders or pre-forms could have been dragged in a straight pathway from source to carving workshops while surmounting all sorts of natural obstacles. Either way, the amount of labor that must have been involved staggers the imagination.

43 (LEFT) This sensitively carved, massive sculpture was found deeply buried in Early Formative deposits at the great Olmec site of San Lorenzo, Veracruz, and is unusually well preserved. As are all other Colossal Heads, it is probably a portrait of a ruler, with helmet-like headgear.

44, 45 Monuments 4 (BELOW LEFT) and 17 (BELOW), San Lorenzo, Veracruz, shortly after excavation. These are two of the smaller Colossal Heads, wearing the typical helmet-like headgear. The nearest source of the basalt from which these were carved lies more than 50 miles (80 km) to the north. Olmec culture, Early Formative period. Hts 5 ft 5.7 in. and 5 ft 10 in. (1.67 m and 1.78 m) respectively.

46 Monument 2, Potrero Nuevo (subsidiary site of San Lorenzo), Veracruz. Two atlantean dwarfs support the top of this basalt throne. Olmec culture, Early Formative period. Ht 3 ft 1 in. (94 cm).

The more than 124 Early Formative sculptures of San Lorenzo include ten Colossal Heads of great distinction (**figures 43, 44, 45**). These heads are up to 9 ft 4 in. (2.85 m) in height and weigh up to 25 tons; it seems likely that they are all portraits of mighty Olmec rulers, with flat-faced, thick-lipped features. They wear helmet-like headgear that probably served as protection in both war and in the ceremonial game played with a rubber ball throughout Mesoamerica. Each of these rulers can be separately identified by the distinctive symbols borne by his helmet, such as jaguar paws, ropes, the head of a bird, eagle claws, or a network of strung, multi-drilled beads.

Also typical of San Lorenzo are the stone thrones: enormous basalt blocks with flat tops that may weigh up to 40 metric tons. The fronts of these have niches, in each of which sits the figure of a ruler, either holding a baby maize god in his arms (probably representing the theme of sacrifice) or holding a rope that binds captives (representing the theme of warfare to take captives for sacrifice), depicted in relief on the sides. One of San Lorenzo's finest thrones was found near the satellite site of Lomas del Zapote, and depicts two pot-bellied, atlantean dwarfs supporting the throne top with their upraised hands (**figure 46**). One royal personage was even able to have his colossal portrait fashioned from a throne recycled from a previous ruler's reign. This might mean that on the San Lorenzo summit, only

47 Stone sculptures of twin young males, which face two seated jaguar sculptures in a tableau from El Azuzul. The site functioned as a main entry on to the central plateau of San Lorenzo. Olmec culture, Early Formative period.

the current ruler's portrait could be shown publicly, with all earlier stone heads and thrones being buried when they died. Most of the Colossal Heads show deep cup-like abrasions and linear furrows, known as striations, all around, suggesting that prior to their burial, they were sources from which powerful essences were repeatedly extracted.

Sculptures could be related in elaborate tableaux, as with the four-piece ensemble uncovered at El Azuzul (**figure 47**). Here, two stunningly carved young male figures are shown kneeling before two seated jaguars. While the jaguars are slightly different in size and treatment, the two human figures resemble each other closely. Stories of twins and jaguars abound in the heroic literature of Mesoamerica, suggesting that basic elements of mythology, as well as such fundamental rites as the ball game, crystallized earliest at San Lorenzo.

In his work at San Lorenzo, Stirling had encountered trough-shaped basalt stones, which he hypothesized were fitted end-to-end to form a kind of aqueduct. In 1967, the Yale team actually came across and excavated such a system in situ (**figure 48**). This deeply buried drain line was in the southwestern portion of the site, and consisted of 560 ft (170 m) of laboriously pecked-out stone troughs fitted with basalt covers; three subsidiary lines met it from above at intervals. There is reason to assume that a drain system symmetrical to this exists on the southeastern side of San Lorenzo, and that both served periodically to remove the water from ceremonial pools on the surface of the plateau. Evidence for drains has been found at other Olmec centers, such as La Venta and Laguna de los Cerros, and they must have been a feature of Olmec ritual life.

One particularly important elite residence on the San Lorenzo summit, the "Red Palace," was fitted with an undulating basalt drain and columns, a sign of the highest prestige in a local setting that lacks stone resources. Attached to the residence were the chief stone-sculpture workshops, where the scarce material was turned into public monuments. According to Ann Cyphers, one of these workshops specialized in recarving stone monuments. Around 1200 BCE, this workshop ceased to function, but not before the sculptors or others had deposited the partially finished works in a line near the shop itself.

Considerable quantities of household debris have come from the San Lorenzo-phase levels, including pottery bowls and dishes carved with Olmec designs, beautiful Olmec figurines and fragments of white-ware "babies," and small mirrors, some of them concave, polished from iron-ore nodes that had been traded in from such distant areas as highland Oaxaca. Also recovered were thousands of obsidian artifacts, mostly razor-like blades but also dart-points and bone-working tools; there is no natural obsidian in the Gulf Coast heartland, but trace-element analysis showed this material to have been imported from many sources in highland Mexico and Guatemala, testifying to immense trade networks that were then controlled by the rising Olmec state.

Owing to the highly acidic nature of the soils at San Lorenzo, plant remains were absent, but occasional pockets of midden contained mammal, fish, and amphibian

48 Part of a deeply buried drain line, formed of U-shaped troughs placed end-to-end and fitted with covers. The entire line is made of basalt brought in from the Tuxtla Mountains. Olmec culture, San Lorenzo, Early Formative period.

remains. The San Lorenzo Olmec were only slightly interested in hunting deer and peccary. The mainstays of their diet were such fish as common snook, and domestic dog. Human bones showing cutmarks and burn marks were also plentiful, possibly an indication of ritual cannibalism carried out on enemy captives. There were also a high number of bones from the marine toad (*Bufo marinus*), a creature that is inedible because of the poison in its skin, but perhaps utilized for its production of bufotenine, a probable hallucinogen. The Olmecs of course had no way of injecting this substance, but they could have smoked the dried skin in powdered form.

Modern scientific analysis of the interiors of pottery vessels has shown that it was the Olmec of San Lorenzo, as well as contemporary Early Formative Mokaya villagers along the Pacific coast of Chiapas and Guatemala, who first discovered the complex process that could turn the seeds of the cacao tree (*Theobroma cacao*) into edible and drinkable chocolate. In Classic and Post-Classic Mesoamerica, this stimulating drink was a prerogative of the elite, and was imbibed in banquets restricted to the king, his court, nobles, high-ranking warriors, and traders linked to the royal house (the *pochteca*, among the Aztecs). This may have been the case among the elite of San Lorenzo.

From the ecological studies carried out by the Yale project—which were undertaken just before the entire area was given over to cattle farming—a great deal was discovered about the economic basis of early Olmec civilization along the middle Coatzacoalcos. The bulk of the early Olmec people were farmers of Nal-Tel maize, raising two crops a year on the more upland soils where rainy-season inundations did not reach; today, these lands are held communally. In contrast, the Olmec elite must have seized for themselves the rich river levees, where bumper crops are secured after the summer floods have subsided. The rise of the first Mesoamerican state, dominated by a hereditary elite class with judicial, military, and religious power, seems to have been the result of two factors: first, an environment with very high agricultural potential due to year-round rains and wet-season inundations of the river margins, along with abundant fish resources; and second, differential access to the best land by crystallizing corporate groups. The parallel with ancient Egypt—the "gift of the Nile"—is obvious. There was nothing egalitarian about San Lorenzo society, as the Colossal Heads testify.

The entire site experienced a significant decline in activity and population toward the end of the Early Formative. Although the specific causes are still unclear, San Lorenzo was never to regain its position as a capital. The shifting river course now bypassed the plateau, possibly causing an upheaval in the distribution systems so important to the San Lorenzo elites. Perhaps there was an uprising from below or outside, although the evidence for this is not as abundant as once thought.

The possibility of hostile, outside military action causing the downfall of the San Lorenzo Olmecs is suggested by the overlying cultural layer, known as the Nacaste phase. Its characteristic pottery is totally non-Olmec: very hard and slipped in white, it has close ties to Chiapa de Corzo, in the Grijalva Depression of Chiapas. But whatever the cause or causes, by 1000 BCE, this great site is finished as a regional power, to be replaced by La Venta (see p. 74).

El Manatí

Archaeologists working in the Olmec "heartland" have long lamented the lack of preservation in the highly acidic soils—the carved wood, the textiles, and almost every other organic material (including human skeletons) have perished without a trace. There was high excitement, then, when the site of El Manatí, only 10 miles (16 km) southeast of San Lorenzo, came to light. It was discovered in 1988 when locals were digging out a pond for pisciculture, at the foot of the western slope of one of the few hills in the region (**figure 49**). The site is thoroughly waterlogged, being bathed by strong springs, and has a highly complex stratigraphy caused in part by modern disturbances.

The waterlogging has resulted in extraordinary preservation of otherwise-perishable Olmec materials, belonging to virtually all phases of San Lorenzo's development, from 1600 to 1200 BCE. An archaeological team directed by Ponciano Ortiz Ceballos of the University of Veracruz and María del Carmen Rodríguez of the National Institute of Anthropology and History (INAH) found eighteen wooden figures in situ, all "baby-faced" just like Olmec hollow clay figurines, and each just under 20 in. (50 cm) high; all were little more than limbless torsos, and most had been carefully wrapped in mats and tied up, before being placed with heads pointing in the direction of the hill's summit and covered with a small rock mound. All the wooden busts were discovered in the most recent levels of the site, and one has been radiocarbon-dated to around 1200 BCE. Other objects included polished stone axes, jade and serpentine beads, a wooden staff with a bird's head on one end and a shark's tooth (surely a bloodletter) on the other, and an obsidian knife with an asphalt handle. The jade offerings were evident from the earliest levels, placing complex Olmec ceremonialism earlier than previously thought. The order

49 Wooden busts emerge from the spring at El Manatí near San Lorenzo. Jades, rubber balls, and other precious items were also delivered as offerings to the spring. The preservation of wooden sculpture from any period is extremely rare in the tropical lowlands. Olmec culture, Early Formative period.

and placement of offerings became more complex and prescriptive as time went on, so that earlier rituals, which included jade objects thrown into the spring, were replaced after 1500 BCE with carefully placed bundles of jade axes or other materials, ending finally in the spectacular series of wooden busts. Most surprisingly, the archaeologists turned up seven solid rubber balls, two of which are from the very earliest activity at the springs; measuring from 3 to 10 in. (8 to 25 cm) in diameter, these are the only examples of this artifact—which must have been very common—to have survived from pre-Conquest Mesoamerica. They confirm that the ball game is at least as old as the Olmec civilization.

Besides the ball game, one further activity at El Manatí has come to light: chocolate drinking. In a project under the supervision of archaeologist Terry Powis and chemist W. Jeffrey Hurst, residues in the bottom of an Ojochi phase (c. 1600–1500 BCE) bowl were found to contain theobromine, the signature alkaloid in chocolate, providing firm proof that the complex process for producing the drink was already known by the Olmecs and their predecessors. More recently, a more substantial sample of 156 potsherds and whole vessels from every occupation phase at San Lorenzo itself has demonstrated that the Olmecs were avid chocolate drinkers.

El Manatí, with its sacred hill and spring, was clearly a long-term pilgrimage destination for the people of San Lorenzo, lying only a half-day's walk from the capital city. It is proof that pilgrimages to holy places are a very old tradition in Mexico—and they have survived until today, with such events as the annual pilgrimage to the Virgin of Guadalupe in Mexico City. Even today the waters of El Manatí receive flower offerings from the local inhabitants.

The Middle Formative Olmecs of La Venta

After the downfall of San Lorenzo at the end of the Early Formative, its power passed to La Venta, Tabasco, the largest of all known Olmec sites, although now mostly demolished by past oil operations. It is located on an island in a sea-level coastal swamp near the Tonalá River, about 18 miles (29 km) inland from the Gulf. The island has slightly more than 2 sq. miles (5 sq. km) of dry land. The main part of the site itself is in the northern half, and is a linear complex of clay constructions stretched out for 1.2 miles (1.9 km) in a north–south direction (**figure 50**). It was extensively excavated—before its desecration by air strips, bulldozers, and parking lots—first by Matthew Stirling of the Smithsonian Institution, and later by the University of California under Robert Heizer. The major feature at La Venta is a huge pyramid of clay, 110 ft (34 m) high. While the building was once thought to have imitated the form of volcanoes nearby, work on its south side by Rebecca Gonzaléz-Lauck has shown that it was in fact a rectangular pyramid, with stepped sides and inset corners. The idea behind such enormous mounds is of interest here, for this is the most sizable of its period in Mesoamerica. It may well be that this was a first grandiose-scale attempt at replicating the trope of a "mountain of sustenance"—a place of

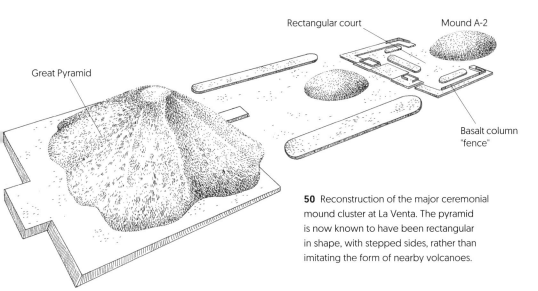

Great Pyramid

Rectangular court

Mound A-2

Basalt column "fence"

50 Reconstruction of the major ceremonial mound cluster at La Venta. The pyramid is now known to have been rectangular in shape, with stepped sides, rather than imitating the form of nearby volcanoes.

bountiful gifts of nature, including maize, which would eventually be released by the Rain Deity for the benefit of people—although other lofty pyramids in Mesoamerica are known to contain elaborate tombs, made during construction of the pyramids themselves. Whether the La Venta pyramid is a funerary monument or not remains to be determined, for although still extant, it has never been penetrated.

To the north of the Great Pyramid are two long, low mounds on either side of the centerline, and a low mound in the center between these. Then, one comes to a broad, rectangular court or plaza that was once surrounded by a fence of basalt columns, each about 7 ft (over 2 m) tall, set side by side in the top of a low wall made of adobe blocks. Finally, along the centerline is a substantial, terraced clay mound.

Robert Heizer calculated that a hinterland population of at least 18,000 people must have supported this elite center; the main pyramid alone probably took some 800,000 person-days to construct. Heizer and his colleague Philip Drucker once wrote that the nearest arable land was an area between the Coatzacoalcos and Tonalá Rivers, and that it was on this that the rulers of La Venta depended for food and labor. This land, however, is relatively poor and eroded, making the proposition unlikely. It would seem far more plausible that the agricultural support area consisted of the rich, natural levees of the tangle of rivers that once flowed in the region of La Venta. This has been borne out by a survey and excavation project directed by William Rust, who has demonstrated that there was a dense occupation of the levee zone beginning at 1750 BCE, and other work has shown incipient agriculture in the region that may date to as far back as the fifth millennium BCE. Concurrently, survey and testing of the La Venta "island" itself makes it clear that this was no empty ceremonial center, but rather a small city.

In its heyday, the site must have been vastly impressive, for different-colored clays were used for floors, and the sides of platforms were painted in solid colors of red, yellow, and purple. Scattered in the plazas fronting these rainbow-hued structures were a great number of monuments sculpted from basalt. Outstanding among these are the Colossal Heads, of which four have been found at La Venta. Sizable stelae of the same material were also present. Particularly outstanding is Stela 3.

51 North end of Throne 5 at La Venta. The two adult figures carry baby maize gods with cleft heads. Overall height of the monument 3 ft 1 in. (94 cm).

On it, two elaborately garbed men face each other, both wearing fantastic towering headdresses. The figure on the right appears to be older, with a goatee and a nose ornament. Over the two men float two sets of smaller, chubby figures directing their gaze toward the central personages. While some wear a buccal mask, or hold a staff, others appear dressed with capes, or seem to point with their fingers to the scene below. The latter may commemorate the hereditary transfer of power between related individuals under the legitimating tutelage of ancestral beings.

Also present at La Venta are stone thrones. The finest is Throne 5, on which the central figure emerges from the niche holding a baby maize god in his arms; on the sides, four subsidiary adult figures hold other little infant maize gods, who squall and gesticulate in a lively manner (**figure 51**). As usual, their heads are cleft, and mouths drawn down in the Olmec snarl.

The excavators at the site encountered a number of buried dedicatory offerings. These usually include quantities of jade or serpentine celts laid carefully in rows; many of these were finely incised with the Olmec Rain Deity and related symbols (**figure 52**). Offering 4 was particularly spectacular: it comprised a group of six celts and sixteen standing figurines of serpentine and jade arranged upright in a sort of scene (**figure 53**). In some offerings were found finely polished ear flares of jade with attached jade pendants in the shape of jaguar canines. Certain Olmec

52 [RIGHT] This flat jade celt from Tomb E at La Venta was carved to represent the Olmec Rain Deity, whose flame-like eyebrows may symbolize lightning. Cinnabar has been applied to highlight the relief. Middle Formative period.

53 [BELOW] Offering 4 at La Venta, Tabasco, consists of a number of figurines and celts of jade and serpentine, arranged in a kind of assembly scene. The bald, reshaped heads are typical of the Olmec style. Middle Formative period.

The Middle Formative Olmecs of La Venta **77**

54 Small jade figurine (also coated in cinnabar) depicting a royal woman seated cross-legged. It was found in Tomb A at La Venta. On the figure's chest she wears a small oval piece of hematite, representing the polished concave mirrors of high-ranking individuals.

sculptures and figurines show persons wearing pectorals of concave shape around the neck, and such have actually come to light in offerings (**figure 54**). These turned out to be concave mirrors of magnetite and ilmenite, the reflecting surfaces polished to optical specifications. What were they used for? Experiments have shown that they can not only start fires by focusing the sun's rays on tinder, but also throw images on flat surfaces in the same manner as a *camera lucida*. They were pierced for suspension, and one can imagine the awe a royal person would have elicited when wearing them.

Three rectangular pavements are known at La Venta, each around 15 by 20 ft (4.5 by 6 m) (**figure 55**). Each comprises about 485 blocks of serpentine, laid in the form of a fringed or tasseled textile, with several signs arranged so as to reference the four world directions and the center. The signs were left open and emphasized by filling with colored clays, and two of them—the cleft element and the "downturned E symbol"—are defining attributes of the Maize God. These were offerings; they were covered with many feet of clay and adobe layers soon after being arranged.

55 Mosaic pavement of serpentine blocks, displaying attributes related to the Maize God; one of three known at La Venta. The pavement was covered over with a layer of mottled pink clay and a platform of adobe bricks.

56 Tomb constructed of basalt pillars at La Venta. The tomb contained several burials accompanied by jade offerings and was covered with an earthen mound.

In the acid soil of La Venta (as at San Lorenzo), bones disappear quickly, and very few burials have been discovered. Of those found, however, the most outstanding was the tomb in Mound A-2, which was surrounded and roofed with basalt columns (**figure 56**). On a floor made of flat limestone slabs were laid the remains of two juveniles, badly rotted when discovered, each wrapped up in a bundle and heavily coated with vermilion paint. With them had been placed an offering of fine jade figurines, beads, a jade pendant in the shape of a clam shell, a sting-ray spine of the same substance, and other objects. Such post-mortem treatment of juveniles strongly suggests hereditary high rank, a hallmark of the centralization of political power. Outside the tomb a sandstone "sarcophagus" with a cover had been left, but other than some jade objects on the bottom, nothing was found within but clay fill.

Although the causes for the demise of La Venta remain unknown, its abandonment occurred at the end of Middle Formative times, around 400 to 300 BCE, for subsequently, once in ruins, offerings were made with pottery of Late Formative cast. As a matter of fact, La Venta may never have lost its significance as a cult center, for among the very latest caches found was a Spanish olive jar of the early European colonial period, and Heizer suspected that offerings may have been made in modern times as well.

Chiapa de Corzo: a La Venta Outlier?

Chiapa de Corzo in the Grijalva Depression of Chiapas began as an Early Formative village, but by the eighth century BCE, it started to participate in the general orbit of La Venta Olmec civilization. This was marked by the construction of a 20-ft (6-m) high funerary pyramid built of clay and rammed earth. Within this was a major royal tomb, found and excavated in 2010 by Bruce Buchand of the NWAF and Lynneth Lowe of Mexico's UNAM. Inside a crypt with wooden roof and floor, a middle-aged male had been laid to rest, accompanied by two human sacrifices, one of them an infant.

The ruler's upper teeth had been inlaid in life with small disks of pyrite and mother-of-pearl, a sign of his exalted status. Over the mouth of the corpse had been placed a bivalve shell. He was adorned with a magnificent necklace of over a thousand jade beads identical to those in La Venta burials, interspersed with jade effigy clamshells, and more jade beads and seed pearls adorned his arms and legs. His entire body had been encased in death with a thick layer of bright-red hematite powder. Adjacent to his crypt was that of his royal spouse, equally rich in jade ornaments, and strewn with red powder.

In pits dug into the plaza at the foot of the pyramid were ritual offerings that included La Venta-style pottery, an adult male sacrificial victim, and over 340 stone axes and celts. Along with these was a polished serpentine celt incised with the lineaments of the Olmec Maize God. In all likelihood this potentate was a provincial ruler with allegiance to La Venta.

Tres Zapotes and the Long Count Calendar

In its day, La Venta was undoubtedly the most powerful and holy place in the Olmec heartland, sacred because of its very inaccessibility; but other great Olmec centers also flourished in the Middle Formative. About 100 miles (160 km) northwest of La Venta lies Tres Zapotes, in a setting of low hills above the swampy basin formed by the Papaloapan and San Juan Rivers. It comprises about fifty earthen mounds stretched out along the bank of a stream for 2 miles (3.2 km) with little marked hierarchy among the architectural groups, suggesting to excavator Christopher Pool that the site was controlled by several powerful lineages of equal rank. Pottery and clay figurines recovered from stratigraphic excavations have revealed an early occupation of Tres Zapotes which was apparently contemporaneous first with San Lorenzo, and later with La Venta, but it was during the Late Formative that the site reached its zenith. Belonging to its earlier horizon are two Colossal Heads, comparable to those of La Venta. But the importance of Tres Zapotes lies in its Late Formative stela, discussed on p. 82.

So far we have said nothing about writing and the calendar in the Olmec heartland. Actually, only a short inscription (on Monument 13) has come to light at

La Venta itself, but no written dates. Nonetheless, several fine jade objects in the Olmec style, now in public and private collections but of unknown provenience, are incised with currently unreadable hieroglyphs. More conclusive evidence that the Olmecs had a script appeared in 1999 at a place called El Cascajal, not far north of San Lorenzo: there, archaeologists Ma. del Carmen Rodríguez and Ponciano Ortiz found that local villagers had recovered a serpentine block from a road cut through an ancient mound; one face of the block was incised with hieroglyphs (**figure 57**). The associated potsherds were almost entirely of the late San Lorenzo phase. The inscription consists of sixty-two signs arranged in more-or-less horizontal lines. Although the signary is derived from Olmec iconography, it bears no resemblance to any later Mesoamerican script and has little likelihood of ever being deciphered.

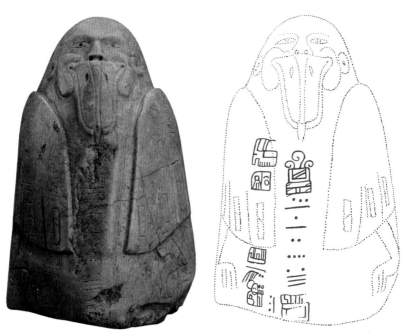

58a, 58b The Tuxtla Statuette, with Long Count date and hieroglyphic texts. Ht 6 in. (15 cm).

It has already been said that Tres Zapotes flourished in the Late Formative, after La Venta had been abandoned. Tres Zapotes has produced one of the oldest dated monuments of the Western hemisphere, Stela C, a fragmentary basalt monument that had been reused in later times. On the front side is a substantial human face wearing an elaborate buccal mask and a headband with the profile view of an ancestral being who wears in turn a headdress topped by a well-sized panoply of feathers. The style of the carving is derivative from Olmec, rather than in the true canon. The reverse side bears a date in the Long Count.

The Long Count system of calculating dates needs some explanation. In Chapter 1, it was mentioned that in use throughout Mesoamerica was a calendar that entailed the meshing of the days of a 260-day divinatory cycle with those of the 365-day solar year. A day in one would not meet a day in the other for 52 years; consequently, any date could be placed within a single 52-year cycle by this means. This is the Calendar Round system, but it obviously is not much help when more than 52 years are involved (just as a historian would not be able to determine from a "'17" record if an event took place in 1917 or 2017), for it would require referencing a year count from an arbitrary point of departure to know in which century the event happened. A more detailed way of expressing dates would be a system that counted days elapsed from a definite starting point: for example, the founding of Rome or the birth of Christ. This is the role that was fulfilled by the Long Count, used only by the lowland groups of Mesoamerica and taken to its greatest elaboration by the Classic Maya. For reasons unknown to us, the starting date was 13 August 3114 BCE (Gregorian), and dates are presented in terms of the numbers of periods of varying length that have elapsed since the reckoning was set in motion. For instance, the longest period was one of 144,000 days, the next of 7,200 days, then 360 days, followed by 20 days, and then 1 day. Coefficients (multipliers for Long Count periods) were expressed in terms of bar-and-dot numerals, the bars having the value of five and the dots, one. A bar and two dots therefore stands for "seven."

In Stela C, the coefficient accompanying the great first period was missing when Matthew Stirling discovered the lower fragment of the monument, but he deduced it as seven. He read the entire date as (7).16.6.16.18, or 3 September 32 BCE in terms of the Gregorian calendar, raising a storm of protests from Mayanists who felt sure that a monument outside Maya territory could not be this old. Stirling was vindicated in 1969 when a Tres Zapotes farmer accidentally turned up the missing top part of the stela, complete with its coefficient of seven. Another date, this time with a fairly long, unread text, is inscribed on a small jade figure of a duck-billed, winged human, in Epi-Olmec style. This is the Tuxtla Statuette, discovered many years ago in the Olmec area, with the Long Count date of 8.6.2.4.17 (14 March 162 CE) (figures 58a, 58b). Since both dates fall in the Late Formative and were found within the Olmec heartland, it is not unlikely that Epi-Olmec or even Olmec literati invented the Long Count and developed the required astronomical observations with which the Maya are usually credited.

The earliest Long Count date of all, however, was found on a reused slab at the site of Chiapa de Corzo, in the Grijalva Depression of Chiapas, outside the heartland proper. It bears a date that can be reconstructed as (7.16).3.2.13 or 8 December 36 BCE, some four years earlier than Tres Zapotes Stela C. Quite possibly, we have not yet discovered the answer to where, when, and why the Long Count was invented.

The Olmecs beyond the Heartland

Notwithstanding their intellectual and artistic achievements, the Olmecs were by no means a peaceful people. Their monuments show that they fought battles with war clubs fitted with chipped lithics or shark teeth and shields, and some individuals carry on both hands what seems to be a kind of cestus, or knuckle-duster, that may have been used as a weapon. Whether the indubitable Olmec presence in highland Mexico represents actual invasion from the heartland is still under vigorous debate. The Olmecs of such sites as San Lorenzo and La Venta certainly needed substances, often of a prestigious nature, that were unobtainable in their homeland—obsidian, iron-ore for mirrors, serpentine, and (by Middle Formative times) quantities of jade—and they probably set up trade networks over much of southern Mexico to get these items. In fact, according to one hypothesis, the frontier Olmec sites could have been trading stations. Kent Flannery has put forth the idea that the Olmec element in such places as the Valley of Oaxaca could have been the result of emulation by groups at the threshold of statehood who had trade and perhaps even marriage ties with the Olmec elite. And finally, the occurrence of iconography based on the Olmec pantheon over a wide area of Mesoamerica suggests the possibility of missionary efforts on the part of the heartland Olmecs.

59 "The Acrobat," a hollow, white-ware figure from Burial 154 at Tlatilco. Early Formative period.

60 Hollow clay figure from Atlihuayan, Morelos, probably representing a shaman in trance wearing the head and skin of a fantastic crocodilian and with harpy eagle brows. It was accidentally discovered in 1948 when highway construction cut through a Middle Formative Olmec site.

Among the sites in central Mexico that have produced Early Formative Olmec objects—principally figurines and ceramics—are Tlatilco and Tlapacoya in the Basin of Mexico (**figure 59**), and the heavily looted site of Las Bocas in Puebla; from the latter have come bowls, bottles, and effigy vases, along with fine, white-kaolin Olmec babies and human effigies. All of these items were probably manufactured at San Lorenzo itself.

Although it is still in the highlands, the state of Morelos, to the south of the Basin of Mexico, is warm and even subtropical, and might well have proved attractive for the Olmecs (**figure 60**). Chalcatzingo is a most important highland Olmec site, and lies in the Amatzinac Valley of eastern Morelos. There, three isolated, igneous intrusions rise over 985 ft (300 m) above the valley floor, and must have been considered sacred in ancient times, as they were by the Aztecs and even the modern inhabitants. At the juncture of the talus slope and the sheer rock cliff of the central mountain has been found a series of Olmec-style bas-reliefs carved on boulders. The most elaborate of these bas-reliefs depicts a woman holding a ceremonial bar in her arms, seated upon a throne (**figure 61**). The bar and the throne are incised with the abstract version of the "Cloud" sign.

61 Relief I, Chalcatzingo, Morelos. A woman ruler is seated within the mouth of the earth which gives off smoke or mist, while raindrops fall from clouds above. Olmec culture, Middle Formative period. Ht 10 ft 6 in. (3.2 m).

The scene itself takes place within the open, profile mouth of the anthropo-morphized earth, as though within a cave, which emits smoke or mist. Above this tableau are three highly iconic rain clouds, from which fall raindrops. The woman must have been a ruler of Chalcatzingo, and the theme is one of power and fertility.

Other sculptures at Chalcatzingo include a relief showing three Olmec warriors brandishing clubs above an ithyphallic captive, and a scene of two rampant felines, each attacking a human. The Feathered Serpent—an important, pan-Mesoamerican deity, depicted as a snake adorned with quetzal plumes—makes an appearance on another boulder, with a man disappearing into its open mouth.

In the 1970s, David Grove and Jorge Angulo directed a University of Illinois project at Chalcatzingo, which cleared up many of the questions posed by the site. The site itself, which consists of platform mounds and terraces below the central mountain, was founded by about 1500 BCE, but reached its height during the Middle Formative Cantera phase, from 700 to 500 BCE, at which time the carvings were apparently made. They are therefore coeval with the apogee of La Venta, which surely was the center from which Olmec influence emanated to Morelos. The Illinois project discovered a table-top masonry throne formed of stone slabs, with a relief of a pair of eyes with cleft supraorbital plaques. Between them are three circles triangularly arranged so as to mimic a cleft. While the form of the eyes is diagnostic of the Rain Deity, the cleft element and the circles are attributes of the Maize God; a child, probably a human sacrifice, had been buried within the throne. The Chalcatzingo elite received elaborate crypt burials, one being accompanied by a greenstone figure in the purest La Venta style; jade earspools, pendants, and necklaces were also present.

Although this part of Morelos is somewhat arid, the Cantera-phase farmers did little irrigation, but planted their crops on artificial terraces. Deer and cottontail rabbits were hunted, but the most prominent food animal, as in most Formative sites, was the dog.

Grove is skeptical, as is Flannery, about whether such a frontier site as Chalcatzingo actually represents an invasion or takeover by Gulf Coast people, and he too favors the idea of Olmec influence coming in through long-distance trade and marriage alliances. In his view, the monuments, many of which depict the Chalcatzingo rulers, have no local antecedents and may well have been carved by artists imported from the heartland to explain the Olmec belief system to the local people.

Zazacatla, located to the south of Cuernavaca in the municipality of Xochitepec, Morelos, must have been another major Olmec center of the Middle Formative. Badly destroyed by modern road building and urban development, it once covered no less than about 1 sq. mile (about 2.5 sq. km). Rescue operations carried out by INAH archaeologists uncovered several huge platforms built of rammed earth faced with horizontally laid limestone slabs. In niches, four modest-sized stone monuments had been placed, two of which are powerful representations of the Olmec Rain Deity.

Guerrero is a mountainous, extremely dry state lying south of Morelos, on the way to the Pacific Coast. Many of the most beautiful blue-green Olmec jades have come from this rugged region, leading Covarrubias to the often-revived but poorly founded claim that this is where the Olmec must have originated. Three exceptional sites show that the Olmec were here, however. Juxtlahuaca Cave had been known for many years; it lies east of the Guerrero capital, Chilpancingo, near the community of Colotlipa, in one of the most arid parts of the state. The cave—the importance of which was first revealed by the Princeton art historian Gillett Griffin and by Carlo Gay, a retired Italian businessman—is a deep cavern. Almost a mile in from the entrance is a series of extraordinary Olmec paintings in polychrome on the cave walls. One of these shows a tall, bearded figure in a red-and-yellow striped tunic with a black cloak, his limbs clad in jaguar pelts and claws; he brandishes with one hand the lower leg of a bird of prey, held by its talons, and the other hand clutches a rope with which he holds in front of him a lesser figure, perhaps a captive, with a black face (**figure 62**). Nearby is the undulating form of a red-painted plumed serpent, with a panache of green feathers on its head (**figure 63**). Deep caves and caverns were traditionally held to be entrances to the Underworld in Mesoamerica, and Juxtlahuaca must have had a connection with secret and chthonic rites celebrated by the frontier Olmec.

62, 63 Polychrome paintings on the walls of Juxtlahuaca Cave, Guerrero. (LEFT) A bearded ruler seemingly subduing a captive. (RIGHT) Red-painted serpent with a feathered crest on the head. Olmec style, Early or Middle Formative period.

Shortly after the Juxtlahuaca paintings were brought to light, David Grove discovered the cave murals of Oxtotitlan, not very far north of Juxtlahuaca. These paintings are in a shallow rockshelter located on a cliff face, rather than a cavern, and are dominated by a polychrome representation of an Olmec ruler wearing the mask and feathers of a bird representing an owl, the traditional messenger of the lords of the Underworld. He is seated upon a throne with the image of the anthropomorphized earth, very similar to that on Throne 4 from La Venta. It is extremely difficult to date rock art, but it is possible that Juxtlahuaca may be contemporary with San Lorenzo, and Oxtotitlan with La Venta.

The third site was being sacked by looters in the early 1980s before archaeologists from the National Institute of Anthropology and History moved in to excavate it properly. The site was given the Nahuatl name Teopantecuanitlan ("The Place of the Temple of Jaguars") by the director of the team, Guadalupe Martínez Donjuan, and lies near the confluence of the Amacuzac and Balsas Rivers in the extreme northeast of Guerrero, in a region of dry hills with sparse vegetation. It consists of three groups of ceremonial constructions, spread out over 395 acres (160 hectares). Group A is the most important of these; construction began here with a sunken court of yellow clay, reached by two pairs of stairways on its south side. At the base of the balustrade, each pair of stairs shares a stone block decorated with a schematic face wearing a headdress and with attributes of the Maize God. According to preliminary accounts, this phase has been dated to 1400 BCE, leading some Guerrero enthusiasts to revive the Covarrubias hypothesis of Olmec origins.

Phase 2 of Group A at Teopantecuanitlan, dated to 900 BCE, sees the substitution of construction in yellow clay by travertine blocks; overlooking the sunken court at this time were four stone monoliths with bas-reliefs in straightforward Olmec style. Associated with this phase is the building of a reservoir and canal system, but whether this was for mundane irrigation functions or more religious and ceremonial purposes—along the lines of the San Lorenzo and La Venta stone drains—is yet unclear.

Sites with Olmec carvings and stelae have been found along the Pacific coastal plain of southeastern Mesoamerica: in Chiapas; the Guatemalan south coast; and as far southeast as Chalchuapa, El Salvador, around 500 miles (800 km) from the Olmec heartland, where a boulder is carved with figures holding staffs in their characteristic style. So few Olmec sites have been excavated—and even fewer fully published—that it often remains difficult to be very precise about the nature of the Olmec presence beyond the Gulf Coast. Was this Olmec colonization or not? Perhaps some of these sites were founded by small groups of warrior-traders, similar in kind to the Vikings of Scandinavia two millennia later.

Decisive evidence for a real Olmec colony has been found by David Cheetham of California State University, Long Beach. The site of Cantón Corralito is located in the Soconusco plain, in the heart of the Mokaya zone (see p. 39), about 240 miles (400 km) southeast of San Lorenzo. It was occupied from Archaic times through the Cuadros Phase, when it was buried in river floods and abandoned. Cantón Corralito carved and incised ceramics are overwhelmingly Early Olmec in style and in iconographic content. Neutron activation analysis proved that many of these were imported directly from San Lorenzo, while the rest were locally made, but accurate, imitations.

Some modern revisionists have questioned the reality of an Olmec civilization, and have downplayed the Veracruz-Tabasco "heartland" as the *fons et origo* of the culture. Others have claimed that this was merely a "sister civilization," and not the "mother culture" championed by an earlier generation of archaeologists—but this claim is belied by the precocity of San Lorenzo; during the Early Formative, when this great urban capital flourished, Olmec civilization had no "sisters."

Basing their argument upon Teopantecuanitlan, there are even those who claim that the Olmec pattern of life began in Guerrero, a position contradicted by the severe environmental constraints posed by that region. Such disagreements as this are compounded by the fact that we have no readable written documents for the Olmec, leaving the subject wide open to different interpretations and even unfounded speculation.

Yet whatever we call it, it can hardly be denied that during the Early and Middle Formative, there was a powerful, unitary religion that had manifested itself in an all-pervading art style, and that this was the official ideology of the first complex society or societies to be seen in this part of the Americas. Its rapid spread has been variously likened to that of Christianity under the Roman Empire, or to that of westernization (or "modernization") in today's world. Wherever Olmec influence or the Olmecs themselves went, so did greater complexity.

Early Zapotecs

San José Mogote remained the most important regional center in the Valley of Oaxaca until the end of the Middle Formative (**figure 64**). By that time, it had full-fledged masonry buildings of a monumental scale, including Building 1, a small acropolis consisting of a huge basal pyramid that supported several temples and elite residences. In a corridor connecting two of these super-structures, Kent Flannery and Joyce Marcus found a bas-relief threshold stone showing a captive as if falling, with the "heart" sign on his chest and a stream of blood flowing from it. The stream ends in two drops that wrap onto the adjacent vertical narrow surface of the stone, mimicking the dripping of actual blood. Between his legs is a glyphic caption, likely representing the name of the captor or perhaps that of the sacrificial victim, "1 Eye" in the 260-day ritual calendar. Since the stone was in situ but broken

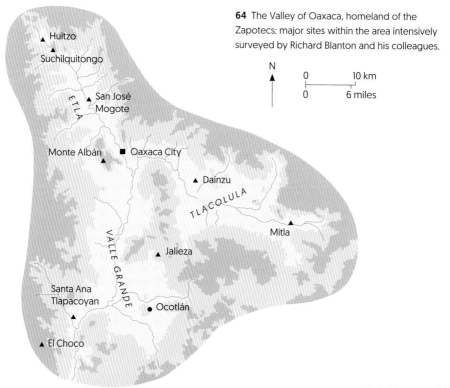

64 The Valley of Oaxaca, homeland of the Zapotecs: major sites within the area intensively surveyed by Richard Blanton and his colleagues.

and incomplete, it was reused from a previous context, perhaps at the footstep of a temple where human sacrifice was enacted.

Toward the close of the Middle Formative, the Zapotec of the valley were practicing several forms of irrigation. At Hierve el Agua, in the mountains east of the valley, there has been found an artificially terraced hillside, irrigated by canals coming from permanent springs charged with calcareous waters that have in effect created a fossilized record from their deposits.

Monte Albán is the greatest of all Zapotec sites, and was constructed on a series of eminences about 1,300 ft (400 m) above the valley floor, near the close of the Middle Formative, about 500 BCE, when it replaced San José Mogote as the valley's most powerful center. The founding of the city took place in a rapid, deliberate episode. The choice to settle here was probably due to the sacred nature of the eminences and the strategic hilltop location at the juncture of the valley's three arms. It lies in the heart of the region still occupied by the Zapotec; since some of the early calendrical signs depict what sixteenth-century Zapotec day names meant, archaeologists feel reasonably certain that the inhabitants of the site were always speakers of that language.

Building L-Sub at Monte Albán

Most of the constructions that meet the eye at Monte Albán are of the Classic period. In the southwestern corner of the main plaza (which is laid out on a north–south axis), however, excavations have disclosed a building called L-sub. This is a stone-faced platform contemporary with the first occupation of the site, which archaeologists call the Danibaan phase. Large stone slabs are set into the platform and covered in bas-relief figures. These are nude men with slightly Olmec-like features (for example, the down-turned mouth), and shown in strange, rubbery postures as though they were swimming or dancing in viscous fluid. Because of this position they are often called *Danzantes* ("dancers," **figure 65**). Some are represented as old, bearded individuals with toothless gums or with only a single protuberant incisor (**figure 66**). About 300 of these strange yet powerful figures are known at Monte Albán, and it might be reasonably asked exactly what their function was, or what they depict. On this subject archaeologists remain in disagreement. The most accepted opinion is that the distorted pose of the limbs, the open mouth, and closed eyes indicate that these are corpses: chiefs or kings slain by the earliest rulers of Monte Albán. In a couple of individuals the genitals are delineated: this stigma was usually laid on captives in Mesoamerica, where nudity was considered scandalous. Furthermore, there are cases of sexual mutilation depicted on the figures, blood streaming in flowery patterns from the severed part.

While the Building L-sub figures have long been interpreted as killed captives, an alternative opinion is forwarded by Javier Urcid, who argues that the figures reference ritual enactments of a warrior group practicing penis self-mutilation.

65 Bas-relief figure, often called a *Danzante* or "dancer," from the facade of Building L-sub. The name glyph of the personage appears in front of his mouth.

66 Bas-relief of a bearded figure from Building L-sub.

67, 68 Hypothetical reconstruction of the grand narrative in Building L-sub, Monte Albán. [ABOVE] Southern end of the basal façade with rows of vertically and horizontally placed figures. The former proceed in zigzag from bottom to top; the latter face north. The glyphs on the corner stones face south, but the texts also read in boustrophedon [opposite directions from one line to the next]. Since the inscriptions follow a well-known format, the initial and ending signs on the missing blocks [shown in gray] are predictable. [BELOW] Examples of three additional groups of carved blocks that include vertically and horizontally placed figures in their hypothesized architectural context atop the platform. The sets include personages with oval-shaped pendants (n=24), figures wearing the buccal mask of the Rain Deity (n=15), and elders (n=11).

Rather than being seen as sprawling dead bodies, Urcid sees the nude figures as forming a procession in a sequence, as if the figures were climbing the platform (**figures 67, 68**). He argues that in other ancient visual narratives of conquest and victory in battle, the vanquished are always shown subdued by the captor, and yet, of the 219 currently known carved figures that appear to have been part of Building L-sub, none can be identified as the victorious. Marks of seniority, such as the addition of the toothless, bearded figures with wrinkles and hunchbacks, are not found on the lower facade of the carving, and to Urcid suggest markers of rank, with seniors representing a council of elders at the highest echelon.

Identifying the carving as depicting dead captives or a procession of warriors depends on what contextual evidence is brought to bear, be it archaeological from other regions, ethnographic, or historical. The continued debate over the depictions of these reliefs demonstrates how much more there is to establish about the symbolic lives of people in the Formative Period.

69 Building J at Monte Albán, a structure that throughout its architectural history underwent at least three major enlargements.

Building J at Monte Albán

Monte Albán was surely the capital of a burgeoning state during this Late Formative period. The city was able to do several things associated with later Mesoamerican states: develop a distinctive art style along with a script—both associated with the necessary proclamations of power and sacredness—and gather a substantial population around the urban center. Two investigators, Richard Blanton and Stephen Kowalewski, give its population as 10,000 to 20,000, and the first Monte Albán palaces seem to appear at this time to meet the administrative needs of the local and valley-wide citizenry.

The development was gradual from the establishment of the site to the end of the Formative at about 150 BCE to 150 CE (called the Nisa phase). Near the southern end of the main plaza of the site was erected Building J, a stone-faced construction with a triangular ground plan pointing southwest (**figure 69**). The exterior of the building is set with over forty reused inscribed stone slabs, all bearing a very similar text format. These Nisa-phase inscriptions generally consist of an upside-down head with closed eyes and elaborate headdress, below a stepped glyph for "mountain" or "town"; over this is the name of the place, seemingly given phonetically in rebus fashion (**figures 70, 71** [p. 94]). In its most complete form, the text is accompanied by the symbol for year and the name of the year. There are also various yet-undeciphered glyphs. Such inscriptions were interpreted by Alfonso Caso as records of town conquests, the inverted heads being the defeated kings.

This obsession with recording victories over enemies characterizes early civilizations the world over, and the rising Formative states of Mexico were no exception. It speaks for a time when state polities were relatively small and engaged in mutual

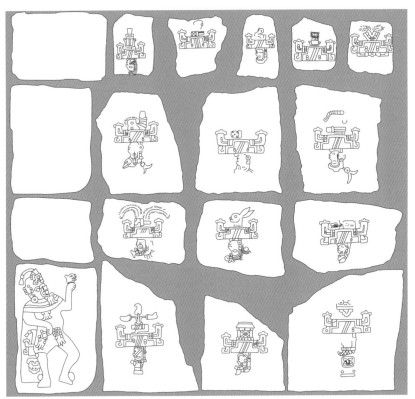

70 (ABOVE) Hypothetical reconstruction of the facade of what would have been a platform decorated with finely inscribed slabs. The location of this building within the Main Plaza of Monte Albán remains unknown.

71 (RIGHT) A finely incised slab, broken and incomplete, from a Late Formative building that was eventually dismantled. The slab was later reused in the second version of Building J at Monte Albán. It exemplifies the monoliths that were written with emblematic texts. Ht 3 ft 9.2 in. (1.15 m).

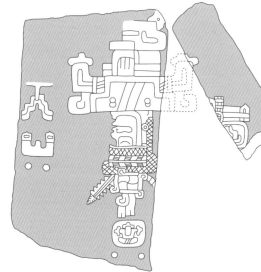

warfare, when no ruler could extend his sway over a territory vast enough to be called an empire.

The theme of warfare in these emblematic inscriptions is explored in other interpretations, including Urcid's. He posits that the "Hill" signs, which consistently contain the depiction of nose ornaments, make reference to "Hill of the Lords," the name of the main plaza recorded in the seventeenth-century map of the nearby community of Xoxocotlan. The headgears of the inverted heads form categories, and one of the most elaborate seemingly depicts a war club with triangular blades, suggesting that upside-down heads and the glyphs above the "Hill" signs name deceased heroic warriors of a hierarchically organized group. In this way, instead of recording conquests, Urcid argues that the monuments memorialized warriors who fought at the service of the state. The emblematic text format is also present on what appears to have been a cornerstone of the original commemorative building (bottom left of **figure 70**); it seemingly depicts a ruler enacting human sacrifice by holding a jaguar's decapitated head, as well as the "Hill" sign, partially revealed on the cape worn by the sacrificer, a glyph that is centerpiece in the inscriptions on the other blocks.

While alternative interpretations argue as to whether power was exclusionary and expressed through the representation and listing of captives and conquered cities, or inclusionary through the registering of dead heroes, it appears that Monte Albán's regional footprint was increasing. As we will see in Chapter 6, by the Classic period the Monte Albán elites succeeded in expanding their territorial domains and instituting divine kingship, boasting new hieroglyphic programs and military prowess to legitimate their power.

Later Life of San José Mogote

After losing regional primacy toward the end of the Middle Formative, San José Mogote became largely depopulated. But some 500 years later, as Monte Albán had already become a sizable urban center, the community grew again, and the small acropolis in Building 1 saw the construction of several temples. One of them, Temple 35, yielded the earliest materialization of the account—documented ethnographically even today in many parts of Mesoamerica—of how the Rain Deity released bountiful wealth from within a "mountain of sustenance" and gave maize to humans (**figure 72**). Underneath the center and against the back wall of the inner sanctum of the temple was a stone cist with a most remarkable tableau comprised of a small enclosure made with stone slabs, inside of which was the skeleton of a quail, and a bowl—similar

72 Tableau of ceramic effigy vessels showing the Rain Deity about to open the "mountain of sustenance" to give maize to humans. Offering under Temple 35, Building 1, San José Mogote. Late Formative. Length of the main effigy 9.05 in. (23 cm).

73 An effigy spouted jar, provenience unknown. The vessel has the representation of a crouching masked and bearded personage. His face is an early form of the glyph that in the Zapotec script would eventually reference the 4th day of the calendar. Middle to Late Formative period. Ht 7.4 in. (18.8 cm).

to the simple serving vessels found in domestic contexts—containing a small effigy vessel. Its size, form, and attributes are typical of effigy vessels that in other contexts are known to be embodiments of maize; other such vessels reference different personifications (**figure 73**). Laid on top of the slab that covered the enclosure was another much more sizable effigy vessel of a prone personage wearing a cape, this one with all the attributes of the Rain Deity, including those held in the hands: a rod to break the enclosure containing maize, and a swirling serpent, symbol of lightning. Behind the stone-slab enclosure, arranged in a single row, were four female impersonators of the Rain Deity; these are the assistants who in the account help to disseminate the richness within the "mountain of sustenance" to the four corners of the world. Present in the tableau were also a pair of deer antlers, similar to the ones described by Father Sahagún to have been used as instruments with which to play the *ayotl* (turtle carapace) during the festivities in honor of the Aztec rain deities.

The Rio Verde Drainage in Coastal Oaxaca

In an effort to determine if the tropical lowlands elsewhere in Mesoamerica had a precocious development toward social complexity, as was the case with the Olmec heartland, archaeologists David Grove, Marcus Winter, Susan Gillespie, and Raúl Arana conducted in 1986 a project in the lower drainage of the Río Verde, on the

74 Siltstone mask representing the Rain Deity. From an offering under Structure 1, in a restricted sector of the ceremonial center at Cerro de la Virgen, Rio Verde, Coastal Oaxaca. Late Formative. Ht 7.2 in. (18.5 cm).

Pacific littoral (shore) of Oaxaca. Being the most substantial river drainage to discharge onto the Pacific Ocean, its diverse and rich ecology is similar to that of the Southern Gulf Coast region, with rivers, floodplains, lakes, estuaries, and mountain habitats. Surprisingly, their study recovered little evidence of occupation prior to the Middle Formative period. Yet, there was a hint of rapid population growth and increased social complexity during the Late Formative. There is now a better understanding of this process of change as the result of a subsequent long-term, multi-disciplinary project lead by archaeologist Arthur Joyce.

As of now, the evidence suggests the presence of few small sedentary communities during the Early Formative (1800–1000 BCE), including La Consentida, a small settlement of agriculturalists covering 2.6 hectares. Toward the end of the Middle Formative (700–400 BCE), the largest settlement in the lower Rio Verde drainage, Charco Redondo, grew to 62 hectares, and the landscape became dotted by a host of other smaller communities, including Rio Viejo, Cerro de la Cruz, and San Francisco de Arriba. By the early Late Formative (400–150 BCE), Charco Redondo remained the largest settlement, although San Francisco de Arriba experienced a veritable boom in size and monumentality, suggesting that it was on the verge of becoming urban. The smaller Late Formative occupation at Cerro de la Cruz extended through 1.5 hectares and yielded evidence of densely occupied residential terraces, community feasts, high-ranking burials with grave offerings, and a public burial ground with fifty-eight interments of mostly adults and without offerings.

It was toward the end of the Late Formative (150 BCE–150 CE) that the lower Rio Verde drainage saw the emergence of an urban center at Rio Viejo. At its height, the site covered some 255 hectares (almost a third the size of Olmec San Lorenzo), and was dominated by a massive acropolis estimated to have a construction volume of some 560,000 cubic meters. The ensemble, which rises some 17 meters above the level of the floodplain, includes a huge basal platform that supports two sizable substructures with additional edifices on top, five smaller buildings, a plaza, and a sunken courtyard. Rio Viejo and its satellite communities, like Cerro de la Virgen (**figure 74**)

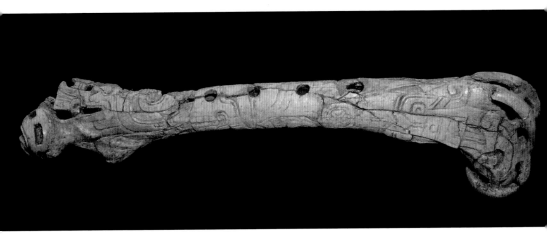

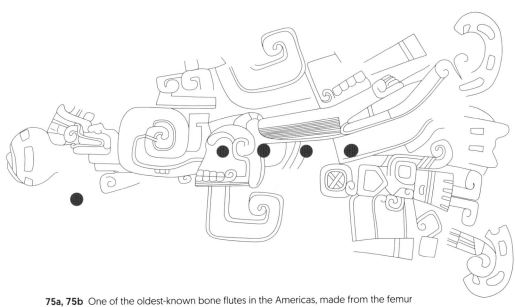

75a, 75b One of the oldest-known bone flutes in the Americas, made from the femur of a deer and elaborately incised and carved out. The imagery is that of a half-fleshed, half-skeletal figure. It was found in a communal burial ground, placed as an offering to a fifteen- to seventeen-year-old adolescent. Yugüe, Rio Verde, Coastal Oaxaca. Terminal Formative (100–250 CE). Length 9.2 in. (23.5 cm).

and Yugüe (**figures 75a, 75b**), were linked to interregional networks of exchange that brought foreign materials to be exquisitely crafted into objects of great value. During the second century CE, both Rio Viejo in the coast and Monte Albán in the Central Valleys of Oaxaca were among a handful of cities in southern Mexico. Yet, except for the local acquisition of grayware pottery from the highlands, there is no evidence for interaction between the Central Valleys of Oaxaca and the Rio Verde drainage.

By 250 CE, the acropolis of Rio Viejo fell into disuse and the settlement dramatically shrunk in size, covering slightly more than a third of its former extent by the fifth century CE. Although the reasons for the political and economic demise of Rio Viejo in the third century CE are unknown, evidence of widespread burning suggests social unrest or local conflict. Yet, as will be discussed in Chapter 7, Rio Viejo experienced resurgence once again during the Epiclassic period (600–900 CE). What has been perhaps most revealing of the investigations conducted by Arthur Joyce in the Rio Verde drainage is that the timing in the development of social complexity may have been in part related to environmental change. Geomorphological and paleo-environmental data indicates that during the Early and Middle Formative periods, the lower Rio Verde drainage experienced increased sediment load and discharge of the river due to erosion in the highlands caused by demographic and agricultural expansion in the Mixteca Alta. Paradoxically, while this environmental impact made the lower drainage unattractive to earlier occupants, it provided a propitious setting for the rapid societal transformations of the Late and Terminal Formative.

Izapa

Another culture of the Formative period upon which we will touch is of high significance. This is the civilization centered on the site of Izapa, located in the southeastern part of the state of Chiapas on a tributary stream of the Suchiate River, which divides Mexico from Guatemala. It is situated in a broad coastal plain: one of the most unbearably hot, but at the same time incredibly fertile, regions of Mexico. Izapa is a vast site, with numbers of earthen mounds faced with river cobbles, all forming a maze of courts and plazas in which the stone monuments are located. There is possibly a ball court, formed by two long, earth embankments. Samples of pottery taken from Izapa show it to have been founded in the Early Formative, and to have reached its height in the Late Formative, persisting into the Proto-Classic period.

The art style as expressed in bas-reliefs is highly distinctive. Although obviously derived from the Olmecs, it differs in its use of substantial, cluttered, baroque compositions with several figures, as opposed to the Olmec focus on the single figure of the ruler. Several of these multi-figure Izapan compositions are concerned with the sacred stories of Mesoamerican divine heroes; many of these stories were still recounted when the Spanish arrived almost 2,000 years later. Izapan style appears on stone stelae that often are associated with "altars" placed in front of them, the latter crudely carved to represent giant toads, which are symbols of rain. The principal gods are metamorphoses of the old gods of the Olmecs, the upper lip of the deity now tremendously extended to the degree that it resembles the trunk of a tapir. Most scenes on Izapan stelae take place under a sky band in the form of stylized teeth, from which may descend a winged figure on a background of swirling clouds. On Stela 3, a serpent-footed deity brandishes a club, while on Stela 1, a "Long-lipped God"—a prototype of the Maya Rain God Chahk—is depicted with feet in the form of reptile heads, walking on water from which he dips fish to be

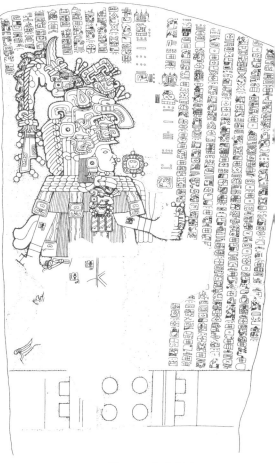

76 Stela 1, Izapa, Chiapas. At the top are a sky band and an ancestral figure holding a serpent. Below, a personification of the Rain Deity is dipping fish from the water with a net; he carries a bottle-shaped creel strapped to his back. Izapan style, Late Formative period. Ht 6 ft 4 in. (1.93 m).

77 Stela 1, La Mojarra, Veracruz. End of Late Formative period. Ht 7 ft 8.1 in. (2.34 m).

placed in a basketry creel on his back (**figure 76**). Most interesting of all is Stela 21, on which a warrior holds the head of a decapitated enemy; in the background, an important person identified by the calendrical name "9 Lord" is carried in a litter, the roof of which is embellished with a crouching jaguar.

The real importance of the Izapan civilization is that it is the connecting link in time and space between the earlier Olmec civilization and the later Classic Maya. Izapan monuments are found scattered down the Pacific Coast of Guatemala and up into the highlands in the vicinity of Guatemala City. On the other side of the highlands, in the lowland jungle of northern Guatemala, the very earliest Maya monuments appear to be derived from Izapan prototypes. Moreover, not only did the Maya adopt the stela-and-altar complex, the "Long-lipped Gods," and the baroque style itself from the Izapan culture, but the priority of Izapa is also quite clear-cut in the very important adoption of the Long Count: the most ancient dated Maya monument reads 292 CE, while a stela in Izapan style at El Baúl, Guatemala, bears a Long Count date 256 years earlier.

La Mojarra and the Isthmian Script

Chance finds can often lead archaeologists in new directions. Such has been the case with the La Mojarra stela, accidentally discovered in November 1986 beneath the waters of the Acula River, in the Veracruz lowlands about halfway between Tres Zapotes and the Classic site of Cerro de las Mesas. This 4-ton monument is of fine-grained basalt, and depicts an imposing, standing figure, richly attired in Izapan style, with a towering headdress formed of multiple masks of a bird with an incurved beak—known for the Zapotec and Maya Late Formative—and topped by a fish creature that has been identified as a shark.

But it is the accompanying hieroglyphic text that caused a sensation among Mesoamerican epigraphers: arranged in twenty-one beautifully carved columns are about 400 signs, the longest inscribed text known so far for Mesoamerica. The script is clearly the same as that inscribed on the Tuxtla Statuette (see **figure 58**, p. 82), but otherwise unknown, and has been dubbed "Isthmian" by specialists. Intensive study by John Justeson and Terence Kaufman has resulted in a proposed decipherment of Isthmian, in which the script is identified as a mixed, partly logographic (semantic), partly phonetic system that reproduces the proto-Zoquean language; this would fit in with the known distribution of the Mixe-Zoquean linguistic family in this area. This proposed decipherment has, however, not received general acceptance, a situation that will continue until a larger body of "Isthmian" texts comes to light, or even less likely, a bilingual inscription in Isthmian and Maya scripts.

There are two Long Count dates on the La Mojarra stela: 8.5.3.3.5 and 8.5.16.9.7, corresponding respectively to 21 May 143 CE and 13 July 156 CE (the latter only six years earlier than the Tuxtla Statuette) (**figure 77**). This places the stela, and the Isthmian script, toward the end of the Late Formative. There are obvious connections here with both the Izapan civilization of the Pacific Coast and the Guatemalan highlands, and with the early Maya civilization then taking form in the Petén-Yucatan lowlands, but until further Isthmian texts are found and studied, the script will remain undeciphered and its external relationships will continue to be a mystery.

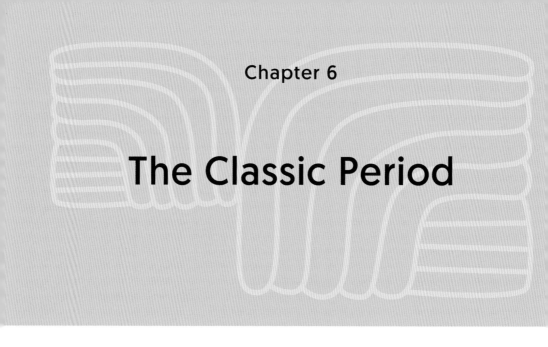

Chapter 6

The Classic Period

The Great Urban Centers

By any criteria, the period from about 150 to 650 CE was the most remarkable in the whole development of ancient Mexico. Cities were founded and grew throughout the area. One of these cities, Teotihuacan, grew larger than all others and became a central point of communication and commerce for all of Mesoamerica. This era is called the Classic, and it is at this time that the people of Mexico further developed state institutions, expanded interregional trade routes, and pursued different forms of political authority ranging from divine kingship to corporate forms of governance (**figure 78**).

The Classic era began at different times in other areas of Mesoamerica. The Classic span is given in most books as 250 to 900 CE, based upon the period during which the lowland Maya were inscribing Long Count dates on their stone monuments. Central Mexico, however, began the Classic in the second century CE and possibly even earlier, when urban construction began at the great city of Teotihuacan. And Teotihuacan itself had fallen into ruins long before the last Classic Maya city was abandoned.

By the Classic period, literacy may have been pan-Mesoamerican, with three major hieroglyphic scripts—that is, writing systems that recorded the spoken language. These scripts encompassed southwestern Mexico (the Zapotec tradition), the Isthmus region (the Isthmian tradition), and southeastern Mesoamerica (the Maya tradition). Although no books still survive from the Classic, we have every reason to believe that many groups with specialized roles possessed them. Dates were generally recorded in terms of the 52-year Calendar Round, but the Long Count was used in the Gulf Coast. What for, if not to write their own history?

This calendrical system was also related to the extensive pantheon of deities shared across Mesoamerica. The genesis of the divinities of Mexico came in the

78 Distribution of Classic- and Epiclassic-period centers. The dark-green shading indicates the core area of influence of Classic Teotihuacan and its peripheral extensions in Mexico. The light-green shading indicates other key Classic civilizations and their interactions with Classic Teotihuacan.

Formative period, as seen in Chapters 4 and 5, and the pantheon, in all its bewildering variety, was fully established by the Classic period. Deities were closely associated with powerful natural forces, so that most groups had a rain deity, a water goddess, a fire god, and divinities associated with the sun and moon. Maize, the staff of life, was often conceived as a young, beautiful deity whose sacrifice and resurrection (read harvest and planting) was of paramount importance. The Feathered Serpent, known to the later Aztecs as Quetzalcoatl, combined bird and serpent characteristics and was often associated with the planet Venus. When necessary, the combined aspects in such imagery could just as easily be split and given separate identities—another way of conveying the multifaceted nature of Meso-american deities.

There must have been many more people in Mexico during the Classic than formerly. Ruins are everywhere in central and southeastern Mexico, and most of them are Classic. In the Basin of Mexico alone, a monumental survey carried out by William Sanders and his associates has shown that by the end of this period, there were forty times as many inhabitants of the area as in the Middle Formative, with the great majority of people living in Teotihuacan.

Using a technology that was based on stone, wood, and vegetable fibers (for metals were generally unknown until after 800 CE), the Mexicans raised remarkable numbers of buildings, decorated them with beautiful polychrome murals, produced pottery and figurines in multitudinous quantity, and covered everything with sculptures. Even mass production was introduced, with the invention (or importation from South America) of the clay mold for making figurines and ceramic braziers. Behind this abundance was the same economic theme that had been emphasized by their predecessors: farming of maize, beans, squash, and chile peppers, reflected in the continued importance of nature deities in the Mesoamerican pantheon. In the Teotihuacan Valley and elsewhere in the arid highlands, agave plants and their products were very important. Some authors have claimed that the Classic achievement could only have resulted from utilization of some form of irrigation, but this was of primary importance only in the drier regions of Mexico, for example the Tehuacan Valley and the Valley of Oaxaca.

Very clearly, the Classic period saw the intensification of sharp social divisions throughout Mexico, and the consolidation of elite classes. It was long assumed that the mode of government was theocratic and that the many figures in Classic art were star-gazing priests who exercised power. Evidence from both the imagery and archaeology at Teotihuacan indicates a more complex picture, with certain social positions having simultaneously administrative, ritual, and military roles. That city's sizable urban working class, mostly devoted to the craft of goods, was unusual. Across Mesoamerica, below the powerful elite groups were diverse groups with specialized knowledge (religious, administrative, scribal, and military); a great variety of craft producers; carriers; and, supporting them all, a rural peasantry.

It may never be known how extensive the sway of each state was over surrounding territory; we have this kind of information only for the Maya. There is, however, evidence of warfare in the area by the beginning of this period, and only a hundred years later (by 250 CE) there is incontrovertible evidence for warrior cults. In reality, there has never been a civilization that did not engage in warfare, including the Classic Maya. In this connection, the sudden spread of the art styles and products of some Classic civilizations has quite justly been interpreted as the result of conquest, although prestige and its attendant emulation were also at play. For the Classic period, Teotihuacan had no rival in the extent of its influence or the intensity of its contacts with the rest of Mesoamerica. Only the Post-Classic Aztec capital of Tenochtitlan would rival the size and reach of the great Classic city.

Teotihuacan

Cities laid on a grid of the order of those in the Eastern hemisphere were rare anywhere in the Mesoamerican Classic. Of the few that did exist, the greatest of all was ancient Teotihuacan (**figure 79**), the most important site in the whole of Mexico: even Moteuczoma Xocoyotzin (the ninth Aztec ruler, known to the Spaniards as "Montezuma") himself made frequent pilgrimages on foot to its ruins. Memories of its greatness persisted in Aztec myths recorded after the Conquest, for it was then thought that the civilization that had begun at Tamoanchan had been transferred to Teotihuacan. There the deities met to decide who was to sacrifice himself so as to become the new, fifth, sun and bring light again to the world:

79 Oblique air view of Teotihuacan from the northwest. In the lower left is the Pyramid of the Moon. The Pyramid of the Sun lies at left center. The furthest visible group is the Ciudadela ("Citadel"), connected to the Pyramid of the Moon by the Avenue of the Dead. The city was laid out on a grid plan, and present-day field boundaries correspond roughly to old foundation walls.

> Even though it was night,
> even though it was not day,
> even though there was no light
> they gathered,
> the gods convened
> there in Teotihuacan.[2]

The most humble god of them all, Nanahuatzin, the "Purulent One," cast himself into the flames and became the sun. But the heavenly bodies did not move, so all the deities sacrificed themselves for mankind. Finally, government was established there; the lords of Teotihuacan were "wise men, knowers of occult things, possessors of the traditions." When they died, pyramids were built above them. The most sizable of the pyramids, those of the Sun and Moon, were said by tradition to have been built by the giants that existed in those days (and so the legend poetically says, "It is not unbelievable that they were made by hand").

The Teotihuacan Valley is actually a side pocket of the Basin of Mexico, comprising about 190 sq. miles (490 sq. km) of bottom land lying to the northeast of the

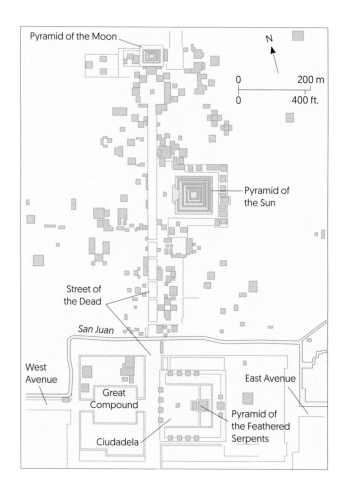

80 Plan of the central core of Teotihuacan, showing some of the numerous smaller structures around the major monuments revealed by René Millon's great mapping project.

Basin proper and surrounded by hills. Of this about one half is suitable for farming. Springs produce copious water that could have been used by the Teotihuacanos for farming, and there is some evidence for irrigation. These natural resources do not explain, however, the movement of most cultivators from throughout the Basin of Mexico to Teotihuacan between 150 BCE and 200 CE. For this we must turn to evidence from the city itself.

The detailed mapping project carried out by René Millon of the University of Rochester gives an idea of the gigantic size of this metropolis, the most expansive city of the Pre-Columbian world (**figure 80**). It covered over 8 sq. miles (20 sq. km), which were densely urbanized. Teotihuacan was laid out in the first century CE on a grid plan that is consistently oriented to 15 degrees 25 minutes east of true north, evincing that the planners must have been sophisticated surveyors as well. Various astronomical explanations have been advanced for this alignment, none of them completely convincing. Perhaps the strangest fact regarding this great city plan is that there is absolutely no precedent for it anywhere in the Americas.

Teotihuacan's major axis is now known as the Avenue of the Dead, which used to be thought to end at the so-called Ciudadela ("Citadel") in the south, a distance of 2 miles (3.2 km) from its northern terminus at the Pyramid of the Moon. It is now known that the avenue is twice this length, and that it is bisected in front of the

Ciudadela by an east–west avenue of equal length, so that the city, like the much later Aztec capital, was laid out in quarters. Everything built at Teotihuacan conformed to the orientation of the main axis. Three monumental structures anchor these sacred ways, and indeed all of Teotihuacan (see below).

The question is (and it must be admitted that no definite answer can be given): who were the people of Teotihuacan? Who built this city, and from where did they come? The early Spanish historian Torquemada tells us that the Totonac claimed the honor, and it is true that a few of the earliest Classic Teotihuacan buildings show a certain decorative influence from Veracruz, the Totonac homeland. But there is little evidence that the Totonac were in Veracruz until much later, during the Epiclassic period. Some scholars claim an Otomí occupation of the city; others hold for the Popoloca. In view of the strong continuities—both sacred and secular—between Teotihuacan and the Toltecs and Aztecs, Nahua affinities would appear to be the most probable. On this question we are little wiser than were the Mexican people at the time of the Conquest, who thought that giants or deities had built Teotihuacan.

The Great Pyramids

Three great pyramids define the center of the city: the Pyramids of the Sun and Moon in the north, and the Pyramid of the Feathered Serpents in the south. All three major pyramids are found directly adjacent to the main thoroughfare, the Street of the Dead. The Pyramids of the Sun and Moon are truly gargantuan structures, with their bases covering several acres and summits rising 200 ft (61 m) (Sun) and 140 ft (43 m) (Moon) over the city (**figure 81**). The Pyramid of Feathered Serpents is considerably smaller, but has the most elaborate sculptural decoration and serves as the center of the Ciudadela, an impressive complex near the center of the urban sprawl. Each of the buildings was the object of complex dedicatory rites consisting

81 View south along the Avenue of the Dead from the Pyramid of the Moon. The Pyramid of the Sun is visible on the left, echoing the shape of the mountain behind.

of human and animal sacrifice as well as the deposit of valuable and aesthetically charged objects. In addition, two of the three (Sun and Feathered Serpents) contain human-made tunnels where elaborate underground rituals were held directly beneath the pyramid.

All three pyramids were raised between 1 and 250 CE, or fairly early in the city's history. The Pyramid of the Sun was the first to be completed, about 100 CE. The building of this most massive of all Teotihuacan sacred structures was inaugurated by a rich deposit of obsidian, ceramics, and animal sacrifices. Similar deposits would characterize most subsequent monumental building at Teotihuacan. Eleven ceramic vessels with imagery of the Teotihuacan Rain Deity, together with what may be child sacrifices—which are very often associated with this deity—suggest that the Rain Deity was central to the meaning of the building. Three greenstone figures were also placed in this deposit, including one small mask of the type that was to be so important to later Teotihuacan art (see **figure 84**, p. 111). The carving on this mask is particularly fine, with rounded features and a rather naturalistic approach to the face, especially when compared to the larger, and probably later, masks associated with Teotihuacan. The interior fill is formed entirely of more than 41,000,000 cu. ft (1,175,000 cu. m) of sun-dried brick and rubble. On the exterior, a stone stairway, in part bifurcated, led to a now-destroyed temple on its lofty summit.

The city's population increased dramatically at the same time the Pyramid of the Sun was being built. In the two centuries before the structure's construction began (c. 150–1 BCE), the city had gone from a hamlet to a city of perhaps 20,000 people—a significant population for the time. During the building of the Pyramid of the Sun, however, the city grew to perhaps three times that size, with an estimated population of 60,000, in the space of a single century. What drew so many people to move to Teotihuacan? Further, given the need for significant human labor to build such an edifice, what convinced so many to work on the pyramid? It is probable that a charismatic leader was needed to bring the society together behind such a huge enterprise, although that leader is not easily identified in Teotihuacan art or writing. Rulers in several adjacent regions of Mesoamerica, including Oaxaca, the Gulf Coast, and the Maya area, insisted on memorializing themselves in public art and inscriptions, which makes the Teotihuacan reticence to use similar artistic strategies even more intriguing.

Discovered by accident in 1971, an extraordinary passageway underneath the Pyramid of the Sun runs approximately 20 ft (6 m) below the central axis of the pyramid, beginning near the main staircase and continuing for 330 ft (100 m) in an easterly direction, finally ending in a multi-chambered terminus shaped not unlike a four-leafed clover. The Pyramid of the Sun tunnel is one of two long ritual tunnels at Teotihuacan; the other is found underneath the Pyramid of the Feathered Serpents, which will be discussed and compared on p. 111. We will never know what these inner chambers contained, as they were emptied in antiquity. Doris Heyden and René Millon noted that throughout pre-Conquest Mexico such chambers were symbolic caves or wombs from which such deities as the Sun and the Moon, and the ancestors of humankind, emerged in the deep, mythological past. We have only to

82 In its day, Teotihuacan was the largest city in the Western Hemisphere. Here we see the Pyramid of the Moon, lying at the northern terminus of the Avenue of the Dead. The *talud-tablero* structures in front of it are considerably later than the pyramid itself.

recall the Aztec tradition that placed at Teotihuacan the creation of the Sun, Moon, and even the present universe to get an idea of how important the memory of these particular chambers was to the later inhabitants of central Mexico.

This subterranean passage is not the only unusual feature to have been found associated with the Pyramid of the Sun. Eduardo Matos Moctezuma discovered an approximately 10-ft (3-m) wide canal that once surrounded the Pyramid of the Sun on three sides. The combination of water and pyramid was for later central Mexicans a literary couplet meaning "city" (*altepetl* literally means "water mountain"). It is possible that such a central metaphor goes back to this building early in the Classic period, or perhaps back even earlier, to Formative pyramids.

The Pyramid of the Moon, which contains six earlier versions inside its massive bulk, was broadly similar to that of the Sun, although smaller, and was built primarily during the next phase, Miccaotli, at the beginning of the Classic (**figure 82**). The pyramid contained no cave in its interior nor moat around its perimeter. It does, however, echo the form of the sacred Cerro Gordo, the major mountain to the north, and may have been conceived by the Teotihuacanos as a replica of that natural feature, which to this day is considered a female deity. Adding to these associations is a rare monumental sculpture of a female deity in the vicinity. Perhaps the Aztecs were right to connect the building with the Moon, which was invariably considered female in Mesoamerica.

Recent work by Rubén Cabrera Castro and Saburo Sugiyama has detailed six previous constructions and three dedicatory offerings in the interior of the pyramid. The building began as a small platform in the last century BCE, but by the completion of the Pyramid of the Sun 200 years later, the Moon was also a monumental pyramidal structure. To inaugurate this important construction phase, a sacrificial offering of felines, eagles, finely chipped obsidian and carved greenstone, and one human victim was laid in the foundation in a pattern similar to the first offering seen in the Pyramid of the Sun. It is only at this point that the Pyramid of the Moon was brought into line with what was to become the orientation of the city. The building was enlarged three more times, with two of these construction episodes marked by elaborate offerings and sacrifices.

Around the year 350 CE, immediately before the penultimate phase of the building, Teotihuacanos buried three males at the summit of the pyramid and seemingly behind what would have been the monument's temple, dressing them up elaborately. Unlike the rest of the deposits, these individuals were seated with their hands free, and as such do not appear to have been treated as captives. They were buried with a rich array of grave goods, including jade items directly related to the Maya elite (**figure 83**), including a figurine carved in a style closely related to Maya work of the same period (distinctly different to the style of the offerings in the tunnel beneath the Pyramid of the Sun, **figure 84**). According to the oxygen and strontium signatures in their teeth and bones, these individuals were probably originally from the southern Maya highlands, an area that is also the source of the precious greenstone objects they wore. One of these Maya had relocated to Teotihuacan early in his life, but the other two appear to have stayed in the Maya area much longer.

In 1937 and 1943, Carnegie Institution of Washington archaeologists, led by Alfred V. Kidder, excavated a series of richly stocked Early Classic tombs, at the great Teotihuacan-influenced site of Kaminaljuyu, near Guatemala City in the Maya Highlands (see p. 124). The occupants, all male and some quite elderly, had been buried seated in exactly the same posture as those in the Pyramid of the Moon. It is therefore probable that the Pyramid of the Moon captives had once lived at Kaminaljuyu, and had the misfortune to end their days in the hands of their Teotihuacano captors. We know that immigrants from several regions were important to Teotihuacan, so the material wealth in these offerings may signal not only the high rank of the sacrificial victims but also the overall importance of the offering in the dedication of a major pyramid.

Workshops in the area of the Pyramid of the Moon produced the razor-sharp obsidian blades and dart points used by the Teotihuacan military. The production of these key military items in the area around the pyramid makes clear the close relation between the city's rulers—those who controlled the pyramids and their environs—and military power. These same obsidian objects with martial associations were central to the ritual deposits laid into all three major Teotihuacan pyramids.

The third building in the triumvirate of Teotihuacan architecture, the Pyramid of the Feathered Serpents, is considerably smaller than the two monumental pyramids discussed above (**figure 85**). What it lacks in size, however, it makes up for with its central location, lavish offerings, and the wealth and importance of its facade decoration. The structure is a seven-tiered stepped pyramid with typical *talud-tablero* facades located within an impressive plaza enclosed by platforms of 435 yards (400 m) on each side. The entire ensemble that includes platforms, plaza, elite residences, and the Pyramid of the Feathered Serpents is called the Ciudadela. This space would have been one of the chief ritual spaces in the city, and its history and the lavish deposits and decoration attest to this importance.

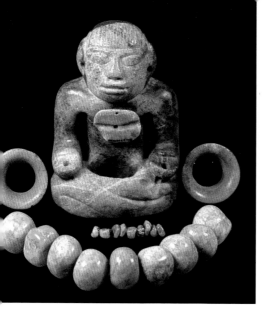

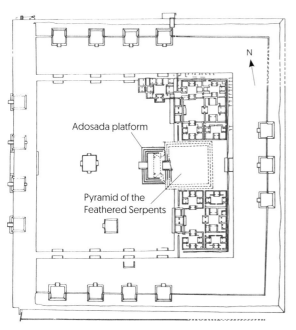

83 (ABOVE LEFT) Jade objects associated with burials near the summit of the Pyramid of the Moon, Teotihuacan. The human figure is carved in a style closely related to Maya work of the same period, and the jade itself may have been imported from the Maya area.

84 (ABOVE RIGHT) Greenstone mask with pyrite eye inlays, deposited in the tunnel underneath the Pyramid of the Sun during construction. Ht 4.3 in. (10.8 cm).

85 (LEFT) Plan of the Ciudadela and the Pyramid of the Feathered Serpents, Teotihuacan. Classic period.

N

Adosada platform

Pyramid of the Feathered Serpents

The Ciudadela had been transformed into sacred ground two hundred years earlier, at the same time that the Pyramid of the Sun was constructed, during the first century CE. At this time a smaller building, decorated with serpents in a watery environment, served as the center of activity. This serpent building was paired with a structure that probably served as a substantial ball court for the playing of the rubber-ball game. The entire area was fitted with drains that allowed for the control of water throughout the space, a concern that was to remain important throughout the history of this area.

Archaeologists recently discovered a substantial tunnel in the vicinity that was originally constructed around the time of the first serpent building. Similarly to the

86 Central pair of greenstone figures found directly below the center of the Pyramid of the Feathered Serpents, at the end of a man-made tunnel.

tunnel under the Pyramid of the Sun, this tunnel began in a plaza to the west of the central building. Oriented east–west, it was approximately 330 ft (100 m) long and ended underneath the center of the building. Unlike the tunnel under the Pyramid of the Sun, which was only about 20 ft (6 m) below the surface, this one reached down to the water table—55 ft (17 m) below the surface—for a good portion of its length. Toward the end of the tunnel would originally have been an offering of five greenstone figures, of which four remained upon archaeological discovery. The central pair consisted of a sizable, elaborately clothed female and a smaller nude male (**figure 86**). The female wore a jade-bead necklace, and both carried bundles with jade earspools and pendants along with mirrors made of pyrite. Both figures exhibit the idealized facial features that were standard at Teotihuacan for the next several centuries. Two other female greenstone figures were found fallen nearby. These also carry bundles of jade and pyrite ornaments. In a small chamber behind the figures, the Teotihuacanos created a mountainous landscape in miniature, with liquid mercury representing the flow of water down the mountains. Around this tableau of human figures and mountains with flowing water were placed dozens of spiral shells, hundreds of slate and pyrite mirrors, skulls of great felines, a dozen rubber balls, and hundreds of serpentine and jade beads. Sergio Gómez Chávez, the archaeologist who explored the tunnel, points out that the entire feature converges on this tableau of greenstone figures with offerings. He also argues that the figures at the center of the tableau could represent the founding figures of Teotihuacan, given that ancestor figures are later shown carrying such bundles, pointing the way to the sacred spot around which the polity would be organized.

The early structure decorated with watery serpents was built directly over the greenstone-figure tableau. The tunnel remained open as that building was replaced with the final version of the Pyramid of the Feathered Serpents at the beginning of the third century CE. The tunnel was then promptly closed and filled with rubble. Only much later (after approximately two centuries) did the Teotihuacanos go back into the tunnel, and even then they chose not to disturb the central offering.

The Pyramid of the Feathered Serpents was the last monumental public structure built at Teotihuacan, completed early in the third century CE. Around the tiers of *talud-tableros* (**figure 87**) (for more on which, see p. 115), plumed rattlesnakes carry images of the Fire Serpent wearing mosaic headdresses. Elsewhere at Teotihuacan this headdress is shown on warriors, and was probably specific to that office. Effigy seashells are sculpted in the background, suggesting that the scene is taking place in a watery environment. As this building was completed, the Teotihuacanos closed and filled the drains they had constructed earlier to control water in the plaza. From this point forward, the plaza was regularly flooded, as evidenced by sand and silt layers deposited in the area. An account from the Maya highlands suggests that we have here another version of the first moment of creation, with an opposed pair of serpents—one representing life, greenness, and peace; and the other heat, the desert regions, and war—cavorting or conversing in the primal ocean (**figure 88**).

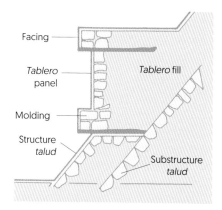

87 Cross-section to show the typical *talud-tablero* building style, as used at Teotihuacan.

88 [BELOW] West facade of the Pyramid of the Feathered Serpents, Teotihuacan. Transition between the Late Formative and Early Classic periods. The *tableros* are decorated with undulating plumed serpents amid shells and bivalves (mollusks with two-part hinged shells); their heads peer out and alternate with Fire Serpent heads. The latter protrude from near the serpents' tails. The narrow *taluds* are embellished with profiled undulating feathered serpents surrounded by shells and bivalves.

Excavations within and around the pyramid, carried out by Rubén Cabrera Castro, Saburo Sugiyama, and George Cowgill, revealed that it had been built in a single episode during which more than 200 individuals had been sacrificed in elaborate dedicatory rites. Young adults with their hands tied behind their backs had been dispatched in two groups of eighteen individuals (the number of months, each twenty days long, in the year), each group being interred in a substantial burial pit on the north and south sides of the pyramid (**figure 89**). More sacrificial victims were interred on the east–west axis of the building. Christine White and her colleagues have analyzed the oxygen-isotope ratios in the bone and dental enamel of these victims and found that the majority of them did not grow up in Teotihuacan, although most had lived there for some time. By contrast, the young female victims buried in adjacent pits did spend their childhood in the city. These results suggest that most of the sacrificial victims may have been enslaved former warriors, probably gifted for the massive dedicatory offerings to the building by their captors. Investigations made in 1925 showed that in addition to this great slaughter, a single slain victim had been placed at each of the pyramid's four corners, in a practice that goes back to the original monumental construction of the Pyramid of the Sun. In the center of the pyramid, directly above the tunnel offerings already described, was the richest offering of all, with twenty victims and thousands of pieces of jade, shell, and other materials. By using such sacred numbers as eighteen and twenty and by placing these offerings in each of the major world directions, the Teotihuacanos were mirroring the symbolism of Mesoamerican creation epics. The presence of sacrificial victims from throughout Mesoamerica speaks to the very real political power of the city, even at this early date.

The exact mode of sacrificial death has not yet been established, but in the absence of obvious signs of violence on the bones, slitting of the victims' throats without involving the cervical vertebrae seems likely. The scale of this consecration, unique so far in the archaeology of any Mesoamerican group, including the Aztecs, is highlighted by the necklaces that many of the victims wear: strings of human jaws, upper and lower, sometimes real, sometimes crafted from shell. The actual human jaws can be traced to several different areas of Mesoamerica through oxygen isotopic signatures. Organized violence was celebrated throughout the pyramid: on the facade with the headdress of a military office, as well as in the interior through the original role of the sacrificial victims.

Sometime after 300 CE, the pyramid's front facade was covered by a plain *talud-tablero* structure (see opposite), preserving the original decorated facade underneath. Sculptures on the other three sides were desecrated and left in disrepair. There is also evidence of looting in the interior of the pyramid around this time. We believe that the desecration of the sculpture, as well as the looting, were carried out by the Teotihuacanos themselves. Groups who had a very good idea of what was inside the pyramid were able to clean out two burial pits in the center, leaving only the slimmest of clues as to what was originally placed there. One of the groups was on the exact centerline of the structure and contained a feathered-serpent baton, surely a signal of very high rank. It is highly likely that the temple

89 (ABOVE) One of several burials with high numbers of tied captive warriors. The arm bones under the vertebral column and the presence of back mirrors and dart points indicate that the victims were sacrificed at the dedication of the Pyramid of the Feathered Serpents, Teotihuacan. Classic period.

90 (RIGHT) Representation of a temple on a Teotihuacan pottery vessel. Early Classic period.

structure at the summit of the pyramid was burned and razed at this time. We do not know what caused the Teotihuacanos to treat this most important structure with such violence, but at the very least this episode points out the controversial nature of the social institution embodied by this building.

Classic Teotihuacan architecture is based on a few simple principles. Wall cores of small stones are faced with broken-up volcanic stones set in clay and covered with a smooth coat of lime plaster. Alternatively, in lower-status areas a mixture of mud and clay could be poured into a mold to form the walls. The typical architectural motif is that known as *talud-tablero*: a rectangular panel with inset is placed over a sloping wall (see **figure 87**, p. 113). Buildings from the humblest family shrine to large temples are decorated with this motif throughout the city, and it is even replicated in pottery decoration from the time (**figure 90**). The panel area is often painted, and in the Pyramid of the Feathered Serpents it serves as the support for elaborate sculptural decoration. Interestingly, the *talud-tablero* form itself seems to be an emulation from the Puebla-Tlaxcala region, but is used to such an extent by Teotihuacanos that it often becomes associated specifically with the metropolis.

Most of what we see today at Teotihuacan was built after the completion of these three great public structures by the early third century CE. By the early fourth century CE, the city had reached the height of its population, estimated by René Millon at a probable figure of 125,000, but possibly reaching 200,000 at its maximum.

Palaces and Apartment Compounds

A major finding of the Teotihuacan Mapping Project was that most of the city consisted of walled residential compounds divided internally into apartments (**figure 91**). Most, if not all, apartment compounds were built after the completion of the monumental pyramids; we know little of how the already substantial population lived before the onset of apartment building. The few entrances to each compound suggest that access was carefully controlled. Compounds measure from 4,300 to 75,000 sq. ft (400 to 7,000 sq. m), although the majority fall near the middle of this range. The differences in construction, decoration, and room size indicate a substantial range of wealth and status.

The city was cosmopolitan: in its western part there was a Oaxaca ward, in which Zapotecs carried on their own customs, while on the east there was one made up of people with strong connections to the lowland Veracruz and Maya areas. Isotope analysis of skeletal remains from the Oaxaca ward has shown that throughout their lives, many individuals moved back and forth between Teotihuacan and their place of origin, suggesting their role as merchants and their maintenance of social ties and identities. These individuals would then return to Teotihuacan's Oaxaca barrio to live out the rest of their lives. It appears that this practice began rather early in Teotihuacan's history.

91 A corner in the patio of the Quetzalpapalotl ("Quetzal-Butterfly") Palace, Teotihuacan. The great city had many luxurious apartment compounds, but most had painted mural decoration, rather than the carvings we see here. The ornaments on the roof represent royal headbands.

92 Ceramic brazier assembled from multiple mold-made pieces. Found in an offering in the apartment compound of Tetitla. Apartment-compound members engaged in religious practices that involved such elaborately decorated ceramic braziers as this for the burning of incense. Probably meant to commemorate a deceased warrior, this brazier mimics a mortuary bundle, framing the funeral mask in the center with butterflies drinking nectar from flowers (top), and alligator eyes wearing a royal headband (below). Classic period. Ht 26.9 in. (68.2 cm).

Typical of the compound layout might be Tetitla, a 196 by 196 ft (60 by 60 m) square complex of several dozen rooms and nine temple structures, all organized around courts. Each court was open to the sky, sometimes with a small altar in the center. Triadic temple arrangements, found at Tetitla and throughout the Classic city, consist of a single raised platform containing the central temple joined to two flanking temples at 90-degree angles. This form is found already at Late Formative Tetimpa, Puebla, as well as at the earliest occupations at Teotihuacan. While windows were lacking, several of the rooms had smaller sunken courts open to the sky, very similar to the Roman *atria*, into which light and air were admitted through the roofed corridors, supported by surrounding piers. The rainwater in the sunken basins could be drained off by means of stone-lined underground canals. All known compounds were one-storied affairs, with flat roofs built from beams and small sticks and twigs, overlain by earth and rubble. Doorways were rectangular and covered by a cloth.

It is estimated that the Tetitla compound would have housed sixty to one hundred people. Each Teotihuacan compound must have been a rather tightly organized social group, given the specialization and planning essential to compound life. Males in the compound seem to have been more closely related to one another than the females. Most compounds had one or two rich burials, suggesting that founders or important lineage members, particularly warriors, were especially honored (**figure 92**).

93 Mural 3 from the south *tablero* in the basal platform of sub-structure 2 of the Building of the Feathered Shell-Trumpets, underneath the Quetzalpapalotl Palace, Teotihuacan. The mural depicts an eagle emitting from its beak a stream and drops of water onto a sign for "Reed." Early Classic period. Ht 1 ft 3 in. (40 cm).

The sophistication and artistry of the Teotihuacanos can be seen in the magnificent murals that adorn the walls of the palaces and apartment compounds (**figure 93**). Many of these are highly repetitive, with rows of human figures whose bodies disappear under their elaborate ritual attire. In the porticoes of one of the buildings in the White Patio at Atetelco are depicted processions of jaguars and coyotes, painted in various shades of red, and perhaps symbolizing key social institutions of this warlike society (**figures 94, 95**).

The most famous of the compound murals are those at Tepantitla; following their discovery, these were interpreted by Alfonso Caso as a depiction of the Paradise of the Rain God, or to use the Nahuatl term, Tlalocan. But the deity dominating the scene, once thought to be the Rain God himself, is now accepted as female, following the work of Esther Pasztory and others. Karl Taube has further shown that this goddess has the mouth parts (fangs and palps) of a spider and that she was a central deity—perhaps the chief one—in the Teotihuacan religious system. While other Mesoamerican urban cultures certainly had female deities, few, if any, gave them such a central role.

The larger and more richly decorated residences, mainly found grouped around the Avenue of the Dead, were surely the residences of the lords of the city. These qualify as true "palaces" in that they are significantly finer than the great majority of the other 2,000 compounds found throughout the city. Two central palace structures flanked the Pyramid of the Feathered Serpents, and it has been suggested that these served as the royal apartments. A particularly fine palace situated between the Sun

94 (ABOVE) Prowling coyote with a feathered crest, from a mural painting at Atetelco, Teotihuacan. The painting is executed in subtly contrasting values of red. A "speech scroll" curves from the mouth of the beast, and below the mouth is the symbol for the human heart, dripping blood. Early Classic period.

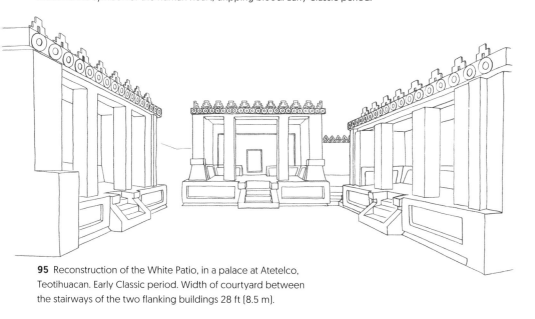

95 Reconstruction of the White Patio, in a palace at Atetelco, Teotihuacan. Early Classic period. Width of courtyard between the stairways of the two flanking buildings 28 ft (8.5 m).

and Moon Pyramids, dubbed "Xalla" by archaeologists, was ten times the size of the average apartment compound. To further emphasize the importance of this group, a raised road was constructed between Xalla and the plaza in front of the Pyramid of the Moon to provide direct communication with the central ritual precinct. Xalla's religious shrines were stocked with exceptional sculptures, including greenstone stelae and a life-sized human figure in marble. Although these and many other palaces fell to the torch at the end of the Classic period, vestiges of their sumptuous decoration in paint and stone are found everywhere (see **figure 99**, p. 125).

If palaces alone had been built in ancient Teotihuacan, this would have been a peculiar sort of city. Some idea of the way more ordinary people lived is given by the compound called Tlajinga 33, in the far south of the city, studied by Rebecca Storey and Randolph Widmer. Although the general layout is comparable to the finer residences in the center, the builders used cheaper materials and did not decorate the residence with murals. An important early burial contained a male with accompanying warrior symbolism, including the goggles associated with elite warriors elsewhere at Teotihuacan. Even though the compound participated in the city's warrior symbolism, fairly humble artisans occupied this compound throughout its history, and it seems that as time progressed, they became poorer and had less control over their crafts. There must have been an immense multitude of traders, artisans, and other non-food producers living in quarters of this sort. Mexico was to see nothing of this kind again until the Aztecs built their capital Tenochtitlan.

The Teotihuacan Pantheon

In the view of several scholars, the presiding deity of the Teotihuacan pantheon was female. Depictions of related female deities, or perhaps aspects of a single goddess, include a colossal statue representing the Water Goddess (in Nahuatl *Chalchiuhtlicue*, "Her Skirt Is of Jade"). An even more massive statue, weighing almost 200 metric tons and now situated in front of the Museum of Anthropology in Mexico City, was found in an unfinished state on the slopes of Tlaloc Mountain. It is identified in the popular Mexican consciousness with that male deity, the Rain God, but wears abstracted versions of the female garments seen on the Water Goddess. It is likely that these and other female entities formed a closely related deity complex, in a similar way to the female deities of the Aztec. Many of the other deities of the complete Mexican pantheon are already clearly recognizable at Teotihuacan. Here were worshipped the Rain God ("Tlaloc" to the Aztecs) and the Feathered Serpent (the later "Quetzalcoatl"), as well as the Sun God, the Moon Goddess, and Xipe Totec (Nahuatl for "Our Lord the Flayed One"), the last-named being the symbol of the annual renewal of vegetation with the onset of the rainy season. Particularly common are ceramic braziers of the Old Fire God, a creator divinity widely known before the rise of Teotihuacan.

Tradition holds that Teotihuacan was a sacred burial ground. Particularly important burials have seemingly been discovered only by professional looters, but underneath the floors of the palaces and apartment buildings have been encountered a number of slab-lined graves and simple pit burials. Similarly to the later Aztecs, the Teotihuacanos favored cremation of the dead, the body first being wrapped in a bundle. Around the remains were placed fine offerings of all sorts, particularly well-crafted and graceful vases, obsidian artifacts, and such perishable items as textiles. Beliefs about the hereafter are recorded in a Nahuatl song:

And they called it Teotihuacan
because it was the place
where the lords were buried.
Thus they said:
"When we die,
truly we die not,
because we will live, we will rise,
we will continue living, we will awaken.
This will make us happy."[3]

Arts, Production, and Trade

The Teotihuacan art style, as revealed in frescoes, sculpture, pottery, and other productions, could be tremendously elegant and refined, as well as highly stylized and ordered. Even when artisans were less careful, there is a grave, minimal quality to the art, and the best work is monumental and still, no matter its size (**figure 96**). Sculpture is best represented in the austere stone masks—fashioned from greenstone, basalt, jade, andesite, and other materials, each of which once had inlaid eyes of mussel-shells or obsidian—as well as in a few pieces of a huge scale, for example the Water Goddess. Murals filled the walls of many of the more opulent apartment compounds, where they were applied in "true fresco," with the diluted pigments applied to a fresh coat of lime plaster. A silicate, such as mica, was often added to the pigment dilution to increase the paint's sheen, and after drying, the whole was carefully burnished.

96 The rather austere beauty of this mask is typical of Teotihuacan. The serpentine stone from which the mask was carved was highly valued from Olmec times onward. The yellowish tinge around the eyes is probably the result of decayed iron-pyrite inlays. Classic period.

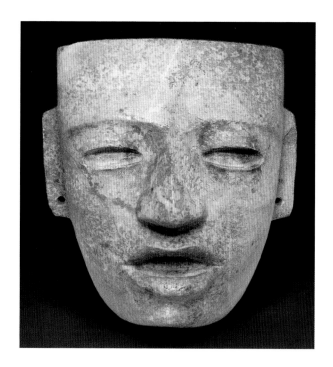

97 Ceramics from Classic burials at Teotihuacan. a)–b) Cylindrical tripods decorated in carved-relief technique; c) long-necked container; d) pitcher; e) jar with face of the Rain Deity; f)–g) blocks with two holes; h)–i) Thin Orange ware. Scale: 1/4.

A hallmark of Teotihuacan culture is the cylindrical pottery vase with three slab-shaped feet (**figure 97**). Adapted in the fourth century CE, perhaps from earlier experiments on the Gulf Coast, this ceramic form became associated specifically with the metropolis. These vases usually have fitted lids on top, some with handles in the form of a bird. On the basis of similar vases in contemporary Maya tombs, they may have served to hold the chocolate drink. Other characteristic forms in clay include vessels in the shape of flower vases. Decoration on these luxury items, found in graves and far away as trade pieces, may be plano-relief, a technique in which the motif is modeled or incised, or painted on a thin coating of lime, the latter executed in the same manner as the wall frescoes. A fine ware known as Thin Orange was manufactured in southern Puebla, an area that may have been under Teotihuacan control, and appears as bowls with annular bases, boxes with lids, or effigies of little dogs.

Polychrome ceramic braziers were the central ritual objects throughout Teotihuacan society and are often found in key spaces in apartment compounds (see **figure 92**, p. 117). To construct these, stamped clay plaques and other mold-made

98 Hieroglyphs from a patio floor in the La Ventilla section of Teotihuacan, dated to 300–450 CE. The placement of the glyphs on the floor and their organization in a grid pattern are unique. There are suggestions that the glyphs may be toponyms (place names) or titles, but they remain undeciphered.

ceramic pieces were attached to a plain ceramic base. Archaeologists have identified a major workshop for the making of these ceramic braziers near the Pyramid of the Feathered Serpents. This central location suggests that those who controlled the Feathered Serpent cult (presumably the Teotihuacan state) also controlled the production and distribution of ceramic braziers. Other objects of clay include mold-made figurines of men and deities, as well as small two-holed ceramic blocks, the function of which remains undetermined. More utilitarian ceramics include storage vessels (*ollas*) and griddles (*comales*). Clay pellets were carefully shaped for employment as blowgun missiles, and we know from a scene on a vase that this tool was used to hunt birds.

Obsidian chipping reached new heights of elaboration, with the production of dart-points as well as undulating serpent bodies (symbols of lightning) and little human effigies of that material. Many obsidian items associated with the military were produced in workshops near the Pyramid of the Moon under the control of Teotihuacan elite, as described on p. 110. Workshops scattered throughout the city produced obsidian blades for everyday use. The Teotihuacan state controlled the great deposits of green obsidian near Pachuca, Hidalgo; and the 100 obsidian workshops known to have existed in the city were part of the thriving mercantile sector.

Bone needles and bodkins testify to the manufacture of clothing and basketry, and the charred remains of cotton cloth with weft pattern, coiled baskets, and twilled sleeping mats or *petates* have been found. Paintings show that men wore a loincloth and/or kilt with sandals, and women the pull-over *huipilli* (a traditional square-cut blouse) and underskirt.

Although none have survived, manuscripts must have been in both ritual and administrative use, for the Teotihuacanos had writing. Teotihuacanos knew of the Maya writing system but did not use it; instead, they used their own writing, mainly to render names or locations accompanying an image. An example is the fascinating patio found in the La Ventilla area, where forty-two glyphs fill a floor in a regular grid pattern (**figure 98**).

Cooking took place in kitchen areas within the compounds, over clay, three-pronged braziers. Pre-Columbian cooks used ceramic pots for stews and *comales* (round ceramic griddles) for making tortillas. Charred vegetal materials and animal bones give some idea of the citizens' diet: they subsisted on a small-cobbed maize, common and runner beans, squashes and pumpkins, husk tomatoes, prickly-pear cactus, agave (century plant), avocados, and amaranth, along with wild-plant foods. The important food animals were deer, dogs, cottontail rabbits and jackrabbits, turkeys, wild ducks and geese, and small fish. Much ink has been spilled over the problem of the agricultural base of Teotihuacan civilization. William Sanders was certain that there was a local irrigation system in the outskirts of Teotihuacan. On the other hand, there is some evidence of *chinampa* cultivation, for relict *chinampa* plots show up on the Millon map of the city, and it is suggestive that the well-known *chinampa* systems in the southern part of the Basin of Mexico, for example the one at Xochimilco, have the same orientation as Teotihuacan itself.

Yet it may be fruitless to look at the valley of Teotihuacan alone for the secret to the capital's remarkable success, for the city held sway over most of the central highlands of Mexico during the Classic, and wielded significant influence over much of Mesoamerica. Other groups came from throughout Mesoamerica to participate in the city's economy and society, forming such cosmopolitan neighborhoods as the Oaxaca barrio discussed above. Similarly to the later Aztec state, it may have depended as much on long-distance trade and tribute as upon local agricultural production. Elegant vases of pure Teotihuacan manufacture or showing pronounced Teotihuacan influence are found in the burials of nobles all over Mexico, and elements of the area's style and symbolism were incorporated into the art of many other Mesoamerican civilizations. The apogee of Teotihuacan influence on other Mesoamerican elites seems to have been between 375 and 500 CE, when interest in all fine Teotihuacan things was at its peak.

Especially interesting is the contact with the Maya on the other side of Mesoamerica. Some 650 miles (1,040 km) southeast of Teotihuacan, the highland Guatemala site of Kaminaljuyu contains elite tombs stocked with luxuries from Teotihuacan as well as even more items that were locally produced but bore the stamp of Teotihuacan style and symbolism (see p. 110). Two elite burial mounds employed the *talud-tablero* architectural style foreign to this region but closely associated with the metropolis. The great majority of those buried there were local lords, however—when they were not sacrificial victims. Four skulls in a single deposit (probable victims of decapitation) contain chemical signatures indicative of the lowland Maya area. Only the principal occupant of the earliest tomb (A–V) in these mounds may have actually spent time at Teotihuacan, and only as a visitor or pilgrim during childhood. At the same time, no Kaminaljuyu commoner seems to have had anything to do with Teotihuacan goods or practices, nor was there any attempt to organize the city in a Teotihuacan-style grid plan. Instead, Teotihuacan relationships here were centered around prestige goods and symbolism intended solely for the elite.

On 16 January 378 CE, the native ruler of Tikal in northern Guatemala—one of the greatest and oldest Maya cities—and his dynasty were overthrown by an invasion from the west, and a new dynasty put in place, by a foreign personage known as Sihyaj K'ahk' ("Fire is Born"). The new arrival appears to have been the liege or general of an otherwise-unknown but important ruler of Teotihuacan bearing the pictorial glyphic name Spearthrower Owl. Similar dynastic disruptions followed during subsequent decades in many other Maya lowland cities, such as Copan, instigated sometimes by central Mexican foreigners, sometimes by native-born Maya imbued with Teotihuacan-inspired military iconography. It seems that mighty Teotihuacan had become a hegemonic empire, controlling much of southern Mesoamerica through military garrisons. One such is depicted by a mural at La Sufricaya, not far from the Guatemala-Belize border; this shows row upon row of seated and fully armed Teotihuacan warriors.

The new Maya rulers and their successors apparently never forgot Teotihuacan's domination over the Maya lowlands, for their kings proudly wore Teotihuacan military headdresses and other gear until the very end of the Late Classic.

The Fall of a City

Teotihuacan met its end by the close of the sixth century CE through the deliberate destruction of palaces and associated elite art. In one example from the Xalla palace, a rare monumental marble figure of a darted sacrificial victim was smashed, the bits scattered, and the entire area burned in what was clearly a desecration of the piece (**figure 99**).

99 Monumental standing figure from the Xalla palace in central Teotihuacan. Such stiffly posed, rather impersonal standing figures as this one were placed in several key caches and must have been important to commemorate sacrificial practices at Teotihuacan. This figure was smashed during the destruction of the Xalla palace in the sixth century. Ht 4 ft 2 in. (1.28 m).

Similar elite anthropomorphic sculptures, including one found adjacent to the Pyramid of the Feathered Serpents, were also smashed and scattered. All three of the major palaces mentioned above, as well as many more along the Avenue of the Dead, were burned to the ground in a targeted conflagration and the art associated with these palaces and their temples was systematically destroyed. This precise and conscious destruction of Teotihuacan's elite and its symbolism suggests a group or groups within Teotihuacano society. Other evidence that the Teotihuacan elite system was on the wane includes the cessation of ceramic brazier production and the closing of the central obsidian workshops. Some internal crisis or long-term political and economic malaise, perhaps the disruption of its trade and tribute routes and the siphoning of migrants by such new polities as the rising Xochicalco and Cacaxtla states, may have resulted in the downfall. Whatever the reasons, direct Teotihuacan influence over the rest of Mesoamerica had ceased by 600 CE.

Along with political and economic factors, stress on the physical environment could have played a minor role in the decline of the metropolis. George Vaillant proposed that the destruction of the surrounding forests necessary for the burning of the lime that went into the building of Teotihuacan resulted in a precocious erosion and desiccation of the region. A related factor might have been the increasing aridity of the climate all over Mexico during the Classic, which apparently was at its most severe in the Basin of Mexico.

Whatever the causes, the luxurious palaces of Teotihuacan were now in ruins, and its major temples abandoned. But away from the Avenue of the Dead, the city continued to live for another two centuries; this reduced occupation is called Coyotlatelco, a name derived from the simple red-on-buff pottery characteristic of the period. (An example of Coyotlatelco pottery is shown in **figure 124**, p. 154.) Through a probable combination of people leaving the city and high infant and child mortality, the population of Teotihuacan had sunk to only a quarter of its former total. Atzcapotzalco, a Teotihuacan-related center west of the great lake, futilely carried on a late survival of their old culture.

The Great Acropolis of Cholula

At the same time that the Teotihuacanos were building the Pyramids of the Sun and Moon, the people of Cholula in the adjacent Valley of Puebla were building a rival monumental acropolis (**figure 100**). Surrounding groups left their smaller centers and flocked to the new monumental core and the burgeoning city around it, although this depopulation of the countryside was less pronounced than at Teotihuacan and its environs. The eruption of the Popocatepetl volcano around the middle of the first century BCE helped drive people of the area to Cholula. The same eruption may have provided an impetus for the growth of Teotihuacan. It is certain that the areas closest to the volcano in both the Basin of Mexico and the Valley of Puebla were abandoned at this time.

100 View from the south of the acropolis of Cholula, Puebla, crowned with a church from the European colonial period. This great adobe-brick construction, which covers some 16 hectares and rises 180½ ft (55 m) above the surrounding plain, is the most massive structure in the Pre-Columbian World.

The first monumental structure at Cholula was a complex arrangement of terraces and plazas capped by an enclosed plaza at the summit. The upper terraces were defined by *talud-tablero* architecture, a style shared with Teotihuacan (see p. 115), which can be traced back to the Formative period at Tetimpa in the Cholula area. Also similar to Teotihuacan was the use of painting to adorn the *tablero* element. Several of the Cholula structure's *tableros* were decorated with murals depicting a series of human skulls in polychrome against a black background. Other elements of the building, and especially the complex plan with plazas and terraces, were decidedly unlike the contemporary monumental architecture of Teotihuacan. The next extensive building phase enveloped the original structures with an edifice that had multiple levels and stairways on its four sides so as to give direct access to all the partitioned spaces in the acropolis.

A 165 ft (50 m) long polychrome mural with life-sized human figures, said to be Early Classic in date (around 100 CE) but bearing no similarity to the Teotihuacan mural tradition, decorated an external wall of one of the many platforms adjacent, on the south side, to the acropolis. Known as "the Drunkards," the scenes on the mural are indubitably ones of drinking and inebriation, perhaps referencing a mythic account of social deviance, a ritual inversion of moral norms applied to elders and young warriors, or an actual historical episode of social factionalism unfolding in a context of an attempted alliance.

During the height of Teotihuacan (around 500 CE), the acropolis of Cholula was already a massive stepped complex at the end of an avenue 1.2 miles long that defined the south–north axis of the city. The avenue led to a plaza in front of

101 Stela 2 from the Patio of the Altars, south side of the acropolis of Cholula. Ht 9 ft 6.1 in. (2.9 m).

the south staircase to the acropolis, a broad open space with stela-altar sets on its eastern and western flanks. These two dual monuments appear to have remained in these locations while the plaza, now known as the "Patio of the Altars," underwent further alterations, but eventually, probably by 600 CE, they were purposefully smashed, and some of the fragments scattered.

The east set (Stela-Altar 1) is comprised of two substantial multi-tone blocks. The stela has a frame carved with volutes and interlaced scrolls, embellishments that are present on the three visible shallow, vertical surfaces of the altar. The west set (Stela-Altar 2) included a great, heavy altar, yet the stela is of smaller proportions than its counterpart from the east set and is pointed at the top (**figure 101**). While this stela is decorated with a frame carved with scroll-like patterns, the three visible shallow, vertical surfaces of the altar depict two pairs of plumed serpents crawling and twisting in opposite directions, with their belly scales up and entangled with scrolls. A carved double line that seemingly defines a frame on the top surface also characterizes the altar.

The blank fields of both stelae are so smooth that it seems likely that they were originally stuccoed and painted with a figural representation. This type of dual monument is common in the Maya region but not in the Mexican central highlands, and as noted by archaeologist David Peterson, the stelae's placement flanking pyramid staircases resembles those at such sites as the Temple of the Jaguars in Tikal. Peterson also argues that these rare monuments from Cholula may have been the stages on which holders of the dual political-religious offices of the Tlalchiac and Tlaquiach, known from later sources, may have sat and stood during important rituals; perhaps as the officials' backdrop, the stelae would have shown the painted representation of a former, prestigious set of dual rulers.

Cerro de las Mesas and Classic Veracruz

Further east, on the Gulf Coast plain, new Classic civilizations appeared that in some respects reflect continuity with the old Olmec and Isthmian traditions of the lowlands, as well as some intrusive elements ultimately derived from Teotihuacan. The site of Cerro de las Mesas lies in the middle of the former Olmec territory, in south-central Veracruz, approximately 15 miles (24 km) from the Bay of Alvarado, on a broad band of high land above the swamps of the Río Blanco. The site is at the center of an area dotted with earthen mounds, that is, the remains of ruined houses. Cerro de las Mesas was occupied from Middle Formative through Late Post-Classic times but attained its apogee during the Classic.

A number of stelae encountered there by Stirling exhibit continuity with earlier Olmec and Isthmian traditions in the region. Similarly to the Isthmian La Mojarra stela (see Chapter 5), several Cerro de las Mesas stelae show a ruler figure combined with columns of hieroglyphs in the Isthmian writing system. Two of the monuments contain readable Long Count dates, one being 9.1.12.14.10 (468 CE) and the other 9.4.18.16.8 (533 CE), well within the Classic period (**figure 102**). Other sculptures

102 Stela 6, Cerro de las Mesas, Veracruz. The vertical column on the left records the Long Count date 9.1.12.14.10 (468 CE). The headdress of the richly attired figure on the right is derived from an Olmec prototype. Ht 5 ft 10.8 in. (1.80 m).

103 (ABOVE) Thin human head of stone, or *hacha*, with headdress in the shape of a crane, designed to fit the front of a stone yoke. Late Classic period.

104 (ABOVE RIGHT) Stone yoke in Classic Veracruz style representing a stylized toad, covered with scrollwork patterns. Depth about 15.7 in. (40 cm).

105 (RIGHT) *Palma* stone in Classic Veracruz style. Ht 20.1 in. (51.1 cm).

include a figure of a duck-billed human closely resembling the Isthmian Tuxtla Statuette (see p. 82), which itself was found not very far from Cerro de las Mesas. A fantastically rich hoard of jade, with many heirloom pieces from the region as well as pieces from other parts of Mesoamerica, was assembled and buried at some time in the Classic, a testament to both the cultural continuity and the power of the site.

Significant changes in the area may be seen in the nearby Tuxtla Mountains, at the site of Matacapan. At some point in the fourth century CE, the site was founded in what had been a sparsely inhabited region. It soon established ties with groups having some association with Teotihuacan, and eventually a Teotihuacan-style *talud-tablero* pyramid was built in the center of the city. By this time (450–650 CE), Matacapan was a burgeoning trade and production center that deftly mixed Teotihuacan and local cultures. Toward the end of this period, Teotihuacan cultural elements and relationships waned and eventually the site declined in importance.

A considerable number of fine stone objects found on the Gulf Coast plain are carved in a very distinct style that has become known as "Classic Veracruz." The majority of them are from the northern and central parts of that state, a zone in which are located several great elite centers that shared in the same art tradition. This style can be mistaken for no other in Mexico. All subject matter in Classic Veracruz style is bound to a complex ornamental motif: linked or intertwined scrolls with raised edges, perhaps derived from the cloud scrolls of the Izapan style.

The Classic Veracruz style commonly appears on a complex of enigmatic stone objects, the so-called "yokes," "*hachas*" ("axes"; thin stone heads), and "*palmas*" ("palms"; broad, leaf-like stones with carved scenes) (**figures 103, 104, 105**). (These misnomers were applied by archaeologists for the objects' formal, but not functional, resemblance to such items.) The two former objects were made in the Classic period, with the *palma* appearing only in the Epiclassic. Modern research has shown that all three are associated with the ritual ball game, as bas-reliefs and figurines depict them being worn in that connection. The yokes are stone replicas of the heavy protective leather belts worn by the players. They are U-shaped and often intricately carved to represent stylized animals covered with convoluted scrolls and human faces. They are found beginning in the Late Formative in central Veracruz, and continue to be made through the Epiclassic. The *hachas* and the *palmas* probably were markers placed in the court to score the game, but they too could be worn on the yoke. In its formative phase, the Classic Veracruz style can best be seen in slate backs for circular mirrors of pyrite mosaic (**figure 106**)—these are certainly Classic in date, as are many of the yokes.

The ethno-linguistic name "Totonac" has often been inappropriately applied to these carvings; while it is true that the Totonacs now occupy most of the zone in which such remains are found, it may or may not have been they who made them. Archaeologists prefer caution in these matters. Nevertheless, Classic Veracruz

106 Carved slate back for a circular mirror found in southern Querétaro. The reverse side was the reflecting surface, consisting of a layer of polygonal pyrite plates. Early Classic period. Diameter 6 in. [15 cm].

107 Classic Veracruz stela with standing figure holding a staff or standard and wearing an elaborate feathered helmet with two serpent profiles.

influence is very perceptibly present in the beginnings of Classic Teotihuacan, and some are inclined to accept Torquemada's statement that the Totonacs built that city (**figure 107**). On the other hand, reciprocal influence from the highlands is also present on the Gulf Coast.

Classic Monte Albán

The civilization of Monte Albán in the Valley of Oaxaca during Classic times was, as in the Formative period, the product of Zapotecan-speaking groups. The changeover from the Late Formative appears to have been marked by social turmoil, with elites increasingly monopolizing institutions of governance and authority and coopting the acropolis at its summit. Intense interregional interaction with the Maya area, as suggested by certain similarities in ceramic wares (potstands and painted stucco decoration of pottery) gave way to a new series of cultural elements, with a particularly strong relationship with Teotihuacan. Immigrants from Monte Albán and its environs were numerous at Teotihuacan, certainly facilitating interchange between the two capitals. It has even been suggested that Teotihuacan directly controlled Monte Albán at some point during the Classic period, although the evidence for this is thin. What is becoming increasingly clear is the interest of the Teotihuacan elites in obtaining large plaques of mica, the mining of which at Ejutla, south of the Central Valleys of Oaxaca, may have been controlled by Monte Albán. The imported plaques were transformed at Teotihuacan into small geometrically shaped, iridescent pieces used for a variety of embellishments. Throughout the Classic, Monte Albán became a major seat of regional power, and from there the ruling elites controlled a considerable number of sites throughout the Valley of Oaxaca and beyond.

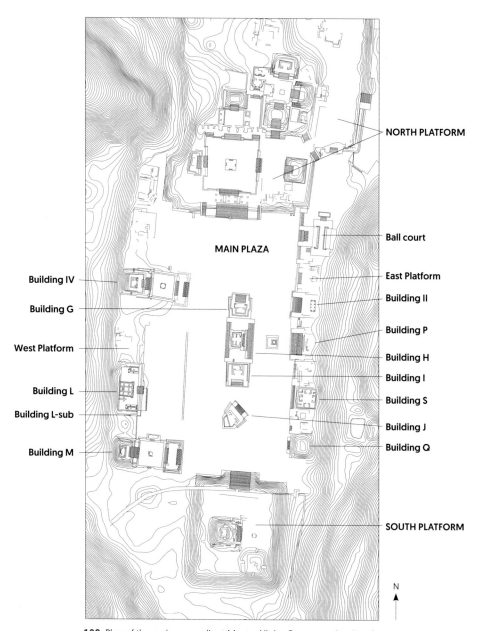

108 Plan of the main acropolis at Monte Albán, Oaxaca, as it existed in the 9th century CE, during the height of the city's development.

The core of the urban center was developed around a very well-sized and long plaza (**figure 108**). Bigger constructions were raised on rock nuclei that remained after the hill was leveled off. Among the buildings of this epoch are stone-faced platforms, fronted by stairways with flanking balustrades. Something similar to the *talud-tablero* architecture of Teotihuacan is evident, but the entablature has a double recess. These and other buildings were once completely stuccoed; some were given additional painted and sculpted decoration. A hint of the latter type of architectural embellishment is deduced from a series of sizable carved stones

109 (LEFT) A carved stone found reset into the South Platform at Monte Albán. Originally, it was part of a narrative commemorating the enthronement of a ruler named 13 Owl. The block shows one of the captives dressed as a jaguar.

111 (RIGHT) Plan of the acropolis of Atzompa, a barrio of Monte Albán. The architectural seat of a high-ranking lineage, it includes a Temple-Plaza-Altar (left), a residential complex with a subsidiary funerary structure (top), and a ball court.

110 (BELOW) Section of the painted walls of Tomb 104 at Monte Albán, Oaxaca. A man named 1 Lizard proceeds toward a large glyph at the back wall of the crypt, c. 500 CE. Ht of wall 5 ft 3 in. (1.6 m).

that, although found re-used in the corners of the South Platform, had previously formed one of the facades of a building that commemorated the enthronement of a ruler. The narrative shows the lord—dressed as a jaguar and seated on a throne while holding a lance—overseeing a procession of six captives, all with their arms tied behind their backs (**figure 109**). A series of short hieroglyphic texts identify him as 13 Owl, reference a series of ritual performances related to his enthronement, and provide the names of the conquered towns from which the captives originated.

Also present among the buildings surrounding the Main Plaza are a majestic sunken plaza and associated structures (the North Platform), where the ruling elites conducted state-related administrative tasks, as well as a small and enclosed

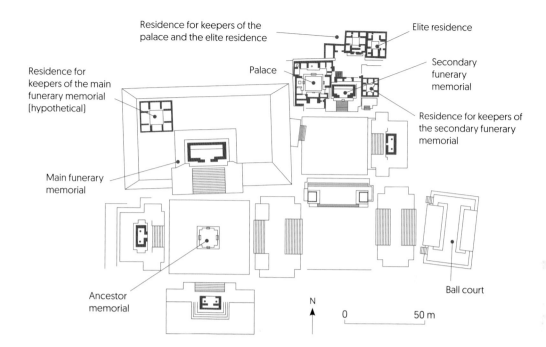

Residence for keepers of the palace and the elite residence

Elite residence

Residence for keepers of the main funerary memorial (hypothetical)

Palace

Secondary funerary memorial

Residence for keepers of the secondary funerary memorial

Main funerary memorial

Ancestor memorial

Ball court

N

0   50 m

quadripartite architectural complex—at the highest point of the acropolis—that bears all the marks for being the place where the paramount lords were buried. (Tombs of other nobles can be found throughout the city [**figure 110**; see also p. 136].) A grand masonry ball court with a ground plan like a capital "I," a form that was replicated at other important valley centers, was built in the northeast corner of the Main Plaza. Even more indicative of Monte Albán culture was the building form identified by Marcus Winter as Temple-Plaza-Altar complex, which is found in Buildings M and IV as well as on hilltops throughout the valley where Monte Albán held sway.

As with the acropolis of Monte Albán, these architectural complexes are often associated with an important residence and a ball court. Recent work at Atzompa, a barrio of Monte Albán perched on a separate hilltop, has exposed its main Temple-Plaza-Altar complex, allowing a better understanding of the function of such complexes (**figure 111**). Undoubtedly the seat of the paramount lineage at Atzompa, the main plaza group appears to have had temples where the patron deities and founding ancestors were venerated. Adjacent on the east side were the residences of the main and branching lineages, together with a secondary funerary temple that had three tombs in its interior, at different stratigraphic levels. Here and there, both peripheral to the temples and the elite residences, were the abodes of supporting personnel in charge of maintaining the temples and the palaces. Further east was the ball court, where mock-battles disguised as a ball game were performed as a prelude to the sacrifice of war captives. This architectural facility signals the ability of the dominant corporate group at Atzompa to conscript an army and fund warring parties, and for its high-ranking members to form part of a military organization.

The slopes of the hills on which Early Classic Monte Albán stands are covered with hundreds of residential terraces, containing an estimated population of 17,000 at the site's Classic apogee. A small number of strategically placed centers

throughout the valley were only slightly less populous than the capital, but the great majority of the over 1,000 valley settlements were significantly smaller. Most of the valley's inhabitants were farmers, irrigating the rich bottomlands for their crops, but they must also have farmed the piedmont zone above the valley.

As with other centers in the valley, residences at Monte Albán varied in size and quality of construction materials depending on the social standing of their inhabitants, but they all conformed to a common layout: an open courtyard surrounded on its four sides by rooms. Very often, the east room had a masonry tomb under its floor, in which multigenerational household heads were buried. Each time these crypts were re-entered, the remains of previous burials were pushed against the back and lateral walls to create space for the new interment. Other members of the household were buried in simple graves, either under the floor of the house's courtyard or under other rooms.

More than 210 tombs have been discovered at Monte Albán alone, some of which were of great magnificence, testimony to the wealth of the nobility. The richest crypts are quite elaborate, often with a corbeled vault, an antechamber, and a staircase leading to the crypt's entrance. Fine murals were painted on the plastered walls, depicting named ancestors as if proceeding toward an apical founder. These genealogical records highlight the important role that ancestral spirits played in legitimating the rights and privileges of noble lineages. Equally, the centrality of founding ancestors accounts for the enormous amount of artistic capital spent

112 [LEFT] Tomb 104 was found in 1938 by Mexican archaeologist Alfonso Caso. This replica can be seen at the Museo Nacional de Antropología in Mexico City. After repeated use, Zapotec tombs became crowded with remains, but this crypt had the single burial of a noble accompanied by a sizable offering. A large effigy vessel of a "Fire Serpent" impersonator and embodiments of maize marking the four corners of the world guarded the entrance.

113 [RIGHT] Cerro de la Campana Tomb 5, facade to the main chamber, Classic period. This tomb, some 5 meters under a room of a palatial house built at the top of an acropolis, is the most opulent crypt ever discovered in the Central Valleys of Oaxaca.

shaping and decorating the crypts. Sometimes, because of tomb re-entry, fresh paintings were applied over existing ones; in this way, some of the murals, as is also the case with those in Tomb 105 at Monte Albán, are palimpsests (traces of earlier writing beneath later inscriptions).

Tomb 104, in the northern part of the city, is certainly among the most spectacular known so far (**figure 112**). Over the facade of the tomb is a niche in the recess entablature with an effigy vessel representing a person wearing a headdress displaying the emblem of the Fire-Serpent, a powerful alter ego associated with the day-name Lizard and with human sacrifice. The door was a single great slab covered with hieroglyphs; within the funerary chamber the only skeleton was stretched out on the floor, surrounded by rich offerings, including a tableau of effigy vessels that replicates the four corners and the center of the world. Polychrome murals grace the walls (see **figure 110**, p. 134), depicting a procession of two figures with elaborate ritual dress advancing toward a substantial calendrical name painted at the rear of the tomb that identifies the apical ancestor of the interred.

Other rich tombs were also built by Zapotec elites outside Monte Albán (**figure 113**). Tomb 5 at Cerro de la Campana, near the modern town of Santiago Suchilquitongo, is a particularly notable example of funerary practices and mortuary art outside the capital, in this instance in the western arm, the Etla Valley. The initial construction of the tomb dates to the beginning of the seventh century, although it was used for at least 200 years thereafter. Looming over the tomb entrance is a monumental name glyph (10 Alligator) framed by an entablature with a double recess. In the jambs below, nobles, elaborately dressed as jaguars and holding staffs, face their female cohorts, who hold incense pouches. The entrance eventually leads to a courtyard that mimics a house layout on a smaller scale and contains yet more costumed jamb figures and murals. While the murals depict the elaborate obsequies of three ancestral married couples, the figures represented in the jambs and facades constitute a long genealogical record. Although little was left in the tomb itself, a small stela was placed there that records an extension of the earlier genealogy. This type of genealogical records on small stelae and portable slabs would become even more central to elites in the subsequent Epiclassic period.

Most effigy vessels—usually found in tombs, but at times placed as offerings under temples—are representations of ancestors who are depicted as deity impersonators, their attributes often signaled by facial features, masks, or defining elements in the headdress (**figure 114**). Such attributes fall into categories that match most of the 20-day names of the calendar, implicating their association with the thirteen core patron deities who presided over or influenced the fate of persons given their day of birth. Such associations suggest that the materialization of ancestral spirits in the urns was integral to scrying practices aimed at interpreting dreams, discovering hidden knowledge and motivations, or foretelling future events. As in Tomb 104 at Monte Albán, and even earlier at San José Mogote (see **figure 72,** p. 95), many effigy vessels were made to form tableaux and reproduce the world order. We have in an old dictionary the Zapotec names of the thirteen deities associated with the sacred calendar, including the Rain Deity, Cociyo; the Maize Deity, Pitao Cozobi, often adorned with actual casts of maize ears; the Sun God, Cozaana, depicted emblematically as a broad-beaked bird; Xipe Totec; the Old Fire God; and, possibly, the Water Goddess. Several of these divinities are shared with other Mexican civilizations and can therefore be identified.

During Classic times, the use of the mold to manufacture effigy vessels was frequent, but the ready-made pieces were combined with ornamentation built up by sharply carved clay strips. Each figure is generally shown seated cross-legged, richly dressed in finery including an elaborate headdress and such sumptuary goods as nose ornaments, earspools, necklaces, wristlets and anklets. At times, such precious materials as shell, coral, jadeite, and obsidian served to highlight in the effigy vessels the eyes or their sumptuary ornaments.

While the mortuary practices based on the use of tombs and effigy vessels are typically Zapotec, the style of Classic Monte Albán frescoes and figural urns adheres to some conventions derived from Teotihuacan. During the Early Classic, some people from the Central Valleys of Oaxaca, if not from Monte Albán itself, had an enclave in Teotihuacan where they maintained their burial customs and scribal tradition, while at the same time cultivating an intimate relation to the techniques and traditions of the Teotihuacanos.

114 Many hundreds of gray-ware effigy vessels have been discovered in Classic period tombs in the Central Valleys of Oaxaca and beyond, usually placed in groups of five to represent the four corners and the center of the cosmos. This fine effigy, found in Mitla, depicts an ancestor wearing a headdress with a great jaguar head topped by a small bird head. The lower lateral motifs allude to budding maize.

The writing and calendric system of Classic Monte Albán exhibit much conservatism and some discontinuities from the Formative base. Although there are no surviving manuscripts, short glyphic inscriptions appear everywhere, both in sculptured relief, on the funerary urns, and painted on walls, at the capital itself and at other Monte Albán centers. The numeration continues to be in the bar-and-dot system. Longer inscriptions typically open with a date in the 52-year Calendar Round. This is given by a Year Bearer: as Alfonso Caso demonstrated long ago, the year was named by one of four days in the 260-day count on which it could begin, along with the numerical coefficient of that day, and a Year sign in the form of a royal headband. The Year Bearer days were in the 2nd, 7th, 12th, and 17th positions within the list of 20 named days. Unfortunately for Mesoamericanists, the Zapotecs never used the Long Count, so inscribed dates cannot be fixed within an absolute chronology. As made more evident in Chapter 5, another complicating factor is that most Zapotec monuments were often reused and moved from their original positions, with the result that texts that once made sense in the context of neighboring inscriptions no longer do so. And lastly, it now appears that many notations in the 260-day count, long interpreted as having chronological significance, are in reality the calendrical names of historical personages.

What kind of script was this? From its origins around 500 BCE through the Classic and Epiclassic periods, there were always about sixty to eighty non-calendrical glyphs; this is far too high for a syllabary, but within the range for known scripts of the logo-syllabic sort: ones in which there is common use of logographic (semantic) and syllabic (phonetic) signs. It remains one of the very few undeciphered writing systems of the world, but progress in cracking it may be possible once linguists reconstruct the proto-Zapotec language, and more inscriptions are found in primary contexts.

While there are no signs of a conflagration, as at Teotihuacan, sometime around 850 CE the abandonment of the capital began and Monte Albán eventually fell into ruins, as did many (but not all) other regional centers in the valley. Later valley inhabitants used the ancient city as a kind of consecrated ground for placing offerings amidst the fallen buildings or burying funerary bundles in abandoned crypts. Some of these later burials—as we shall see—exhibit extreme wealth and were left there perhaps in an attempt to establish their continuity with the dynasties that had ruled at Monte Albán for over a thousand years.

The Classic Downfall

The single most important fact that archaeologists have learned about the Classic period in Mexico is the supremacy of Teotihuacan, its impress being clearly recorded throughout this incredibly varied country and beyond, to other parts of Mesoamerica. As the urbanized center of Mexico, with high population and tremendous production, its power was imposed through political and cultural means not only in its native highland habitat, but also along the tropical coasts, reaching even into the Maya area. That this was a trading and tribute empire entirely comparable with the Aztecs' cannot be doubted. All other states were partly or entirely dependent upon it for whatever achievements they attained at this time, and any solution to the problem of why the Classic developed at all must be approached through the more central problem that Teotihuacan, without local antecedents, presents to puzzled archaeologists.

As Teotihuacan collapsed, populations maintained their sizes and even grew in many areas of Mesoamerica including central Mexico, which would suggest that there was no widespread catastrophe or agricultural failure. Instead, it seems that regional urban centers may have siphoned production, trade, and people from Teotihuacan. Soon, several of these centers would rival and then surpass the old capital in importance. At the same time, much Teotihuacan elite culture was put to the torch in the mid-to-late sixth century by people who may themselves have been Teotihuacanos. And yet, for centuries after its political and economic demise, Teotihuacan continued to be a major source of prestige and many of its symbols of power endured in later sign systems.

In short, the land was ripe for internal revolution as well as a reconfiguration of patterns of interregional interaction, whether based on trade or conquest from outside, and the two forces probably together produced the different way of life that we see in later periods.

Chapter 7

The Epiclassic Period

When Teotihuacan fell in the seventh century CE, the central unifying force in Mexico, and indeed in all of Mesoamerica, was gone. The largest city in Mesoamerica was now reduced to a quarter of its former population, which was still substantial in Pre-Columbian terms. It was never again a major political force, however, and the loss of that centralizing force left a considerable power vacuum in ancient Mexico. Into this vacuum stepped a number of smaller city-states, each vying for power and prestige in the wake of the great capital's fall. Between 650 and 900 CE, these competing polities and their capitals developed new political and trade alliances and eclectic art styles, reconfiguring the political, economic, and cultural systems of ancient Mexico after the loss of its imperial capital.

The Maya Connection: Cacaxtla and Xochicalco

One of the more intriguing Epiclassic developments was the footprint of foreigners, almost certainly from the Gulf Coast lowlands and the Yucatan Peninsula, in the highlands of ancient Mexico. The interrelationship of the highland Mexicans and the Maya has been established by archaeology and epigraphy, especially between 378 and 500 CE, when Teotihuacan-affiliated personages significantly impacted the Maya political landscape at such sites as Kaminaljuyu, Tikal, and Copán. Equally, it is now clear that people affiliated with the Maya resided at Teotihuacan, and that Teotihuacanos were familiar with Maya art and writing. At Classic period Cholula, the local elites emulated the Maya practice of erecting stelae with altars. The Maya probably exerted considerable intellectual and religious influence over the rest of Mesoamerica, and there is some evidence that the dreaded Tezcatlipoca, the great god of war and the royal house in Post-Classic Mexico, was of Maya origin. Moreover, Maya civilization was experiencing its most vibrant stage during this period.

Building activity at numerous Maya centers reached its zenith, as did the mutually destructive strife brought on by the competition between the two great alliances in the area: one centered on Tikal, old ally of Teotihuacan during the Classic period, and the other led by Kalak'mul, the metropolis to the north and heir to a kingdom even older than Tikal. Although we do not fully understand the dynamics, it seems that Maya rivalries and their related search for alliances played a part in the repartitioning of ancient Mexico during the Epiclassic.

Cacaxtla

The site of Cacaxtla contains the most important evidence of Maya-affiliated influence in the heart of central Mexico (**figure 115**). Cacaxtla is one of a number of hilltop sites in the Puebla-Tlaxcala border area, and lies only 15½ miles (25 km) northwest of Cholula. The early chronicler Diego Muñoz Camargo tells us that it was a "seat and fortress" of the Olmeca-Xicallanca, whose capital was then Cholula. The name "Olmeca" (not to be confused with the archaeological Olmecs) means "people of the region of rubber," that is, of the southern Gulf Coast. "Xicallanca" is another Nahuatl name, referring to "the people of Xicallanco (or land of calabashes)" (a type of gourd-bearing tree). Xicallanco was an important trading town in southern Campeche controlled by the Putún: Mayan-speaking seafaring merchants whose commercial interests ranged from the Olmeca country along the coast of the entire Yucatan Peninsula as far as the Caribbean shore of Honduras.

In November 1974, looters were discovered working at Cacaxtla; they had uncovered part of a remarkable mural with colors so fresh that it seemed to have been painted only yesterday. Official excavations have now revealed a palace complex of the seventh and eighth centuries CE, with pilastered rooms arranged around patios and plazas. There is nothing Maya about its flat-roofed architecture, but there are similarities to the coeval palaces of Xochicalco and El Tajín. The known

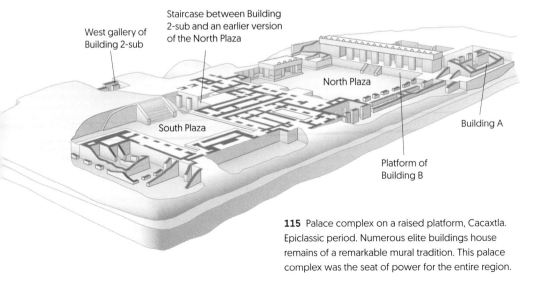

West gallery of Building 2-sub

Staircase between Building 2-sub and an earlier version of the North Plaza

North Plaza

South Plaza

Building A

Platform of Building B

115 Palace complex on a raised platform, Cacaxtla. Epiclassic period. Numerous elite buildings house remains of a remarkable mural tradition. This palace complex was the seat of power for the entire region.

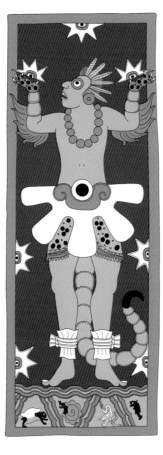

116 Color drawing of the painted piers in a room from the west gallery of Building 2-sub at Cacaxtla, Tlaxcala. A winged woman and a winged man-scorpion hold stars. The shape on their waists is the sign for Venus. Ht 6 ft 10.6 in. (2.1 m).

murals appear on an architectural complex (Building 2-sub) that was subsequently covered by new edifices, on a *talud* of the supporting platform of Building B, and on the interior walls and jambs of Building A.

One of the known murals in Building 2-sub was painted on the piers inside a room along its west gallery (**figure 116**). It depicts a woman and a man gazing upward, with kilts of jaguar pelts, wings on their arms, and blue painted bodies. Placed in a frame with stars, while holding additional celestial bodies with blue jaguar paws, both figures have a large Venus sign superimposed in the area of their waist. Although there is no baseline to the compositions, the figures are bound below by an aquatic band. Notable is the scorpion tail of the man. Several of the signs in these paintings, including the Venus glyphs, the scorpion tail, the seven stars in each pier, the wings of the figures, and the prevalence of the blue color strongly suggest references to celestial phenomena and their relationship to the rainy season.

Impressive as well, and also in Building 2-sub, are the murals flanking a staircase that connects two courtyard groups built at different levels. Although only the bottom half of the staircase remains extant, the painted narrative references a quadripartite landscape—indicated by four maize plants with personified corncobs:

117 Color drawing of a painted wall flanking a staircase in the north gallery of Building 2-sub at Cacaxtla, Tlaxcala. The scene represents a ruler named 4 Dog personifying the Maya god of merchants. To the right is his *cacaxtli* or back-pack; attached to it is his headdress. Ht 6 ft 10.6 in. (2.1 m).

two in each wall—with such fantastic creatures as a toad-jaguar, a jaguar-turtle, and a toad-lizard ascending toward the top of the staircase. The entire composition, framed by an aquatic band, must have depicted two prominent figures standing on imposing plumed serpents: one on the west wall at the top of the staircase (now missing) and the other on the east wall at the bottom of the staircase. The latter is a man, most likely a ruler from Cacaxtla, identified by his calendrical name 4 Dog (**figure 117**). He is shown embodying an old deity known by Mayanists as God L, and as a merchant associated with a cacao tree (emblematic of the coastal lowlands). Propped up beside him is a carrying frame with merchandise strapped to it.

It is indeed probably no accident that the name of the site, Cacaxtla (or Cacaxtlan), means "place of the carrying-frame."

Vividly depicted on the basal *talud* of Building B is a narrative that symbolically conflates a great battle in progress with the immolation and post-sacrificial treatment of captives, highlighting a prominent ruler of Cacaxtla called 3 Deer, shown as a personification of the Rain Deity. While the paintings are characterized by much realism and utter detail given to conveying fierceness and despair (for example a dazed victim seated on the ground holding his entrails in his hands), at the same time, the story is highly coded: jaguar warriors—some of them accompanied by glyphic captions—sport central-Mexican-style profiles and are always victorious, while the defeated bird warriors have Maya-style profiles and are rendered anonymous by the lack of nominative captions. The glyphic captions seem to identify high-ranking warriors by a common title or epithet (the signs of a crossed circle, the upper jaw, and the glyph "Bloody heart") and their personal name.

The murals in Building A—a two-room structure that has a layout almost identical to those of ancestors' shrines at the Maya site of Palenque, Tabasco—were those found by looters, and yet they are temporally the latest. Although the paintings on the back wall of the structure were found much obliterated, those on the intermediate wall and its associated entryway were mostly complete except for the topmost portion and the section of the lintel above the access between the vestibule and the inner room. Originally, the mural above the entryway depicted the face of the Rain Deity, the open mouth of which framed the entrance to the inner chamber, as is also the case with similar "rain deity entrances" in buildings across the Yucatan Peninsula, at such sites as Chicana, Hormiguero, and Hochob. As in the other murals from Cacaxtla, those from Building A display an array of such binary and complementary oppositions as night-day, earth-sky, rainy season-dry season, agriculture-warfare, below-above, north-south, local-foreigner. The central theme is the genealogical reckoning—spanning three generations—of two local lords who seemingly formed a dual form of government at the site.

The genealogy traces the lords' descent from a mythical twin couplet named 7 Alligator and 7 Alligator. The genealogical branch painted on the north jamb and vestibular wall shows two jaguar-clad lords with central-Mexican-style profiles. These are identified hieroglyphically as 2 Lord and 9 Alligator. The branch painted on the south jamb and vestibular wall depicts two lords with black body paint and with Maya-style profiles. These are identified hieroglyphically as 3 Deer (the ruler featured in the older battle-sacrifice murals of Building B) and 9 Alligator (who appears dressed as an eagle). Prominent are the visual references to fertility (ruler 2 Lord waters the earth with a rain-deity jar while a flowering maize plant germinates from his navel) and fecundity (lord 3 Deer holds a sizable *Strombus* shell from which one of the mythical ancestral twins emerges).

The last and most prominent dual lords in the genealogy—one standing on a serpent-jaguar and the other on a serpent-bird—allude to human immolation. This can be deduced as they hold respectively a bundle of darts with water dripping from the tips (a substitution for sacrificial blood) and a substantial sacrificial knife

118 Color drawing of the south wall in the portico of Building A at Cacaxtla, Tlaxcala. The painting shows a ruler named 13 Eagle wearing an eagle costume and standing on a feathered serpent while holding a large sacrificial knife. Aquatic animals and a maize plant frame the scene. Ht 5 ft 8.5 in. (1.74 m).

with dual serpent heads whose tongues are eccentric blades (**figure 118**). These jaguar and eagle lords seem to foreshadow the roles of the Tlalchiac (Nahuatl for "downward, toward the earth") and Tlaquiach ("upward, toward the heights [sky]"), overseers of internal and external political affairs in the Late Post-Classic kingdom of nearby Cholula (documented in the sixteenth century in the Nahuatl-language manuscript *Historia Tolteca-Chichimeca*, in the 1581 Spanish census ordered by King Phillip II, and by Sahagún's interlocutors).

At a later date, stucco reliefs were applied to the frame of the interior doorway in Building A, concealing parts of the open mouth of the front-facing rain-deity image. Each of the added reliefs, which exhibit bilateral symmetry, depicts a figure facing toward the doorway, wearing an imposing serpent headdress and seated on the symbolic representation of a sacred hill. Above each richly clad figure is a descending bat.

The Cacaxtla murals are thoroughly Maya in their style. Both the naturalistic body proportions and the organic, flowing profiles are diagnostic of the Epiclassic Maya painting tradition and contrast with the more blocky, geometric style of Teotihuacan and much of the rest of highland Mexico. Figural poses and facial profiles also strongly recall Maya models. Telling is the use of a vegetable binder to form the paint medium—a technique identified by art historian Diana Magaloni for Maya and Gulf Coast mural artists, but unknown in the Teotihuacan mural tradition, where pigments diluted with water were laid on fresh plaster in the true fresco technique. Art historian Donald Robertson argues for a model of patron-client relationship and emulation of a foreign style at Cacaxtla, which best explains the evidence. Given the intimate relationship between script and identity, the absence of Maya phonetic writing at the site suggests the Cacaxtla murals were not ordered by Maya kings. Robertson posits that local rulers would have commissioned a famed artist or artists with training in the Maya style and techniques; this emulation of a foreign style in the murals would allow the rulers to accrue political power. Their ability to do so was ultimately based on the wealth that came from the control of long distance exchange networks linking the highlands with the Gulf Coast lowlands that stretched from Veracruz through Campeche.

Equally intriguing is the presence of a great number of female figurines in an offering found in the nearby site of Xochitecatl, many of which share important elements with female figures from the southern Gulf Coast. Xochitecatl, which had an important Formative occupation, was reinhabited during the Epiclassic; in this period the major pyramid aligned to the Cacaxtla palace, suggesting that the ceremonial center was controlled by the Cacaxtla elites. The female figurines were deposited around this time. Their raised hands, filed teeth, and pronounced smiles are all traits shared with figures on the Gulf Coast, although the slab-like bodies at Xochitecatl follow local practices. Archaeologist Mari Carmen Serra and her team have interpreted several ritual and political offices for the figures, suggesting the important role of females and gender symbolism at these closely related sites; this is also the case in Epiclassic southern Veracruz, especially at such sites as El Zapotal.

Cholula

Following the withdrawal of Teotihuacan's political sway from central Mexico, nearby Cholula appears to have shrunk in its urban dimensions and consequently in population. Another eruption of the Popocatepetl volcano further strained the region's economy, and even though the city never became completely abandoned, it took until the beginning of the tenth century CE for the settlement to regain regional primacy. Yet, during the Epiclassic, the acropolis fell into disuse and was slowly reclaimed by nature so that by the time of the Spanish Conquest, this majestic architectural mass of the Classic period looked similar to a natural hill covered with trees and vegetation.

Indigenous and European-colonial-era sources claim that the continuous occupation of Cholula was attributed to the same newcomers who built Cacaxtla, called the Olmeca–Xicallanca. Muñoz Camargo's writings from the mid-sixteenth century concerning the political and economic control of the "Olmeca-Xicallanca" in the Valley of Puebla-Tlaxcala, and their eventual replacement in Cholula by the "Tolteca-Chichimeca," are most likely eponyms lingering in the social memory of the time in which he wrote (thirteen centuries later!) rather than historical references to wholesale ethnic and population movements and replacements. The designation "Olmeca-Xicallanca" would have meant to reference local highland elites with strong ties to cultures and economic interests from the southern Gulf coast of Tabasco and Campeche (easterners), while the name "Tolteca-Chichimeca" would have implied a change of alliances by subsequent local elites who established strong relations with cultures and economic interests from the Basin of Mexico and beyond (westerners). What is evident is that in the sixteenth century, the Nahuatl and Mixtec names of Cholula, Tlalchihualtepetl (human-made hill), and Ñundiyo (stairway place) still alluded to the past glory of the largest acropolis ever built in Mesoamerica, despite it having been mostly abandoned around the seventh century CE.

Xochicalco

Another regional center that reached importance with the twilight or disappearance of Teotihuacan's hegemony is Xochicalco, strategically placed atop one of a string of defensively terraced hills in western Morelos. This cosmopolitan trading center has been mapped by Kenneth Hirth of Pennsylvania State University, who finds it to be the hub of a well-planned network of stone-surfaced causeways with access to the city via well-guarded ramps. Founded before 700 CE and active throughout the Epiclassic, Xochicalco had extensive foreign contacts, especially with the Mixteca Baja, the Central Valleys of Oaxaca, the central Gulf Coast lowlands, and the Maya area.

Its most striking structure, the Building of the Feathered Serpents, is a *talud-tablero* platform, but the *talud* element is very high compared with the *tablero* (**figure 119**). On the *taluds* are sculpted reliefs of eight huge, undulating Feathered Serpents amid cloud signs, reminiscent of those on the Pyramid of the Feathered Serpents at Teotihuacan. Between the folds of the serpents' bodies, the figure of a man appears ten times; he is seated cross-legged on a cushion, with a headdress sporting the imagery of an alligator. Also between the folds of the serpents are six oversized glyphs with the calendrical name 9 Alligator, capped by the representation of a precious nose ornament. Unique to the north and south halves of the western *talud* is the presence of two short, hieroglyphic texts that recount historical events: one that took place on a year 13 Flint, again featuring 9 Alligator as well as a second personage named 2 Earthquake, and another event that occurred on a year 6 Reed involving the capture of a prisoner named 12 Monkey by a captor called 10 House.

The lower *tablero* of the basal platform, most of it destroyed by stone mining operations in the sixteenth century, depicted thirty-two figures, all seated and accompanied by short hieroglyphic captions. Common to all the personages were their goggled eyes (implying their personification of the Rain Deity) and a headdress that symbolizes "royalty." Facing toward the west side of the building—where the staircase yields to an upper level—the figures initiate two branches at the center of the east side, and wrap around the structure. While the first two personages on each branch hold paraphernalia used in self-bloodletting and are identified by their calendrical and personal names, the remaining figures carry incense bags and are identified by their personal name and—much as in the battle-sacrifice mural at Cacaxtla (p. 145)—by a common title or epithet (the signs of a crossed circle and an open jaw). Furthermore, the cheeks of the staircase display two seated warriors identified by their calendrical names. Nothing remains of the *tablero* in the upper

119 Building of the Feathered Serpents at Xochicalco. A ruler named 9 Alligator is depicted several times seated within the serpent's undulations.

level of the building, but the few extant portions of the corresponding *talud* depict several seated warriors identified by their calendrical and personal names. The same applies to the jambs flanking the entryway to the upper structure, except that in this case the warriors on each side are shown standing and facing toward the exterior.

In the balustrades of the staircase, three-dimensional versions of the serpents shown on the facades are replicated in stone. The belly scales were visible, as if the serpents were swirling upward in an upside-down position, similarly to the ophidians carved on Altar 2 of Cholula. The heads (at the top of the basal platform) and tails (extending onto the floor of the plaza in front of the building) are now lost, but must have been assembled sculpted blocks.

The multiple meanings of the narrative in the Building of the Feathered Serpents at Xochicalco undoubtedly include references to an apical ancestor, 9 Alligator, and to the genealogies—recounted through the male line—of two corporate groups that appear to have shared power at Xochicalco when the building was commissioned. The wealth of the city must have come through trade and war, and the building became a grand testimony of the power that smaller Epiclassic polities were able to amass.

120 Xochicalco Stela 1. The subject matter of the four inscribed surfaces includes the genealogy of a ruler named 7 Alligator (depicted in the front surface), and references to two rituals of enthronement (rendered in the back surface). Ht 4 ft 11 in. (1.5 m).

It is likely that the Xochicalco building was an attempt to recreate that great central monument of Teotihuacan power, only now with seated lords and historical accounts. The convention for representing the ancestor 9 Alligator in the facades of the building appears to have been inspired by small, portable jade plaques, showing seated lords, that were manufactured in the Maya region and avidly exchanged during the Epiclassic throughout central Mexico. The visual facing off of the two genealogies rendered on the lower *tablero* is reminiscent of the genealogy on Copan's Altar Q, including the depth of sixteen generations. And the raised edges of the Xochicalco bodies recall reliefs found at El Tajín, in the Gulf Coast lowlands. Other dates and calendrical names based on the 260-day count are found elsewhere at Xochicalco, and, as do those of Cacaxtla, show resemblances to both Teotihuacan and Ñuiñe scripts—yet they foreshadow several of the conventions that would eventually, during Post-Classic times, become the norm through highland Mesoamerica (**figure 120**). The elites of Xochicalco, like those of Cacaxtla, were drawn to the script

121 Monumental ball court at Xochicalco with the remains of two stone rings, originally embedded in the walls to mark the middle of the playing field.

and imagery of the illustrious past (Teotihuacan) as well as to those of the powers in the present (from Oaxaca, the Maya area, and the Gulf Coast)—a situation that led to the eclectic nature of Epiclassic styles and scripts.

There are numerous caves in the hill on which Xochicalco was built that could have been used for storage purposes by the local population, as Kenneth Hirth suggests. Directly adjacent to the main ceremonial plaza, and not far from the Building of the Feathered Serpents, is a cave that has been transformed into an underground observatory: a human-made vertical tube leads up to the surface, and on the two days a year when the sun is at its zenith, or directly overhead, a beam of sunlight penetrates the shaft to the cave floor. This underground zenith observatory is the descendant of recently discovered underground chambers at Teotihuacan, where the same celestial phenomena were marked.

Xochicalco seems to form a kind of bridge between Classic and Post-Classic central Mexico. Xochicalco's main ball court, for instance, with its I-shaped layout, has exactly the same dimensions as the northern ball court at Tula of the Toltecs, which must be several centuries later (**figure 121**).

The Mixteca Baja and the Ñuiñe Script

The Mixteca Baja region, a transitional ecological zone of low-lying altitude, hot climate, and rugged topography, extends into what are now the southwestern portion of the State of Puebla, the northwest portion of the State of Oaxaca, and the northeastern part of the State of Guerrero. During the heyday of Teotihuacan, the

122 Carved stone with Ñuiñe hieroglyphs. Monument 2 from Cerro de la Caja, near Tequixtepec del Rey, Oaxaca. Carved on a red basalt, it depicts a jaguar devouring a small figure to symbolize a ruler enacting human sacrifice. Ht 5 ft 1.4 in. (1.56 m).

Mixteca Baja was dotted by several kingdoms, the capitals of which were perched on top of bluffs and higher hills, and was part of the economic secondary hinterland of the great central Mexican metropolis. It is known, for instance, that "Thin Orange," a luxury ware used in Teotihuacan, was produced in the Mixteca Baja, and that at times, the local potters tailored their products according to the stylistic tastes of the inhabitants of Teotihuacan. Yet, well before the political collapse of Teotihuacan, the region saw the creation of a distinctive script, dubbed Ñuiñe (a word in the Mixtec language meaning "hot land") by archaeologist John Paddock (**figure 122**). Used mainly in monumental architecture and funerary contexts, this scribal tradition was undoubtedly an offshoot of the Zapotec writing system. And although it followed many of its graphic conventions, it incorporated key signs common in the Teotihuacan script. Rather than being simply a combination of different scribal traditions, the Ñuiñe script was singularly emblematic, with signs clustered instead of displayed in a linear fashion. Quite likely, the glyphs stood for logograms. As such, the use of the script extended through a region characterized by a linguistic mosaic, with major pockets of Popoloca, Chocho, Triqui, Ixcatec, and Mixtec speakers.

As Teotihuacan influence in the region diminished, the Ñuiñe script continued to be used, including the few, still-prestigious signs that had been borrowed from Teotihuacan writing. Little is known of the political dynamics between the Epiclassic kingdoms of the Mixteca Baja, but their changing interaction most likely involved trade, marriage alliances, and warfare. Many of the carved monuments set in monumental architecture—for example, cornerstones, lintels, and stelae—are

123 Ñuiñe effigy vessel from Cerro de las Minas, depicting a masked old man wearing wings and seemingly holding a tobacco container. Ht 13.2 in. [33.5 cm].

of volcanic origin, including black and red basalts as well as hexagonal pillars that are formed when lava flows cool rapidly. Yet, this material is not evenly distributed throughout the region. To extract heavy blocks of volcanic origin, to mobilize them, and to set them atop citadels required an immense amount of human labor, economic solvency, and political clout. From the tall Peña near Huehuepiaxtla, in southern Puebla; to Cerro de la Flecha near Micaltepec; Cerro del Faisán near Cosoltepec; Cerro de las Minas near Huajuapan de León; or Cerro del Jaguar near Cuquila, in northwestern Oaxaca, the Ñuiñe phenomenon left its mark in other forms. Among them are small, portable slabs found in underground masonry tombs, each one inscribed with the calendrical name of a prestigious ancestor. Other commemorating monuments associated with the crypts, such as lintels or sealing stones, reference genealogical reckonings that are, at times, shallow. Sacred landscapes in the Mixteca Baja were also places where inscriptions were written, mostly using painting as the medium. Most impressive of these are palimpsests on the walls of a majestic through-cave known as Puente Colosal, at the eastern edge of the Valley of Coixtlahuaca. Most of the inscribed day names likely identify the names of people who visited the place to leave offerings.

Equally characteristic of the Ñuiñe archaeological culture are ceramic effigy vessels that depict prominent figures—either as deity impersonators or as mortals identified by their calendrical name—or divine entities (**figure 123**). Common among the latter is a group that shows the embodiment of the Old Fire God, sometimes masked, sometimes bearded, seated cross-legged on a squared base often decorated with volutes and interlaced scrolls. Over the head is a sizable receptacle, probably used to burn incense; the tall wall of the receptacle also displaying interlaced scrolls and volutes.

124 Coyotlatelco ceramic vase, Teotihuacan, Epiclassic period. Example of pottery made at Teotihuacan after the city's decline. Variants of this type are found throughout the region.

Tula Chico

The region of Tula, Hidalgo, some 46 miles (75 km) northwest of Teotihuacan, is often considered only through its Early Post-Classic (after 900 CE) apogee. The Tula region was home, however, to an important Teotihuacan-related site, Chingú, from the 2nd century CE through the end of the Classic period. This regional center covered more than one square mile (2.5 sq. km), reproducing Teotihuacan's layout and architecture at a reduced scale. The beginning of the Epiclassic period in the region saw a number of hilltop sites interacting with a reduced Chingú. The people in this area used Coyotlatelco pottery, related to ceramics found to the northwest in the Bajío region; this is also found throughout the Basin of Mexico during this period (**figure 124**). Their main source of obsidian at this time also came from the north and west, at Ucareo, Michoacan, as Dan Healan has shown. By the eighth century CE, these groups eventually created a densely settled area surrounding a sacred precinct known as Tula Chico. Although the Tula Chico precinct served as the model for the later Early Post-Classic Toltec Tula precinct, Tula Chico itself was burned and abandoned at the end of the Epiclassic and then left in ruins throughout the apogee period at the site.

Cantona

Cantona, unlike the rest of the Epiclassic powers, had an important Classic-period occupation. Angel García Cook, the chief archaeologist at this impressive but

125 One of twenty-four ball courts at Cantona. The typically spare adornment includes three circular plain markers along the central axis.

little-visited and little-known site north of the Oriental basin in the state of Puebla, describes the Classic-period city as founded on a volcanic flow which must have supplied much of the building material. This material was cut and then placed without the use of mortar. Cantona controlled the Oyameles-Zaragoza obsidian source only 6¼ miles (10 km) away, and trade in this product must have been a major resource for the site.

According to García Cook, around the year 600 the site filled suddenly with walled walkways leading to carefully delimited, walled residential compounds. These compounds are not the apartment buildings of Teotihuacan, but groups of house mounds that have been sealed and given one controlled point of entry. Access to the acropolis, where much of the ceremonial architecture was located, was carefully controlled through walkways and entry gates. The entire site became fortified and densely populated, and a moat was constructed at the most vulnerable point. The city was to remain a fortified center until its abandonment around 1000. Taken as a whole, the desire of the Epiclassic Cantona elite to keep enemies at bay was matched only by their desire to control circulation throughout the city itself.

At some point Cantona became a center for playing the rubber-ball game on I-shaped masonry courts (**figure 125**). To date, some twenty-four ball courts have been found at the site, eighteen of which García Cook believes were functioning at one time.

El Tajín

In accord with the importance of ball-court equipment in the art of its inhabitants, there are no fewer than seventeen ball courts at El Tajín, an elite center about 5 miles (8 km) southwest of Papantla, in the rich zone of northern Veracruz. The surrounding land is highly fertile for maize, cacao, tobacco, and vanilla, all of which are still grown. The site derives its name from the belief of the modern Totonac that twelve old men called Tajín live in the ruins and are lords of the thunderstorm (and therefore equivalent to the Rain Deity).

El Tajín was first occupied during the Classic, when it was a village more or less equal to several others in the area. Work by Arturo Pascual Soto in several of these surrounding early sites has revealed a thriving Classic-period culture, with decoration of tripod cylinder vase supports that initially owes much to Teotihuacan. Morgadal Grande, the most important of these outliers, contains a Classic-period ball court with carved relief benches that prefigure El Tajín's central architectural form. Cerro Grande, another outlier, has produced a substantial Classic-period stela fragment, on which a figure in high relief is shown frontally, holding a feathered bag, with feet splayed to either side. Again, echoes of this style and format will appear in some of the earliest monumental art found at El Tajín itself. Sometime in the seventh or early eighth century, El Tajín began the systematic conquest and rebuilding of these important regional sites, and much of the evidence for the Classic culture is found in the fill of Tajín-style Epiclassic buildings.

Epiclassic El Tajín is very extensive, its nucleus covering about 146 acres (60 ha.), but subsidiary ruins are scattered over several thousand acres. The site is

126 Registers with a quincunx [center top] [a pattern with four points forming a quadrangle and one point in the center] and masked figures [sides] in the top murals from Structure I, El Tajín, c. 700–1000.

set among low hills, with a lower area dotted with pyramids and ball courts, and an upper area of elaborately decorated palaces and other structures for elite gatherings (**figure 126**). The decorations in both paint and carved stone are done in the last major manifestation of Classic Veracruz style, as seen in the use of raised outlines and scroll forms throughout the site (**figure 127**).

The central core of the site is defined by the Pyramid of the Niches, a relatively small (only about 60 ft or 18 m high), four-sided structure of refined symmetry,

127 Such *palmas* as this were used in ball-game-related pageantry during the Epiclassic in the El Tajín region. Here, as a backdrop to the front surface, elegant scrolls outline profiled faces above and below a standing person with animal characteristics. Ht 19.31 in. [49.2 cm].

128 Pyramid of the Niches at El Tajín. Epiclassic period. Ht about 60 ft (18 m).

faced with carved stone blocks, rising in six tiers to an upper sanctuary (**figure 128**). A single stairway climbs to the top, flanked by balustrades embellished with a step-and-fret motif. The combination of niche surmounted by flying cornice, seen most strikingly in this building, was certainly emblematic of the site, appearing in other areas of northern Veracruz as El Tajín extended its reach. The Pyramid of the Niches was covered with a layer of stucco and was painted red, as were most of El Tajín's structures (a few, however, were a vivid blue). War standards were raised on sizable rectangular bases at the foot of the structure, and just to the south the most important ball-court activities were held in the main ceremonial court.

Other stone buildings at El Tajín are very similar in their architectural design, the step-and-fret motif (a symbol of lightning in late pre-Conquest Mexico) being particularly common. Palace-like buildings with colonnaded doorways were roofed with massive concrete slabs (utilizing marine shell and sand cement mixed with pumice and wood fragments) poured over wooden scaffolds, rather a solid construction technique.

129 One of four cornerstones from the ball court at Aparicio, Veracruz. Represented is a seated ball player wearing a *palma* and a glove to hit the ball; his head is severed, and intertwined snakes sprout from the neck to symbolize blood. The narrow surface has interlaced scrolls. Ht 3 ft 7.3 in. (1.10 m).

The Building of the Columns is part of the most substantial palace complex at the site. The drums of the columns are carved with scenes of elite ceremonial life. The most interesting of these depicts a procession of victorious warriors bringing stripped captives to the enthroned ruler, a personage with the calendrical name 13 Rabbit; before him lies the corpse of a disemboweled victim. Similar names, taken from the 260-day count, are found here and elsewhere at El Tajín, but with the exception of a small number of short texts on ceramic vessels, writing was used exclusively for naming figures.

Above all, the inhabitants of El Tajín celebrated in their art the ball game, human sacrifice, and death, three concepts closely interwoven in the Mesoamerican mind (**figure 129**). The courts, which are up to 197 ft (60 m) long, are formed by two facing walls, with stone surfaces either vertical or battered. Interestingly, nowhere is the game itself depicted; instead there are references to the complex of rituals surrounding the game. Among these ball-court images, the six in the South Ball Court are the most elaborate, describing a series of rituals glimpsed only in parts

130 Relief panel from the northeast corner of the South Ball Court, El Tajín. The scene shows the sacrifice of a ball player. The action takes place in a ball court, and all the figures wear the proper paraphernalia: yokes, *palmas*, and knee pads. A skeletal figure rises from a vase on the left. Classic Veracruz style, Epiclassic period. Ht 5 ft 1.4 in. (1.56 m).

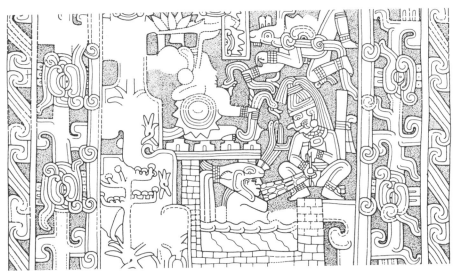

131 Detail of the south-central relief panel from the South Ball Court, El Tajín. A personification of the Rain Deity draws blood from his penis in a Temple-Water, while a person-fish drinks the sacrificial blood. Above, a reclining half-human, half-animal personage hands a rod of lightning to a seated figure with a star sign on its waist. Agave plants can be seen on the left. Ht 6 ft 9.1 in. (2.06 m).

elsewhere in Mesoamerica. The sequence seemingly begins on the northwest panel, where two facing figures, each one with an attendant, speak to each other, indicating their alliance. Later, in the southeast panel, a figure is depicted, dressed for war and being handed spears. A third scene, on the southwest panel, is presided over by a suspended figure—with fleshed head and skeletal body—who oversees a ritual that depicts a reclining personage facing a standing figure dressed as a bird while two musicians play a rattle and a drum. The climactic scene, on the northeast panel, alludes to sacrifice by heart extraction in the ball court itself, and is presided by the suspended figure, but this time shown descending and with fleshed body and skeletal head. On each corner panel, always nearest the center of the court, a skeletal figure rises from a jar depicted amid water (**figure 130**). This probably refers to the "place of the skull" in the center of the court, which the later Aztecs conceived of as a spring that was the origin of agricultural fertility. While the south-central panel depicts a scene of penis bloodletting, with a fish-human seemingly imbibing the sacrificial blood (**figure 131**), the north central panel shows the accession of a ruler who appears personifying the Rain Deity while wearing an "*oyohualli*" shell pendant.

El Tajín's destruction was by fire, traditionally by 1200, but perhaps by 1000 if recent evidence for post-Tajín squatter settlements around that date is taken into account.

Central Veracruz

From central Veracruz comes a lavish ware, known as Tuxtlas polychrome, that hints at the use of highly crafted plates for food servings at feasts and social gatherings at which the display of prestige goods and conspicuous consumption initiated gift-giving, political alliances, and patron-client relations (**figure 132**).

Scholars are still at odds as to the social function of tens of thousands of figurines found in variants throughout the area. These Remojadas-style hollow clay effigies were fashioned in naturalistic poses from which much ethnographic data can be drawn. The roots of the art reach back to the Late Formative, but most production was during the Epiclassic, when Remojadas figurines have close kinship with those of the Maya to the east and some interesting similarities to those of

132 Tripod plate with plumed serpent. The elegant line and firm composition seen here are typical of Tuxtlas polychrome. Los Tuxtlas, 600–900 CE.

133 Wheeled pottery figurine depicting a deer or a dog. Remojadas style, central Veracruz. The snout and eyes are decorated with asphalt. These amusing objects represent one of the several applications of the principle of rotational movement in Mesoamerica. Ht 7.1 in. (18 cm).

134 Pottery figure of a smiling boy, Remojadas style, central Veracruz. The upper teeth of this individual are characteristically filed. Epiclassic period. Ht 20.5 in. (52 cm).

Xochitecatl to the west. Such features as faces were generally cast from clay molds, and asphalt was used to heighten details or to indicate face paint (**figure 133**). The subjects are standing or seated humans, both male and female: curiously infantile boys and girls with laughing faces and filed teeth; ball players; lovers or friends in swings; and warriors (**figure 134**). The deities are also portrayed: Xipe Totec, as represented by a priest wearing the skin of a flayed captive; the Rain Deity; the Death God; and the Old Fire God, often shown as a wrinkled old man.

The most impressive of these hollow ceramic figures are near life-size and descend from the Classic tradition of monumental ceramic sculpture at Cerro de las Mesas, near which several of these were found, at El Zapotal. El Zapotal was a small town with a monumental core of earthen architecture, part of a heavily populated region with scores of similar small settlements including Cocuite, Dicha Tuerta, and Nopiloa. A shallow mound at El Zapotal yielded several construction phases, with an earlier structure that appears to have been a funerary memorial around which some 200 individuals were buried. These burials consisted of both bodies and dry bones exhumed from somewhere else, which were laid to rest over a long span of time, and even continued to be added once the memorial had been covered by subsequent structures. Yet, with each interment, previous burials were impacted, producing a complex clustering of deposits of skeletons with altered anatomical relations and disturbed and broken offerings. The memorial itself, built on a U-shaped platform, is a three-sided enclosure with clay walls that may originally have had a thatched roof.

135 A seated life-size clay representation of the Death God, part skeletal (skull, arms, and rib cage) and part flesh (tongue, hands, legs, and feet), forms the centerpiece of an elaborate funerary memorial at El Zapotal, Veracruz. Epiclassic period.

Inside, the focal point is an astounding sculpture of unbaked clay in the center of the back wall (**figure 135**). Seated on a throne-like bench, the figure is partly fleshed (the tongue, the hands, the legs, the feet), partly skeletal (the skull, the rib cage, and the arm bones). His loincloth is embellished with a glyphic brooch, and other accoutrements include a pectoral, earspools, bracelets, and anklets. The figure also wears an imposing headdress with the imagery of the Rain Deity projecting from the center, while profile views of skulls and Rain Deity heads adorn the tips of the lateral fastenings. The backrest is also adorned with jaguar heads in profile view. On the rear of the throne, openwork reveals part of the vertebral column and the thorax of the skeletal figure.

The interior and exterior of the three walls of the enclosure were painted with murals that are now much obliterated. Nevertheless, enough remains to make out four groups of personages, each one proceeding toward seated skeletal figures, including the one sculpted in clay who—on the interior side—is approached by a personage on either side of the throne. Two other groups are painted on the east and west arms of the enclosure. The fourth group is painted on the exterior of the rear wall.

136, 137 Life-size ceramic figures of women from Mound 2 at El Zapotal, Veracruz. Epiclassic period. Nineteen of these were arranged near the west side of a shrine dedicated to the Death God (**figure 135**, p. 163), as if proceeding away from it.

In front of the enclosure, as if complementing the procession of figures painted on the walls, stood nineteen life-size, hollow ceramic statues facing away from the entrance. These depict standing and seated women (**figures 136, 137**). Most were shattered due to the weight of the fill with which the tableau was covered. Bare-chested, the representations are characterized by their long skirts, each fastened by a belt with double-headed serpents; varied and imposing headdresses; and such personal accoutrements as nose plaques, necklaces, and bracelets. Several of the figures carry a copal bag (copal being an aromatic resin from the copal tree), which is adorned with jaguar or skull imagery. While the seated figures are shown with pensive faces, most if not all of the standing statues have closed eyes and open mouths; this is reminiscent of Xipe Totec impersonators wearing the flayed facial skin of a sacrificial victim.

Central Oaxaca

The Epiclassic in the Central Valleys of Oaxaca saw the apogee of Monte Albán. By the eighth century CE the city reached its maximum extension and a population of some 22,000 inhabitants, and its acropolis took the shape now seen by visitors. Ceramics for daily use and effigy vessels were mass-produced, and highly charged

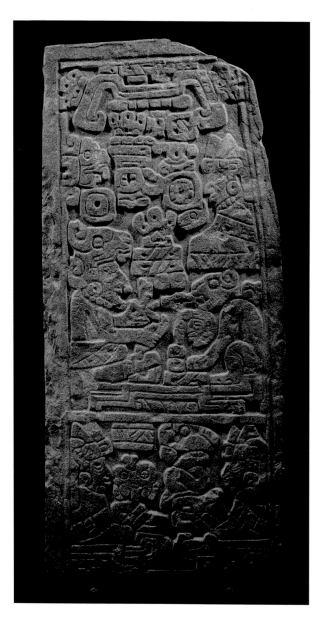

138 Epiclassic monument from the North Platform at Monte Albán, inscribed with genealogical records. Ht 8 ft 10.2 in. (2.7 m).

aesthetic production was confined to a few crafts. Monte Albán maintained long-distance interaction with other regions, especially for the procurement of obsidian. In small quantities and confined to elite contexts is the presence of locally made pottery imitating Balancán Fine Orange, a ceramic associated with the Putún Maya of Tabasco and southern Campeche, and another group of ceramics resembling the "slate ware" of such Maya sites as Uxmal and Kabah in the northern Yucatan Peninsula. Such grand construction projects as the ones in the North Platform—the administrative and funerary hub of the ruling elite—were accompanied by inscribed stone monuments containing genealogical records (**figure 138**). One of these, a stela found by archaeologist Marcus Winter, indicates that during the later history of Monte Albán, several prominent women acted as regents. The stela stood halfway

139 A carved stela recounts three events in the early years of a child named 6 Owl, the heir to the rulership at Noriega, near Monte Albán. In the middle register, rituals are performed around the young boy, while in the top register he accedes to power. The bottom register shows and names his parents. Ht 3 ft 4 in. (1 m).

up one of the loft temples at the highest point of the acropolis, where the royal tombs of the ruling lineages are likely to lie under meters of architectural accretion.

Another commemorative monument, part of one of the few narrative programs still in primary context, was the focal point of a small shrine associated with the ball court in the acropolis. The stones framing the entrance to the enclosure, including the lintel and the jambs, establish the pedigree of a ruler named 8 Reed, and the main inscribed slab shows him performing a preparatory ritual for the ball game. Except for the explicit presentation of a humiliated captive, the scene is practically identical to one of the tableaux from the South Ball Court at El Tajín.

During the Classic period the thrust of monumental art at Monte Albán had been the exaltation of divine rulers, linking them at times to an apical ancestor, but during the Epiclassic the royals and the nobility deployed lengthy genealogical reckonings in their historical records. This was a strategy to legitimate unequal power relations and to contest access to resources, including land, labor, privileges, and key positions in the administrative, religious, and military institutions. This was not solely a tactic of the royals; it was equally pursued by paramount as well as lesser corporate groups and their lineages at many subject communities, even those in the immediate hinterland of Monte Albán. From Noriega, a settlement that was probably subject to the secondary center of Zaachila and located near the southern foothills of Monte Albán, comes a small stela (later re-used to cover a funeral cist), with scenes that anticipate the lengthy narratives that will subsequently characterize the screenfolds from the Late Post-Classic (**figure 139**). The small monument depicts three rituals in the life of a child named 6 Owl who appears to have acceded to power at a young age; it also establishes his prestigious ancestry. While lesser lineages were able to commission only much smaller, portable genealogical slabs, most of them have been found in tombs, already broken and incomplete; this fact indicates their constant circulation and display in contexts of the living.

This apparent increase in the power of the nobility in secondary and lesser towns subject to Monte Albán may have contributed in part to the eventual inability of the capital to maintain its territorial control—and to the eventual fragmentation of its polity into smaller, hostile factions. At Lambityeco, a secondary settlement some 15 km east of Monte Albán, the investigations by archaeologists John Paddock and Michael Lind documented what may have been a widespread process. The excavations of one of the most substantial mounds at the site yielded evidence of how an elite group accumulated wealth through time, apparently from its control of the production of salt from saline marshes at the edge of the settlement. In a span of several generations, the residence of the lineage in question underwent continuous modifications, building subsequent greater residences on top of the remains of previous ones—all of them using the same original tomb to bury their household heads. What was originally a single courtyard with rooms around it and a modest crypt under the east room eventually became a two-courtyard complex, one used as living quarters and the other for public activities. The latter included a room raised on a platform, apparently to conduct business, and an elaborate altar and mausoleum constructed above the tomb, later turned into a two-chambered crypt to house all the accumulated ancestral remains. The entablatures of the mausoleum that faced the courtyard displayed a genealogical record, identifying at least five generations of married couples by their calendrical name. Then, toward the end of the ninth century CE, a grandiose complex bearing the architectural signature of the Monte Albán state suddenly engulfed the lavish residence of the time. A variant of the Temple-Plaza-Altar, with a substantial residence that had its own simple tomb devoid of any genealogical record atop a tall platform, had now obliterated from the landscape the previous house with its prominent mausoleum and multigenerational genealogical record. This evidence suggests that the interests and authority of the ruling elites of Monte Albán were being undermined by the power and influence of a prominent noble lineage from Lambityeco, and the rulers of Monte Albán reacted by curtailing the ambitions of the local elite. Its subjugation by Monte Albán was, however, short lived. By 850 CE, its political decline began, and although the abandonment of the capital was gradual, it eventually became a desolate place visited by people only to deposit offerings amid its ruined buildings. The collapse of the polity led to the abandonment of a score of secondary centers, like Cerro de la Campana (Suchilquitongo), Macuilxochitl, and Lambityeco. The Zapotec script lost prestige, and the practice of inscribing genealogical slabs and manufacturing effigy vessels with embodiments of ancestors and deities ceased.

The Pacific Littoral of Guerrero and Oaxaca

The dramatic descent of the Sierra Madre del Sur into the Pacific littoral does not lead to extensive alluvial plains, as in the Gulf Coast region. Rather, the flowing into the ocean of numerous rivers creates lower drainages of various scales with small deltas and mangroves. The largest fluvial systems have, over time, created more sizable expanses of flat land with much agricultural potential. During the Epiclassic, a considerable swath on this littoral—from central Guerrero to central Oaxaca—appears to have been home to several city-states. Some of these, including those centered at Piedra Labrada, near the Santa Catarina River; Guerrero; and Rio Viejo, near Rio Verde, Oaxaca, became major centers that could have controlled substantial territories encompassing several adjacent river mouths. This area was most likely inhabited by Tlapanec, Zapotec, and Chatino speakers. The key settlements were small urban centers with monumental architecture. Depending on the availability of local materials, great structures were made out of earth, or were built around clay nuclei dressed with stones. Most telling was the memorializing of local rulers in substantial and heavy monoliths, mostly stelae (**figures 140, 141**). These monuments depict richly clad figures identified by their calendrical names. Most of the graphic conventions seem to be Zapotec-derived, but the scribal practices are distinct in that no texts or chronological references to the Calendar Round are yet known.

The site of Piedra Labrada may extend through some 300 hectares, and at least five well-sized mounds are still present. More than twenty carved monuments have been found throughout the site, although only a few are still complete. Monument 3, documented in the 1960s by Román Piña Chan, depicts a jaguar lord named 10 Knot, with blood signs in his mouth and claws: a symbolic reference to human sacrifice.

The Late Formative site of Rio Viejo—which had been abandoned for some 400 years—saw a renewed and vibrant community, which by 650 CE had regained regional primacy. During this period of renewed preeminence, Rio Viejo covered 250 hectares (2.5 sq. km). Although no new building activity took place in the Late Formative-era acropolis, it was in use, and the core of the settlement had shifted by as much as 1 km toward the southeast. As many as thirty-one carved monuments have been found at Rio Viejo, clustered in three zones of the city that gravitate toward elevated features, two of them human-made—including the initial focus of Late Formative monumental architecture and the subsequent acropolis—and a natural hilly ridge. It may be that during the Epiclassic, three high-ranking corporate groups at Rio Viejo pursued a strategy of memorializing lineage heads while vying for power.

Throughout a considerable portion of Coastal Oaxaca, between Manialtepec to the north and Astata to the south, a singular fine-paste ceramic ware dubbed "Talun Carved" was produced and exchanged (**figure 142**). As highlighted by archaeologist Donald Brockington, the ware shows affinities with the ceramic tradition from Río Blanco, in the southern Gulf Coast lowlands, and with the carved slate wares from the Maya lowlands. The vessels are mostly deep bowls, the exterior surface of which is divided into panels featuring scenes that often depict personages presenting or exchanging objects, with their glyphic names accompanying them.

140, 141 Carved stelae from coastal Guerrero and Oaxaca. (ABOVE LEFT) Monument 3 from Piedra Labrada, Guerrero, represents a ruler named 10 Knot dressed as a jaguar with the blood sign in his mouth and claws. (ABOVE RIGHT) Monument 2 from Cerro del Rey, near Rio Grande, Oaxaca, depicts a half-human, half-jaguar ruler named 10 Alligator. The blood sign, allusive to human sacrifice, appears on top of the jaguar's head. Hts 7 ft 5.7 in. and 6 ft 10.6 in. (2.28 m and 2.1 m) respectively.

142 Talun Carved vessel from coastal Oaxaca, depicting a personage with the calendrical name 1 Lord. Ht 4.9 in. (12.4 cm).

Guanajuato and Northwestern Mexico

The void left by Teotihuacan reverberated around the northern regions of Meso-america, in parts of what are today the states of Hidalgo, Querétaro, Guanajuato, and Michoacan. Throughout this northern belt, a host of agricultural societies reasserted their cultural link to the rest of Mesoamerica, and their elites avidly exchanged luxury and prestige goods, including jade figurines, shells from the Gulf Coast and the Pacific littoral, turquoise, and obsidian from the Michoacan source in Ucareo-Zinapécuaro. An important settlement in this region was the site of Plazue-las, in the southwestern portion of Guanajuato. At its height, Plazuelas covered some 35 hectares. Spread over three hilly spurs separated by ravines, the settlement includes such monumental structures as temples, terraces with residences, and two ball courts (**figure 143**).

The paramount building, known now as "Casas Tapadas," was transformed through time, but in its final phase displayed a novel layout comprised of a central plaza with an east–west orientation that has within it, in sequence, a temple erected directly on the floor of the plaza, a main temple supported by a tall pyramidal

143 Ball-court marker from Las Plazuelas, Guanajuato. The emblem of the Fire Serpent, part ophidian, part alligator, with stepped eyebrows to signal luminosity, was a powerful alter-ego of rulers during the portentous moment of human immolation. Ht 2 ft 6.3 in. [77 cm].

144 View from the air of La Quemada, a walled hilltop fortress in Zacatecas, north central Mexico. At the right of the picture is the Hall of Columns. La Quemada was one of the northernmost complex settlements during the Epiclassic period.

platform, and behind it a secondary temple also supported by shallow platforms. These three structures face toward the west. Flanking the entire length of the central plaza are two parallel narrow courtyards bounded by walls, and toward their east end sit temples on platforms that face toward the central plaza. Three converging roads seemingly accessed the entire complex, one from the west (the main entrance), and the others from the north and the south. To some extent, this layout appears to conform, in part, to an old Late Formative template of a triad of buildings facing toward a common plaza. There are, however, also reminiscences of the layout, at a smaller scale, of the Ciudadela at Teotihuacan. Notable is the fact that the low-lying temple in the central axis was embellished at the top of its basal *talud* and cornice by sculpted merlons in the shape of clouds, identical to the decoration of the cornices in the Building of the Feathered Serpents at Xochicalco. Yet, it appears that the sacred, monumental architecture at Plazuelas combined masonry platforms and basal walls with thatched roofs.

While farmers had moved into the northwestern fringes of Mesoamerica by the first century CE, it was not until the Epiclassic that we see substantial settlements in this frontier zone formed by the modern states of Durango, Zacatecas, and Sinaloa. La Quemada, which flourished from 500 to 900 CE, occupies a hilltop 820 ft (250 m) above the surrounding valley floor and is protected by strategically located defensive walls, behind which the bulk of the population lived (**figure 144**). Ben Nelson's work at the site has shown that warfare was a central concern, indicated by the display of considerable quantities of disarticulated bones as trophies, with substantial displays of disarticulated human remains heaped on the floor. Other bone

145 Pyramid at La Quemada. The markedly steep sides and unbroken profiles are unusual in Mesoamerican architecture. A small temple may have been placed at the summit. Epiclassic period.

assemblages were treated with reverence and hung from the rafters, suggesting an ancestor cult. Displays of human bone were important not only at La Quemada, but also at smaller centers in the area. One of the most important architectural innovations is the *tzompantli*, or skull rack; later this building type was important to Mesoamericans as the place to exhibit trophy heads related to ball-game decapitation sacrifice. It is no surprise, then, that at La Quemada and other sites in the region I-shaped ball courts are also found. Other innovative architectural forms include the colonnaded hall, often with an adjoining sunken patio, and the soaring, steep-sided pyramid (**figure 145**).

A series of roadways organizes the immediate area into a set of linked settlements, ruled, rather harshly it would seem, from La Quemada. The Huichol people of adjacent Jalisco recount that at one point an evil priest lived on a "great rock" which was also a fortress, protected by eagles and jaguars. This ruler-priest required tribute in peyote, and would not let the people acquire the items necessary to worship the deities: shells, feathers, and salt. The people appealed to the deities, who then destroyed the leader and his aides with twenty days of heat. This may be an indigenous account of the end of La Quemada, for the fortress was burned around 900 CE and never reoccupied.

Alta Vista, located 106 miles (170 km) northwest of La Quemada, was its contemporary, exhibiting much the same focus on warfare, and several of the same architectural innovations. Unlike La Quemada, which apart from its architecture was singularly poor in its material culture, Alta Vista was a wealthy trading community with an even more impressive architectural tradition. Great quantities of turquoise have been found at the site. Turquoise had first appeared in the Formative period, mainly in west Mexico, and always in small amounts. In Alta Vista there was large-scale processing of the ore into regular tesserae (miniature tiles used in mosaics) for turquoise mosaic objects. Many of these were laid into elite graves at Alta Vista itself.

Although Alta Vista was the center of a vast mining industry focusing primarily on malachite, azurite, ocher, cinnabar, and weathered chert, there are no high-quality turquoise deposits in the area. Trace element analysis, carried out through neutron activation by Garman Harbottle at the Brookhaven National Laboratory, has shown that much of the raw turquoise came from mines in the American Southwest, especially from New Mexico. It is fairly clear that the northwestern frontier was instrumental in the transmission of Mesoamerican traits into the American Southwest, in particular the colonnaded masonry building and the platform pyramid; the ball court and the game played in it; the organization of settlements into a linked hierarchy with roads; copper bells; and perhaps even the taste for turquoise-encrusted objects.

The End of the Epiclassic

Around 900 CE, many of the cities that had forged a post-Teotihuacan order went into their own decline and eclipse. Much of the west Mexican area, including the mining area around Alta Vista and the Teuchitlan Tradition heartland, had collapsed by this date. Certainly two of the sites with substantial Maya connections, Cacaxtla and Xochicalco, were abandoned by this time, and so was Monte Albán in the Central Valleys of Oaxaca. It is probably no coincidence that the central Maya area itself was going through a complete collapse between 800 and 900 CE, the signs of the times being their failure to erect dynastic monuments dated in the Long Count system, clear-cut vandalism and defacement, and the depopulation of centers. As at the fall of Teotihuacan, there must have been much movement of populations, shifting alliances, and a certain amount of social unrest at the end of the Epiclassic. Out of this was to emerge a new order, the Toltec, which was to link the Maya and ancient Mexico yet again, create a new capital, and initiate a new art style.

Chapter 8

The Post-Classic Period: The Toltec State

A Time of Troubles

Following in the wake of the disturbances and migrations that occurred during the ninth century CE came a seemingly new mode of organized life. The Post-Classic continued and heightened the Epiclassic emphasis on militarism by parading seemingly endless lines of warriors throughout public art. There was now an entrenched class of professional warriors, grouped into military orders that took their names from the animals from which they may have claimed a kind of totemic descent: coyote, jaguar, and eagle. At the same time, new alliances and trade relationships were formed across ancient Mexico to the Maya area and even to Central America and the Southwest United States (**figure 146**).

Throughout Mexico, this was a time that saw a great deal of social unrest and movement, with factions amalgamating to form small, aggressive, conquest states, and splitting up as swiftly as they had risen. The Epiclassic saw movement and conquest on a grand scale, but during certain spans of the Post-Classic the rhythm and intensity of these processes increased. Even groups of distinctly different speech sometimes came together to form a single state—as we know from indigenous annals, for we have entered the realm of post-Conquest, historic accounts written in both native and Spanish scripts. Naturally, such new conditions are mirrored in Early Post-Classic art styles, which are characterized by an interest in costume ornament over naturalistic human features and in a hard-edged carving style that is not overly concerned with the niceties of finish.

Metallurgy began being practiced by societies in western Mexico around the 9th century CE. The Early Post-Classic saw the spread of metalworking throughout Mesoamerica along with its importance as an exclusively elite luxury good, namely personal ornamentation (**figure 147**).

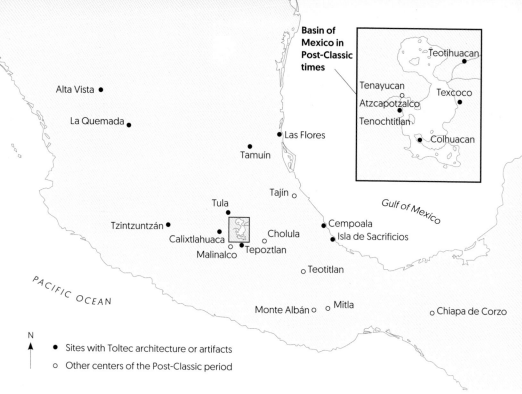

Basin of
Mexico in
Post-Classic
times

Teotihuacan
Tenayucan
Atzcapotzalco
Tenochtitlan
Texcoco
Colhuacan

Alta Vista

La Quemada

Las Flores

Tamuín

Tajín

Tula

Gulf of Mexico

Tzintzuntzán

Calixtlahuaca
Malinalco
Tepoztlan

Cholula

Cempoala
Isla de Sacrificios

Teotitlan

PACIFIC OCEAN

Monte Albán   Mitla

Chiapa de Corzo

N

● Sites with Toltec architecture or artifacts

○ Other centers of the Post-Classic period

146 Distribution of Toltec sites and other important centers of the Post-Classic period.
The inset map is the Basin of Mexico.

147 Copper tools and ornaments, Post-Classic period. The large "axe-money" is from
Mitla, Oaxaca. The awls (center) are from Lake Chapala in Michoacan; the bells (upper
left) and tweezers (top center) are from Mexico and of unknown provenience.

A Time of Troubles   175

Related to the rise of metallurgy was the introduction of turquoise as a precious stone of similar prestige to jade. Both turquoise and metalwork had their origins far to the north and west of central Mexico, but both materials were fervently embraced by much of Mexico, and indeed much of Mesoamerica, during this period. In the realm of both jewelry and turquoise work, the skill of the Mexican craftsman reached heights of great artistry (see p. 186).

The Chichimeca of Northern Mexico

It was not only internal pressure brought by new conquest states that disturbed Mexico. It was both intra- and inter-societal processes that had far-reaching effects, including displacements and migrations into central Mexico of people from the northwestern frontier and other marginal groups on the northern borders of Mesoamerica. The two great northwestern centers of the Epiclassic, Alta Vista and La Quemada, shared such traits as the skull rack and colonnaded hall with Epiclassic Tula Chico, in the region of central Mexico that would later become the Toltec capital. The Epiclassic Tula region also experienced an important influx of people and goods from the Bajío, the northern zone centered on the modern states of Guanajuato and Querétaro. For those living in central Mexico, all these northern groups were subsumed under the designation "Chichimeca," a name meaning something similar to "lineage of the dog." In later Aztec chronicles they are portrayed as bow-and-arrow wielding nomads, an image probably related to their distinction between "foragers" and "agriculturalists." At the same time, Chichimeca are described as obsidian and flint workers, turquoise artists, and feather workers—all things associated with Alta Vista and La Quemada, as well as other northern groups, all of whom were sedentary, urban-dwelling Mesoamericans. Further, several ruling dynasties in the Basin of Mexico were proud to claim Chichimec ancestry, and a group called the "Tolteca-Chichimeca" was instrumental in the conquest or founding of cities throughout the first half of Post-Classic Mexican history.

Given the conflicting images of the Chichimeca emerging from the chronicles, along with the rather complex history of northwest Mexico, who were these people? There is no simple answer to this important historical question, for it seems that many different sorts of groups were subsumed into this category by those who wrote Mexican history. In the account recorded by Father Sahagún, nomadic people were called "Teochichimeca," who lived in natural shelters and clothed themselves in animal skins and yucca-fiber sandals, subsisting on wild fruits, roots, and seeds, and on the meat of such animals as the rabbit. The "Tamime" are described as Chichimeca who emulated the practices and speech of more complex societies to the south; they wore the hand-me-down clothes from the cities and did some farming to supplement their foragers' diet. The portrait of the Teochichimeca is a fairly accurate description of the lifeways of desert-dwelling hunters and gatherers. The "Tamime," if they may be identified with the frontier farmers and urban-dwellers of northwestern and west Mexico, formed more complex societies than those described by Father Sahagún and other chroniclers. Perhaps it was this latter group, those prosperous northwestern farmers and urban-dwellers, who on immigrating to central Mexico brought with them certain innovative cultural traits and whose presence further disrupted the Epiclassic order, who eventually ushered in the Post-Classic.

Tula and the Toltecs

There have been four unifying forces in the pre-Spanish history of Mexico: the first of these was Olmec, the second Classic Teotihuacan, the third Toltec, and the last Aztec. In their own annals, written down in Spanish letters after the Conquest, the Mexican nobility and intelligentsia looked back in wonder to an almost semi-mythical time when the Toltecs ruled, a people whose very name means "the artificers." Of them it was said that "nothing was too difficult for them, no place with which they dealt was too distant." From their capital, Tollan (Tula), they had dominated much of northern and central Mexico in ancient times, as well as parts of the Guatemalan highlands and most of the Yucatan Peninsula. After their downfall, no Mexican or Maya dynasty worth its salt failed to claim descent from these esteemed people.

Like many other Post-Classic states, Toltec society seems to have been composed of disparate groups that had come together for obscure reasons. One of these, which would appear to have been dominant, was called the Tolteca-Chichimeca. The other group went under the name Nonoalca, and according to some scholars consisted of sculptors and artisans from the old urban centers in Puebla and the Gulf Coast, brought in to construct the monuments of Tula. The Tolteca-Chichimeca, for their part, were probably Nahua speakers with a fairly complex northern Mesoamerican culture, like that of the "Tamime" Chichimeca mentioned earlier.

The Toltec Annals

Indigenous writers recorded numerous accounts of the ancient history of Tula soon after the Spanish Conquest. Most of these are especially concerned with the fall of Tula, for by tracing their lineage to the Toltec diaspora, later kings could claim Toltec descent. Yet enough remains of earlier episodes to allow us to piece together a more complete story. Couched in a poetic prose, the accounts tell of political factionalism, diaspora, and military expansionism. Said to have been led by their ruler Mixcoatl ("Cloud Serpent"), who, accounts tell us, was deified as patron of hunting after his death, by the beginning of the ninth century the Tolteca-Chichimeca had entered in contact with the complex societies at the southern extension of the Sierra Madre Occidental, passing through what now comprises northern Jalisco and

148 Feathered Serpent from cornice of north banquette, Courtyard 2 in the Burned Palace, Tula, Hidalgo. Toltec culture, Early Post-Classic period.

southern Zacatecas. It is no easy matter to outline their history from the contradictory accounts that we have been left, but according to the scheme of Jiménez Moreno, Mixcoatl and his people first settled at a place in the Basin of Mexico called Colhuacan. The account tells us that his son and heir was Topiltzin, the most famous figure in all Mexican history. Topiltzin was born in the year 1 Reed (either 935 or 947 CE), and later identified—to the confusion of modern scholars—with the Feathered Serpent, Quetzalcoatl (**figure 148**). As would be expected in the aftermath of the Conquest, this king is described in literature of this period as being of fair skin, with long hair and a black beard.

The first event in the rule of 1 Reed Topiltzin Quetzalcoatl was the transfer of the Toltec capital from Colhuacan via Tulancingo to Tula, the ancient Tollan, a name signifying "Place of the Rushes," but which to the ancients meant something similar to "civilized life." Some years after its founding, according to the annals, Tula was the scene of a terrible internal strife. Topiltzin was supposedly a kind of priest-king dedicated to the peaceful cult of the Feathered Serpent, abhorring human sacrifice and performing all sorts of penances. His enemies were devotees of the fierce god Tezcatlipoca ("Smoking Mirror"), the giver and taker away of life, lord of sorcerers, and the patron of the warrior orders. Conflict arose between the two, the latter perhaps made discontented by the intellectual pacifism of their king.

As a result of this moral struggle for power, Topiltzin and his followers were forced to flee the city. Some of the most beautiful Nahuatl poetry records his unhappy downfall, a defeat laid at the door of Tezcatlipoca himself. Topiltzin and his followers were said to have become slothful, the ruler having even transgressed the priestly rules of sexual continence. Tezcatlipoca undermines his foes by means of various evil stratagems: coming to Topiltzin in the guise of an old man and tricking him into drinking a magic and debilitating potion; then appearing without his loincloth in the marketplace, disguised as a seller of green chile peppers, and inflaming the ruler's daughter with such a desire for him that her father is forced to take him as son-in-law; next, Tezcatlipoca appears as a warrior successfully leading a band of dwarfs and hunchbacks who had been given to him in vain hope that he would be slain by the enemy; making a puppet dance for his enemies, causing them in their curiosity to rush forward and crush themselves to death. Even when they eventually killed Tezcatlipoca by stoning, the Toltecs were unable to rid themselves of his now festering, rotted body.

At last, according to the accounts, Topiltzin Quetzalcoatl is exiled from his beloved city. He leaves after burning or burying all his treasures, preceded on his path by birds of precious feather. As Tula disappears from his sight:

Then he fixes his eyes on Tula and in that moment begins to weep:
as he weeps sobbing, it is like two torrents of hail trickling down:
His tears slip down his face;
his tears drop by drop perforate the stones.[4]

On his way, trickster magicians cross his path again and again, trying to make him turn back. At last he reaches the stormy pass between the volcanoes Iztaccihuatl and Popocatepetl, where his jugglers, buffoons, and his palace pages freeze to death. He continues on, his gaze directed at the shroud of the snows, and eventually arrives at the shore of the Gulf of Mexico. One poem relates that there he set himself afire, decked in his quetzal plumage and turquoise mask; as his ashes rose to the sky, every kind of marvelously colored bird wheeled overhead, and the dead king was transformed into the planet Venus as the Morning Star. Another version of the account, the one claimed by the Spaniards to have been known to Moteuczoma Xocoyotzin, tells us that Topiltzin did not perform an act of self-immolation, but rather set off with followers on a raft formed of serpents on a journey to the east, from which he was supposed to return some day.

It may be evidence of the historical core within this story that a number of Maya and colonial Spanish accounts speak of the arrival from the west, sometime in the tenth century CE, of a Mexican conqueror named in their tongue K'uk'ulkan ("Feathered Serpent"), who with his companions subjugated their country. There is also evidence in the archaeology of Yucatan for a seaborne Toltec invasion, successfully initiating a Mexican period, with its capital at Chich'en Itza.

With the sanguinary rule of the Tezcatlipoca party now dominant at Tula, the Toltec empire may have reached its greatest expansion, holding sway over most of central Mexico from coast to coast. At the height of its power, Tula is pictured in the poems as a sort of idealized fantastical land, where ears of maize were as big as *mano* stones, and red, yellow, green, blue and many other colors of cotton grew naturally. There were palaces of jade and gold, one of turquoise, and one made of blue-green quetzal feathers. The Toltecs were said to be so prosperous that they heated their sweat baths with the small ears of maize. There was nothing that they could not make; wonderful potters, they "taught the clay to lie." Truly, they "put their heart into their work."

The end of Tula approached with the last ruler, Huemac ("Big Hand"). Triggered by a disastrous series of droughts, factional conflicts broke out once more, apparently between the Tolteca-Chichimeca and the Nonoalca. In 1156 or 1168 Huemac transferred his capital to Chapultepec, the hill-crowned park in what is now the western part of Mexico City, where he committed suicide. Some Tolteca-Chichimeca hung on at Tula for another fifteen years, finally themselves deserting the city and moving south to the Basin of Mexico and as far as Cholula, subjugating all who lay in their way. Tula was left in ruins, with only memories of its glories. As the Nahuatl poet tells us:

Everywhere there meet the eye,
everywhere can be seen the remains of clay vessels,
of their cups, their figures,
of their dolls, of their figurines,
of their bracelets,
everywhere are their ruins,
truly the Toltecs once lived there.[5]

The final diaspora had begun, with bands of refugees dispersing along former alliance networks over highland and lowland Mexico, all claiming Tula as their homeland. Even Maya groups from the distant highlands of Guatemala claimed that the Toltecs had legitimated their reign. The Maya rulers of that region claimed they had visited the Toltecs in Tula and there obtained their sacred power objects and their right to rule. In death, as in life, Tula remained a potent force in Mesoamerican thought through its role in the definition of cultural and political ideals. But how do these stories compare with the actual physical remains of the city?

Archaeological Tula

It has been the misfortune of modern scholarship that there are not one, but many places named Tula in Mexico—a quite natural circumstance from the meaning of the original name Tollan, which can be translated not only as "Place of the Rushes," but also as "civilized urban space." The term was therefore applied to such great ancient centers as Teotihuacan and Cholula. Given this premise, the glowing descriptions appearing in native and Spanish accounts have led many an archaeologist, such as George Vaillant, to the erroneous conclusion that the Tula of the Toltecs must have been the admittedly magnificent Teotihuacan. In the late 1930s, however, documentary researches by the Mexican ethnohistorian Wigberto Jiménez Moreno proved that the city of Topiltzin and Huemac was the Tula lying some 50 miles (80 km) northwest of Mexico City, in the state of Hidalgo. This has been borne out by subsequent excavations.

The first serious archaeological work at Tula took place as far back as the 1880s, when the French explorer Désiré Charnay excavated a palace structure and noted close ties between the remains at Tula and those at distant Chich'en Itza. Intensive excavations were begun at the site in 1940 under the direction of Jorge Acosta of the National Institute of Anthropology and History, and continued for another twenty years. Further projects undertaken by Eduardo Matos Moctezuma, Richard Diehl, Alba Guadalupe Mastache, Robert Cobean, and Dan Healan have given us an even deeper knowledge of the Toltec capital.

Tula of the Toltecs had not only been burned and sacked by its destroyers (whoever they might have been), but the later Aztecs had thoroughly looted sculptures, friezes, and offerings, which were reused in Tenochtitlan and elsewhere. Its reconstruction has therefore been extremely difficult, and it is little wonder that it now seems unimpressive as one of the major sites of Mesoamerica, and convinced some (but not all) modern scholars that it was Chich'en Itza that conquered Tula, and not the other way around (see p. 190).

Placed in a defensible position on a limestone promontory, Tula is surrounded by steep banks on three sides. There were small villages here in Formative times, and a more substantial settlement during the apogee of Teotihuacan, when the extensive irrigation system in the broad valley to the northwest of Tula may have been begun.

It is during the Epiclassic, however, that we see the beginnings of what will be Toltec Tula. The inhabitants of the valley (perhaps the Tolteca-Chichimeca of the annals) produced Coyotlatelco pottery and a new, rougher style of monument carving that would eventually characterize Tula and the Toltecs. Their main source of obsidian at this time came from the north and west, at Ucareo, Michoacan, as Dan Healan has shown. As discussed on p. 176, other traits were also shared with the north and west by this time, including skull racks and colonnaded halls. Over the course of the Epiclassic there developed a sizable community of localized artisans specializing in the production of such items as pottery vessels, mold-made figurines, and obsidian blades. A civic-religious center, dubbed Tula Chico, was established in what later became the northeast part of the city. Epiclassic Tula Chico exhibits many of the stylistic and iconographic traits seen later at both Tula Grande and the faraway but related Maya site of Chich'en Itza with striking specificity. Tula Chico elements that predate their appearance at both Tula Grande and Chich'en Itza include halls decorated with sculpted reclining figures with jewelry and back mirrors (very similar to those found in Tula Grande Palacio Quemado, p. 186), as well as architectural panels alternating quadrupeds and birds of prey, the latter similar to those found in Tula Grande Pyramid B (see p. 182). The precocious appearance of these Early Post-Classic traits at Epiclassic Tula Chico suggests that a significant portion of Toltec style and iconography was generated here and later found its way to the more sizable Tula Grande site as well as to Maya Chich'en Itza.

The Tollan phase (900–1200 CE) marks the major occupation of the capital and the construction of a monumental civic-religious center called Tula Grande, south-west of Tula Chico. The traditional dating is based on both archaeological evidence and interpretations of indigenous histories, but most of the radiocarbon dates for this phase cluster in the 900–1000 CE range, as do new dates for comparable Basin of Mexico ceramics and Tohil Plumbate trade wares, suggesting that the apogee of Tula Grande may be slightly earlier than once thought. At this time the city—one of the largest, if not the largest in Early Post-Classic Mesoamerica—covered 5.4 sq. miles (16 sq. km), and contained an estimated population of 30,000 to 40,000. Tula's rulers had decreed a major reorganization of the city, for its streets and avenues, which had formerly been oriented to true north, were now changed to seventeen degrees east of north, very similar to the orientation of Teotihuacan. The old center of Tula Chico was abandoned, never to be reinhabited. Tula Grande was now the sole major civic-religious center during the Tollan phase. It consists of a wide central

plaza bordered on the east by the thoroughly despoiled Pyramid C, the most substantial structure at Tula and as yet unexcavated; on the west by an unexplored ball
court; and on the north by Pyramid B and its annexes (**figure 149**). On the north side
of Pyramid B is a smaller plaza, beyond which is another I-shaped ball court about
120 ft (37 m) long, an exact copy of the prototype at Xochicalco.

Pyramid B is the most impressive building at Tula (**figure 150**). Built in six
successive stages, in its final form this stepped pyramid-platform was fronted by
a colonnaded hall, along the back of which banquettes with polychrome bas-reliefs
of marching warriors were ranged. An ancient visitor would have walked through
the colonnade, climbed the stairway, and passed through the entrance of the temple,
flanked by two composite stone columns in the form of Feathered Serpents, with
their rattles in the air and heads on the ground. The temple itself had two rooms;
the roof of the outer one was supported by four colossal atlantean figures (support-
ive columns in the shape of humans), representing warriors carrying an *atlatl* in
one hand and darts, a war club, and a tobacco bowl in the other—perfect embodiments of Toltec warrior ideals (**figure 151**). The rear room had four composite
square pillars, carved on all sides with warriors accompanied by name captions,

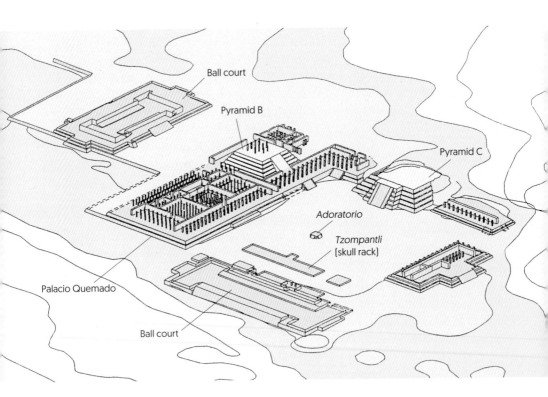

149 Isometric view of Tula Grande, the central part of the city, where
the great majority of monumental public sculpture and architecture in
Tula is found. Elite and non-elite houses, not shown here, surrounded
this monumental core, following a layout in a grid-like pattern.

150 [ABOVE] View from the southeast of Pyramid B at Tula, Hidalgo. This stepped pyramid rises in five tiers and has an overall height of around 33 ft [10 m].

151 Colossal atlantean figures of stone: three of the four from on top of Pyramid B. Each figure is made of four sections of stone and represents a warrior carrying an *atlatl* in one hand and a bowl for tobacco in the other. On the chest is worn the stylized butterfly emblem of the Toltec. Ht 15 ft [4.6 m].

152 Stone *chacmool* from Tula. Reclining figures of this sort are found wherever Toltec influence extended. This *chacmool* wears a nose-plug and carries a sacrificial knife strapped to the upper arm.

including one with a long beard and a feathered serpent glyph (perhaps Topiltzin in his role as Quetzalcoatl) and another with a smoking mirror in place of one foot (Tezcatlipoca, Quetzalcoatl's nemesis in the Tula stories). There, in the sanctuary, once stood a stone altar supported by little atlantean figures. Also in the temple and in other parts of the ceremonial precinct were peculiar sculptures called *chacmools*, reclining personages bearing round receptacles for human hearts on their bellies; one of these had a sacrificial knife strapped to his upper arm (**figure 152**).

Around the four sides of Pyramid B were bas-reliefs symbolizing the social institutions on which the strength of the empire depended: prowling jaguars and coyotes, and eagles eating hearts, interspersed with frontal views of crouching winged human figures with goggled eyes, nose plaques, feathered-serpent helmets (including the bifid tongue) and jaguar claws (**figure 153**).

Adjacent to this pyramid is the Palacio Quemado, or Burnt Palace, which consists of very spacious colonnaded halls with sunken courts in their centers. The columns were built up of rubble over wooden cores. Again, low banquettes extend along the walls, which were apparently frescoed. Reclining figures in low-relief are found in significant numbers, echoing earlier Tula Chico architectural decoration. These halls most likely served for meetings and ceremonies, rather than as palaces.

In fact, two floor plans very closely resembling the apartment compounds of Teotihuacan have been uncovered away from the center of Tula, and these were certainly residences for nobles.

On the north side of the pyramid and parallel to it is a long wall spanning 131 ft (40 m) embellished with painted friezes, the fundamental repeating motif of which is a part-skeletonized, part-fleshed reclining personage entwined with a serpent.

The grim man-at-arms whose features are delineated in stone in the atlantean figures and in many other instances at Tula carried the feather-decorated *atlatl* in the right hand, and a cluster of darts in the left; the bow seldom appeared in the art of Mexico. A heavy padding of quilted cotton on the left arm provided protection against enemy darts. Strapped to the small of the back was the *tezcacuitlapilli*, a round, pyrite mirror backed by a turquoise mosaic representing four encircling Fire Serpents. Headgear consisted of a pillbox-shaped hat topped by quetzal plumes and bearing on its front a bird flying downward. The customary nose ornament was something like a button through the wings of the nose, and a goatee often embellished the warrior's chin. Over the chest was a breastplate worn under a highly abstract butterfly pectoral, both emblematic of warriors. Either the breechclout (*maxtli*) or the short kilt could be worn, while below leg and ankle bands the feet were shod with backed sandals.

153 East side of Pyramid B at Tula, bas-reliefs of coyotes and felines alternate with rows of eagles eating hearts and crouching winged human figures with goggled eyes, nose plaques, feathered serpent helmets (including the bifid tongue) and jaguar claws. Toltec culture, Early Post-Classic period.

154 Mosaic mirror with pyrite, turquoise, and shell inlays. Tula, Burnt Palace. Diam. 13.2 in. (33.6 cm).

A splendid shell breastplate and turquoise *tezcacuitlapilli* back mirror un-earthed at Tula give some idea of how impressive this paraphernalia must have been. The back mirror, which consisted of over 3,000 pieces of finely worked turquoise mixed with shell, was deposited 11.8 inches (30 cm) above the breastplate in the center of a patio in the Palacio Quemado (**figure 154**). Buried with the breastplate in a sizable earthen box were marine shells from both the Gulf of Mexico and the Pacific, which along with the turquoise probably from northwest Mexico or the south-western United States indicates the far-flung nature of the Toltec trading networks.

The most common foreign-trade pottery at the site was the distinctive Tohil Plumbate ware, one of the very few true glazed ceramics of the pre-Spanish Western Hemisphere, produced in kilns on the Pacific coastal plain near the Mexican-Guatemalan border. The ware was made with a slip of clay high in alumina and iron and fired so as to reduce the amount of oxygen to create a vitrified surface with a gray or olive-green color (**figure 155**). Plumbate was probably made to order for the Toltec taste, and one superb effigy was discovered at Tula showing the face of a bearded man with a coyote helmet, all completely covered with small plaques of mother-of-pearl. A storage or cache pit in a room of one house produced five Tohil Plumbate goblets, along with three goblets and a bowl of Papagayo Polychrome, a kind of brightly painted pottery manufactured in quantity at this time in an area extending from eastern Honduras down to northwestern Costa Rica.

The Aztec testimony that the Toltecs were master craftsmen is validated by the breastplate and mirror discussed above. Both objects are exceptionally finely made from precious materials (highly valued shells and turquoise). Archaeologists have also uncovered objects in *tecalli* (also known as "Mexican onyx," a kind of limestone called travertine, deposited by mineral spring) that was highly valued by the elite.

a   b

155 Plumbate effigy jars from Teotihuacan and Tula. Toltec culture. a) bearded warrior in jaguar helmet; b) turkey effigy.

A more common but still highly important material, obsidian, was produced on a considerable scale, similar to that at Teotihuacan, and in the same manner as the Teotihuacanos, during the Tollan phase the Tula Toltec controlled the great mines of green obsidian at Pachuca, Hidalgo. In fact, Richard Diehl estimates that more than forty percent of Tula's inhabitants were engaged in production of obsidian cores, blades, and projectile points for internal consumption and export.

In clay one also finds a small amount of Mazapan pottery, a red-on-buff ware featuring bowls, the interiors of which are decorated with parallel wavy or straight lines applied by a multiple brush; mold-made figurines; and tobacco pipes with flaring bowls and long stems embellished with undulating snakes (**figure 156**). To date, Tula has yielded no metal of any kind, neither copper nor gold, but this is scarcely a surprise, for as yet no fine tombs, where one would expect such valued materials, have been located there. On the other hand, many of the ornaments portrayed in stone are painted yellow, suggesting that they stand for golden or gilded jewels.

156 Mazapan ceramic artifacts, from Teotihuacan. Pottery of this sort underlies the Toltec culture at Tula. a) and b) Mazapan red-on-buff bowls, scale: 1/8; c) female figurine, scale: 1/2.

a   b   c

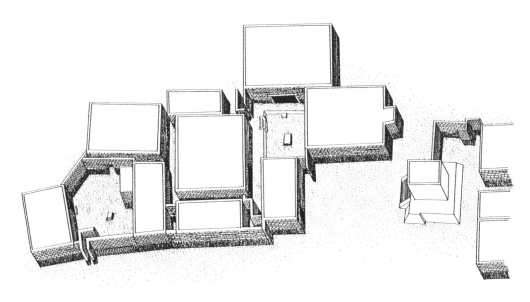

157 Reconstruction drawing of houses and associated small temple at Tula. Toltec culture, Early Post-Classic period.

Representations of deities are seemingly rare but not lacking. Curiously, the supposedly victorious Tezcatlipoca himself is absent, except for one warrior column. Recognizable are representations of several deities worshipped also by the Aztecs, such as Tlaloc (the Rain Deity); Xipe Totec (God of Spring); Centeotl (the Maize Goddess); Xochiquetzal (the Goddess of Love); and Tlahuizcalpantecuhtli (an avatar of Quetzalcoatl as Morning Star). And while the imagery of the Feathered Serpent is most pervasive, many of these representations may not necessarily allude to Quetzalcoatl.

As inheritors of the central-Mexican scribal tradition, scribes at Tula used writing in monumental settings for very specific purposes, including the naming of prominent personages by means of their calendrical or personal names, and to recount brief historical references that include dates in the Calendar Round. The script seems to be predominantly logographic, and could have been read by speakers of different languages. Nominal captions characterize some of the warriors depicted in the squared pillars atop Building B. And from an assortment of stone monuments, many of them later reused and found out of their original context, some twelve of the twenty-day names of the calendar can be identified. In three examples of calendrical statements, a human figure is shown carrying the year glyph as a burden on his back, as if it were a load of merchandise. These dates include the year names House (twice) and Flint.

The practice of human sacrifice at Tula can be surmised from the presence of the *chacmool* sculptures, monuments that served both as stones to facilitate the backward bending of sacrificial victims as well as receptacles for offerings. Also, the base of an actual *tzompantli* (skull rack) was found just to the east of Ball Court II, the most substantial at the site; fragments of human skulls littered its surface.

In accordance with Mesoamerican custom, these were probably decapitated heads displayed as war trophies after captives had played the ball game, simulating a mock battle, and had then been sacrificed.

Richard Diehl's University of Missouri excavations brought to light some of the domestic architecture of the Toltecs. Individual houses were flat-roofed buildings of square or rectangular plan; these formed complexes of up to five houses, each group separated from the others by exterior house walls and courtyard walls (**figure 157**). Each such group had a small altar or shrine in the center of the courtyard. An important part of the rites celebrated there must have been the worship of the Rain Deity, represented by hour-glass-shaped pottery braziers with faces of Tlaloc indicated by clay fillets; there are also openwork ceramic censers with one long handle and two feet for supports. Animal figurines with small wheels—perhaps to animate them—were part of the household cult. The dead were generally buried in a pit beneath the house floor, and accompanied by pots. The general settlement pattern seems to be different from Teotihuacan's, but there is evidence that Tula also had an overall grid plan, organizing these household clusters into wards of around 1,970 ft (600 m) on a side.

Tula is closer to the northern margins of Mesoamerica, and it was also marginal for farming, since summer rainfall is insufficient for effective cultivation, and there are winter frosts. Accordingly, food for Tula's population came from the fields irrigated during the rainy season from small canals running from modest check dams.

All the evidence points to the death of the city through sudden and overwhelming cataclysm: the ceremonial halls were burned to the ground, and the wall with partially skeletonized beings and serpents was toppled over. The fury of the destruction visited on Tula makes one wonder about the hand that performed the act. The mere fact that the subsequent reoccupation of the site was by a people who used so-called "Aztec" II pottery does not mean that the vanquishers of the capital were of the same affiliation. If we take the surviving accounts in the Toltec annals at face value, the demise at Tula would have been primarily the result of an internal strife, although external, regional factors were probably also at play. In later Aztec accounts, when Xolotl and his band of Chichimeca passed by Tula on their way to the Basin of Mexico, they found it already in ruins and spent some days exploring its shattered walls.

Tula and Chich'en Itza

As long ago as 1885, Désiré Charnay had recognized the close relationship between the architecture and sculpture of Tula and that of distant Chich'en Itza, in the middle of the Yucatan Peninsula; and he proposed that the Toltecs had invaded and conquered Yucatan, as the native and Spanish sources had implied. This last hypothesis has had its ups and downs over the subsequent century, primarily caused by the almost total lack of an archaeological culture history or even a radiocarbon-based chronology for Chich'en Itza, in spite of decades of research by the Carnegie Institution of Washington and the Mexican government.

Chich'en Itza has two components. The first of these is native Maya, and consists of a number of buildings in an architectural style known as "Puuc," dated to the Epiclassic and located in the southern part of the city. Guidebooks call this "Old Chich'en." The other component, "New Chich'en," covers the northern part of the site, and is closely linked to Tula of the Toltecs—so closely, in fact, that Richard Diehl has said that "despite the 1,100 km that separate them, these two communities were more alike than any other two archaeological sites in Pre-Columbian America." C. Kristan-Graham has listed some of the more significant of the many traits shared by the two as "feathered serpent columns, atlantids [atlantean figures], chacmools, *cipactli* [crocodile day-sign] glyphs, banquettes decorated with processional reliefs, colonnaded halls, similarly attired profile figures, and low relief images of feathered serpents, composite man-bird-serpent creatures posed frontally, profile raptors, canines and felines." One might add that both have a major *tzompantli* of the same shape and declination placed just east of the principal ball court. Even further, personal names at both Tula and Chich'en Itza are expressed in a logographic system that is Toltec, not Maya.

The greatest novelty for the Maya area is the Feathered Serpent imagery so ubiquitous in Toltec-related Chich'en Itza. This is specifically a rattlesnake covered with quetzal feathers, a symbol totally unknown among the Classic Maya, but ancient in central Mexico (and even among the Middle Formative Olmec). It seems logical to deduce that this was direct appropriation of a major cult coming directly from Tula of the Toltecs, along with several other such specific, non-Maya traits as the *tzompantli* and the colonnaded hall. It may be recalled that these latter two traits began far north and west of Tula, then appearing at Epiclassic Tula Chico well before they were adopted by the Maya far to the east. Given the geography and the close ties between Tula and northwest Mexico and the early appearance of Toltec elements at Tula Chico, it is difficult to believe that these traits originated at Chich'en Itza and then were passed back to Tula, as some scholars have asserted. There may never have been such a personage as Topiltzin Quetzalcoatl—archaeologist and ethnohistorian Susan Gillespie has argued that much of his "history" was fabricated in the early European colonial period—but this has no bearing on the material evidence for Toltec traits at Chich'en Itza.

In a 1961 paper on Chich'en Itza and Tula, the Yale art historian George Kubler proposed that the "Tula first" hypothesis of an older generation was all wrong. He argued that all of the supposed Toltec traits at the admittedly more impressive Chich'en Itza were, in fact, indigenous Maya; there never had been a foreign Toltec invasion from the west; and Tula was influenced by Chich'en Itza rather than the reverse. Over the ensuing half century, Kubler's "Chich'en first" hypothesis was adopted by the majority of North American and European archaeologists and art historians, and especially by Mayanists. In their view, all of Chich'en Itza was Epiclassic—including the famous Castillo pyramid, the Great Ball Court, and the Temple of the Warriors. Tula and Chich'en were "Twin Tollans," with Chich'en being the dominant sibling and influencing central Mexico through appropriation and trade. In its extreme form, some scholars have even claimed that the Toltecs never existed, but were an Aztec myth.

Most of the arguments in favor of the "Chich'en first" hypothesis, however, fail to take into account actual stratigraphic archaeology that was conducted by INAH archaeologists (such as Peter Schmidt) and others in the heart of the site over a period of years. In 2018, Beniamino Volta and Geoffrey E. Brasswell, both of the University of California, and Nancy Peniche May of the Universidad Autónoma de Yucatan published a definitive study of the entire site based on actual stratigraphy, radiocarbon dates, and a more refined ceramic chronology. They came to the conclusion that the older, traditional chronology was correct. The entire northern section of the city ("New Chich'en") rests on a vast platform that was built shortly after 900 CE, and buildings placed on it—such as the Castillo and Temple of the Warriors—therefore completely postdate the southern, Epiclassic part of the city. This means that entire part of the site is Early Post-Classic and contemporary with Toltec Tula.

Peter Biró of the Department of Ancient American Studies, Bonn, and Eduardo Pérez de Heredia of La Trobe University have discovered additional evidence for a Toltec intrusion or invasion of Chich'en Itza from central Mexico. Overlooked by previous scholarship is a substantial stone disk found in the ruins of the building known as the Caracol. It bears a Maya glyphic inscription dating it to around 929–932 CE. In its upper register are six Toltec warriors, richly clad, standing around a smoking, hourglass-shaped brazier. Below are five other figures, one bearing a torch. All eleven are named in the Maya text. The headdresses of two of the figures bear the sign for Tollan, "Place of the Reeds," and two are associated with a feathered rattlesnake. As Biró and Pérez state:

> ...this monument records an important moment in the history of Chich'en Itza and of Yucatan in general: the arrival of the "Mexican-Toltec" people, and the re-foundation of the city under a new social construct that included foreigners and local nobility.[6]

Chapter 9

The Post-Classic Period: Rival States

Late Zapotec Culture at Mitla

When Monte Albán was abandoned at the end of the ninth century, such new centers in the Central Valleys of Oaxaca as Zaachila, Teotitlan del Valle, and Mitla rose to prominence as the result of complex interregional alliances between numerous royal courts that headed small city-states.

Mitla, about 25 miles (40 km) southwest of Oaxaca City, is most famous for its relatively well-preserved buildings. The name is derived from the Nahuatl Mictlan, or "Land of the Dead," but to the Zapotecs it was known as Lyobaá, "Place of Rest." Not very much is known of the archaeology of Mitla, but it has at least Classic, Epiclassic, and Late Post-Classic occupations, corresponding to pre-Teotihuacan, post-Teotihuacan, and Aztec times; it was still inhabited when the Spaniards arrived.

Mitla is one of the architectural wonders of ancient Mexico—not a grandiose, mighty city, admittedly, but of unparalleled beauty. Five architectural groups are scattered over the site, four of which are Late Post-Classic structures, while the remaining one is a Classic-period complex, reused in the Post-Classic. During this latter period a fortified stronghold on a nearby hill guarded the settlement. Into one of the structures is built a colonial church, which destroyed parts of its southern quadrangle. Most remarkable among these buildings is the Group of the Columns (**figure 158**). As is also the case with the others, it has three adjacent quadrangles, each one with a central plaza or courtyard surrounded on all sides by halls and rooms. But this building is the most sizable and most open to public access.

Here and elsewhere at Mitla, long panels and entire walls are covered with geometric stonework mosaics, the intricate designs of which are almost entirely based on the step-and-fret motif (**figure 159**). Each piece of veneer is set into a red stucco background. From the descriptions handed down from the colonial period, it

158 Facade of the North Hall, Plaza E from the Group of the Columns, Mitla, Oaxaca. Late Post-Classic period. Overall height about 26 ft (8 m).

159 East room of the Patio of the Grecas in the Group of the Columns, Mitla, Oaxaca. Late Post-Classic period.

is known that the spacious rooms of the palaces had flat masonry roofs supported by huge horizontal beams of wood.

If we can believe the somewhat sensational but highly detailed account of pre-Spanish Mitla given by the Dominican friar Francisco Burgoa, who visited the district in the seventeenth century, this was once the residence of a High Priest (*Vuijatao*, or "Great Seer") of the Zapotec nation, a man so powerful that even kings bowed to his commands. Fortunately, based on comparative architectural studies with earlier layouts elsewhere, it can be deduced that Mitla's groups of buildings were most likely palaces inhabited by a powerful corporate group whose leading heads oversaw a small kingdom and performed political, military, and religious roles, including divination, oracles, and human sacrifice. It is probable that Mitla served as a gateway community linking the Central Valleys of Oaxaca to the Sierra Mixe and the Gulf Coast, to the Isthmus of Tehuantepec, and to the Sierra Sur and the Pacific littoral.

The Group of the Columns, the paramount palace, includes a substantial plaza surrounded by long halls with roofs supported by monolithic columns. It also includes a small and secluded residence beside the main colonnaded hall, and a secondary plaza adjacent to the administrative complex. This complex was probably dedicated to the ancestors, as it was the only one with underground tombs. The two known crypts, under the northern and eastern halls of the complex, are cruciform in their layout and their walls are embellished with stonework mosaics, as if mimicking the rooms above. Already emptied by the time Father Burgoa made his fanciful account, the size of these tombs suggests they functioned as burial chambers crowded with remains that grew through generations. The northernmost palace, the one partially destroyed by the construction of the sixteenth-century church, still has remnants of bichrome (red and white) murals painted on the massive stone lintels that face the courtyard of its residential quadrangle. The paintings parallel those executed on indigenous manuscripts or screenfolds and, as determined by archaeologist John Pohl, seemingly recount historical narratives that begin in a mythical past and progress forward to tell deeds of those mortals who ruled at Mitla.

The Royal Houses of the Mixteca

"A succession of very small, rather prosperous valleys surrounded by large areas of nearby desert" is how Ignacio Bernal once characterized the homeland of the Mixtec people. This is the rugged, mountainous land in western and northern Oaxaca called the Mixteca. Archaeological survey carried out by Ronald Spores of Vanderbilt University has shown that initially, during the Classic, Mixtec settlements were located on hilltops; but by the outset of the Early Post-Classic, they had moved down into the valleys. There, as John Pohl and Bruce Byland have demonstrated, groups were organized into multiple kingdoms or polities, with no widespread political integration and no substantial cities. Each kingdom was under the domination of one independent

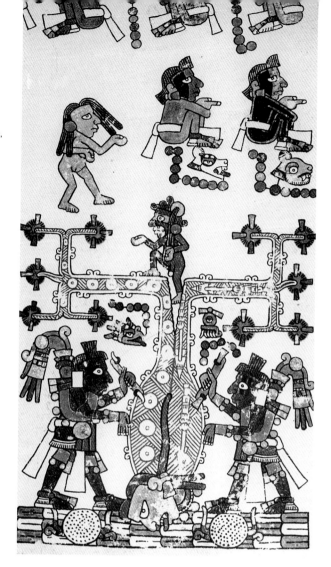

160 Detail of page 37 of the Codex Vienna. Two jeweled artisan lords named 7 Rain and 7 Eagle use their crafting tools to decorate a great female-tree, from which the first woman and the first man emerge. The foundational scene takes place on a feathered mat (symbol of a valley), with balls of burning tobacco. Mixtec culture, Late Post-Classic period.

lord. Since arable land was scarce in this precipitous landscape, there was fierce competition for it along the borders between kingdoms, and warfare was endemic.

Miraculously, there have survived four pre-Conquest manuscripts and a handful of *lienzos* (large sheets of fabric) which, through the research of Alfonso Caso, Mary Elizabeth Smith, John Pohl, Marteen Jansen, Bas van Doesburg, and Manuel Hermann, among others, have carried Mixtec history back to a time beyond the range of any of the annals of other Mexican, non-Maya cultures. Analysis of the manuscripts by Emily Rabin has established that they cover a 600-year time span beginning about 940 CE. These manuscripts are bark-paper or deerskin screenfolds in which the pages are coated with gesso and painted; they were produced late in the Post-Classic by the Mixtec nobility. As Jill Furst notes, "they are concerned with historical events and genealogies, and present records of births, marriages, offspring, and sometimes the deaths of native rulers, and their conflicts to retain their lands and wars to extend their domains." The one exception is the front, or "obverse," of the Codex Vienna (**figure 160**), which she has found to be a land document that begins in the mythical "first time" (when the ancestral Mixtecs emerged from a tree at a place called Apoala), and establishes the rights of certain lineages to rule specific sites through the approval and sanction of the deities and sacred ancestors.

The reader is taken through these primarily pictorial texts by means of red guidelines (generally horizontal), but there is no standard layout in all the manuscripts: in some, the texts proceed from right to left, and in others from left to right. Dates are given only in the 52-year Calendar Round; the year itself is given with a sign that morphed from the old Teotihuacan "Royal headband" symbol, accompanied by Year Bearers 3-8-13-18 (i.e. 7 House, 3 Rabbit, 12 Reed, 1 Flint), followed by the day in the 260-day count. There is no attempt at portraiture, and there was no need for it, for each personage in the histories is indicated by his or her birthdate in the 260-day count, plus an iconic personal name, so there is little ambiguity. Each individual received further specificity through detailed renderings of costume, which often identified precise offices or ceremonies.

Compared with the Maya script, and with the Zapotec writing system from which it may have derived, Mixtec writing has a strong pictorial component, complemented at times with signs that stand for words—but relying on puns based on terms that sound the same yet mean different things (this is known as homophony) as well as signs that code for meaning but are not read (these are known as semantic determinatives). This was a deliberate strategy used to communicate beyond the Mixtec language area. Neighboring and distant royal houses with speakers of Chocho, Zapotecs, and Nahua could understand the core of the narratives using their own primary language.

In addition, a great deal of information was encoded in the images. Here the emphasis was on rather schematic human figures with clearly delineated costume and jewelry that spoke to the figure's identity and status. Although the art style is often referred to as "Mixtec" or "Mixteca-Puebla," its origins are still hotly debated. It is certain that variations on this style, now preferably known as the "Late Interregional" style, could be found across ancient Mexico and much of the Maya area by the fourteenth century, allowing elites from those areas to share information effectively across a considerable portion of Mesoamerica. This style and symbol system achieved an even wider distribution than the earlier Toltec system.

Since there were several powerful lords ruling in the Mixteca at any one time, expansionist policies could spark profound, mutually destructive strife. To counter this, the Mixtec nobility shared an adherence to certain oracular shrines as well as other cult practices that served to establish alliances and cement their relationships. By the time the Spanish arrived, the Mixtec nobility was so thoroughly intertwined that all could claim descent from a handful of common ancestors whose exploits, often centered around the shrines and cult practices that bound the Mixtec elite, made up a heroic saga known throughout the region.

The heroic sagas come down to us by way of the four pre-Conquest manuscripts mentioned above. These relate that by the beginning of the Post-Classic period, the leading power in the Mixteca was a town called Hill of the Wasp, a Classic-period hilltop settlement in the southern Nochixtlan Valley, where it is still

161 Detail of page 52 of the Codex Nuttall, which records scenes from the life of the Mixtec king, 8 Deer "Jaguar Claw." Here, 8 Deer has his nose pierced for a special ornament in the year 1045 CE. Other scenes in the manuscript include 8 Deer going to war (page 49 of codex) and a record of the town "Curassow Hill," which was conquered by 8 Deer (page 46 of codex).

referred to today by its codical name in Mixtec, Yucu Yoco. When it was conquered in the late tenth century, its rulers were sacrificed, and an epic cycle of conflict referred to as the "War of Heaven" commenced. According to the manuscripts, three Mixtec factions fought for sixteen years, eventually founding the Mixtec political landscape of the Post-Classic period. Scenes of these battles in the manuscripts are highly schematized, with the act of capture indicated by the grasping of hair, and defeat by the darting of place names. Mortuary bundles also figure in key scenes. The bundles were very important to the elites, for it was through access to the divine ancestors in the form of bundles that family tradition and prestige were upheld. Such other-than-human figures as the Mixtec-culture hero 9 Wind also played an important role in the indigenous account, thereby divinely sanctioning the results. The War of Heaven ends with the establishment of a first dynasty of Tilantongo (its Mixtec name means "Black Town"), which jointly ruled several valleys from a place called Xipe Bundle, until it too fell.

In the second dynasty of Tilantongo, the manuscripts have much to tell about a renowned warlord named 8 Deer "Jaguar Claw," who lived during the Calendar Round that began in 1063 CE and ended in 1115 (**figure 161**). When he rose to power, he attacked a town known as Red and White Bundle, located to the east of Tilantongo, sacrificing both the lord of that place and his wife Lady 6 Monkey, who had been a princess of Mountain of the Place of Sand. In 1097, 8 Deer "Jaguar Claw" seems to have made a journey to Cholula (another Tollan, "place of the rushes," or "place of legitimacy," comparable to Tula, Hidalgo, described in Chapter 8), where he was invested with a nose ornament (akin to a kind of coronation) under the auspices of the Toltec king himself, a man called 4 Jaguar. This probably marks 8 Deer's accession to the throne of Tilantongo, with the ruler of Cholula fulfilling the same function as the pope who crowned the Holy Roman Emperor.

We follow in the screenfolds the machinations of 8 Deer "Jaguar Claw," as he tries to bring rival statelets under his sway: marrying no fewer than five times, all his wives were princesses of other towns, some of whose families he had subjected to pre-sacrificial darting rituals and ultimately to the sacrificial knife. "Who lives by the sword dies by the sword," goes the European saying, and this formidable warrior was ultimately killed by Lady 6 Monkey's son. This latter personage became ruler of a town called Place of Flints, and married the daughter of 8 Deer "Jaguar Claw" himself. The exploits of 8 Deer were so fundamental to Mixtec history that they still served to legitimize claims for several Mixtec royal houses when the Spanish arrived, 400 years later.

By approximately 1350 CE some Mixtecs began to occupy lands in a small kingdom in the Valley of Oaxaca by the usual method of state marriage. Mixtec

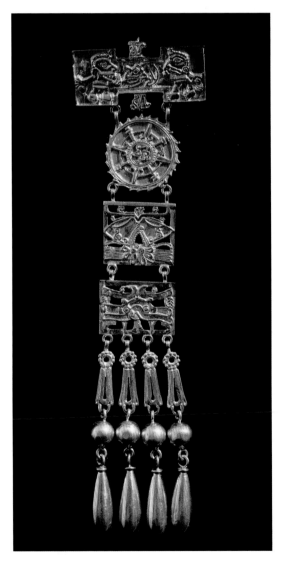

162 Gold pendant from Tomb 7, Monte Albán, Oaxaca. The pendant was cast in one piece by the lost-wax process. The several elements represent, from top to bottom: a ball court with two players and a skull in the center, a solar disk, a double-headed personified flint knife with open mouth, and the side view of an alligator with open jaws (symbol of the Earth). The piece ends with four dangling feathers, each one anchoring a tinkling bell. Late Post-Classic period. Length 8.7 in. (22 cm).

royal brides insisted on bringing their own retinues to the Zapotec court. By the time the Spaniards arrived, a number of royal houses in the Valley of Oaxaca had mixed Zapotec and Mixtec ethnicities, and were powerful enough to commission gifted artists, including some of the finest goldsmiths and workers in turquoise mosaic in Mexico. The wealthy funerary accoutrements from Tomb 7 at Monte Albán are eloquent testimony (**figures 162, 163**). Here, in an abandoned and ruined Classic-period tomb at some point in the mid-fourteenth century, members of a multi-ethnic royal house from nearby Saayucu (now Cuilapan de Guerrero) or Zaachila re-deposited several male and female funerary bundles that were clad with rich sumptuary goods, leaving as well objects related to divination and oracular performances. Accompanying the central bundle were magnificent objects of gold, cast in the lost-wax process, and silver; turquoise mosaics; necklaces of rock crystal, amber, jet, and coral; thousands of pearls, one as big as a pigeon's egg; and sections of jaguar bone carved with mythological, calendrical, and historical scenes. While Alfonso Caso and his team had identified the central skeleton as male, other evidence, especially the presence of a weaving kit with battens, picks, spindle whorls, and spindle bowls, suggests strong female associations. Because of cognatic affiliation (tracing descent from either the male or female line), native groups of Oaxaca had a tradition of politically powerful females, and several of these are featured in the manuscripts, but there is as yet little firm evidence to corroborate that the skeleton was female. It is likely, however, that the central figure was a male impersonating a female deity. Both the Mixtecs and the Aztecs had important political and ritual posts based on female deities, the costumes of which often contained spinning and weaving implements.

Zaachila became a major capital after the demise of Monte Albán, and had a Zapotec king, but its elite culture was multi-ethnic. Two of its residences have produced four tombs with astonishing material wealth, almost equal to that in Tomb 7, including some of the most remarkable polychrome pottery ever discovered in the

163 Two miniature bone weaving battens from Tomb 7, Monte Albán, Oaxaca. One (no. 71, above) has a sequence of six animal heads, five facing to the left and one to the right. Interspersed by diagonal bands with the 'Mat' sign, they include a dog (reference to Xolotl, twin of Quetzalcoatl), a quetzal, a Fire Serpent, an eagle, a jaguar, and a serpent. The other (no. 169) represents two deities, each followed by two animal heads that stand for world directions. All emerge, amidst scrolls of breath, from a rope that ends in a flower, starting with Quetzalcoatl, rabbit (south), eagle (east), Xipe Totec, serpent (west), and jaguar (north). Late Post-Classic period.

164 Polychrome ceramic cup with the effigy of a hummingbird on its rim. Tomb 1 under an elite residence in the acropolis of Zaachila, Oaxaca. Ht 2.99 in. [7.6 cm].

Americas: the ceramic gem in this case is a beautifully painted cup with the three-dimensional figure of a blue hummingbird perched on its rim (**figure 164**).

Not only to the south, but also as far north as Cholula, multi-ethnic artistic influence was felt, resulting in the hybrid Late Interregional style that produced some of the finest manuscripts, sculpture, pottery, and turquoise mosaics of latter-day Mexico. Although, as with several other rival states in Mexico, the Mixtecs, Chochos, and Cuicatecs were marked down for conquest in its aggressive plans, they were never completely vanquished by the Aztec empire. The Mixtecs united successfully with the Zapotecs against the intruder and in so doing avoided the fate of so many other once independent polities of Late Post-Classic Mexico.

The Huastec

Another important Post-Classic group was the Huastec, located in northeastern Veracruz and adjacent regions, where they continue to live. The Huastec speak a Mayan language, although all other major Mayan languages are found far to the south and east in Guatemala and the Yucatan Peninsula, making Huastec an interesting linguistic outlier.

The Huastec had their own material and artistic culture from at least the Late Formative. During the Classic period they continued to develop the ceramic vessels and figurines that first appeared in the Formative, but we know of little monumental architecture and art that may be firmly dated to this period. Toward the end of the Epiclassic it is clear that groups with Huastec culture were visiting the regional capital of El Tajín and exchanging fine ceramics with that site.

Late Post-Classic Huastec elites would wear shell ornaments including finely carved shell pectorals with imagery rendered in a local variant of the Late Interregional style. In one of the most aesthetically charged pendants, a figure engages in the same auto-sacrificial ritual seen on a relief panel found at the ball court at El

165 Cut out and incised shell object worn on the chest. The elaborate imagery recounts a foundational event, with two deity impersonators on top of the maws of serpents (the Earth). The male on the left is bleeding his penis, while the female on the right offers him a bundle of weapons. Below a "Place of Reeds" appears a kneeling captive. Length 7.7 in. (19.6 cm).

166 [BELOW] Section of bichrome murals in a rounded altar at El Consuelo, Tamuín, San Luis Potosí. Ht 1 ft 8.4 in. (52 cm).

Tajín (**figure 165**). In addition to the theme of self-sacrifice, another major trope in this type of ornament is that of the victorious warrior, depicting a fierce combatant subduing a captive and symbolically offering him in sacrifice to the earth, the latter rendered as a serpent-alligator with its open jaws.

The Huastec site of Tamuín is well known for its rich artistic remains, including striking Late Post-Classic murals (**figure 166**). These, also rendered in a local variant of the Late Interregional style, are exclusively red on white and depict figures with deity markings and elaborate costumes. Some deity markings are reminiscent of the shell pectoral imagery referred to above. Tamuín was also the source of the famous Post-Classic sculpture of a young man with extensive body paint or tattooing, called the "Adolescent," now in the National Museum in Mexico City

167 Stone sculpture of a tattooed young person carrying on his back a miniature figure, the pose of which is similar to that in which the female earth deity is depicted in Aztec art. The earspools and the objects held in the main figure's hands were probably made out of wood. From Tamuín, San Luis Potosí. Ht 4 ft 7 in. [1.45 m].

(**figure 167**). The contrast between the style in which the statue is carved and that of the painted murals from Tamuín is stark, suggesting that in the Late Post-Classic, Huastec artists pursued different stylistic choices. For instance, at Castillo de Teayo, which was likely an Aztec garrison with a resident Nahua enclave, Aztec sculptural cannons prevailed (**figure 168**). But at Huilozintla, just 16 km northeast of Castillo de Teayo, artists adhered more to the conventions to render the human body much in the same manner as the sculptural program at Tamuín. The archaeology of Huilozintla is under-reported, and early in the twentieth century the site was subject to looting and pillage. Three outstanding carved stelae from there were dispersed to a nearby estate and to Xalapa (the capital of the modern state of Veracruz) and eventually ended up in museums. While one is but a fragment, the other two are complete and relatively well preserved. They all depict tattooed personages (similar to the Tamuín "Adolescent") identified by their calendrical names, performing self-sacrifice by piercing their tongues with long, pointed sticks (**figure 169**). These figures appear as impersonating the deity Ehecatl-Quetzalcoatl, as can be surmised by the cut-shell pectoral, the awls for auto-sacrifice embedded in their coiffures, or the characteristic beaked profile of the deity represented in their headdresses.

Closely related to this sculptural artistic production is a distinctive black-on-white ceramic ware that comprises effigy vessels, many of them spouted (**figure 170**). Whether the effigies are those of animals or humans, the vessels' surfaces are covered by designs similar to the tattoos seen on the Tamuín "Adolescent" or the rulers depicted on the Huilozintla stelae.

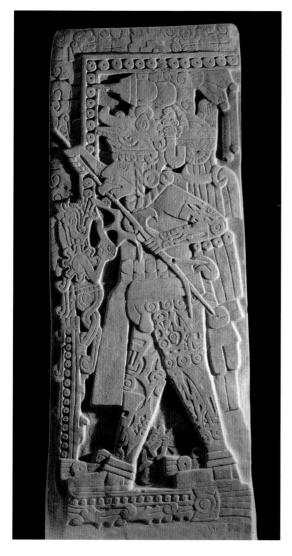

168 (TOP) Monument 41 from Castillo de Teayo in northern Veracruz carved in Aztec style. It depicts the male and the female versions of the Rain Deity holding maize plants and staffs. Ht 6 ft 0.7 in. (1.85 m).

169 (LEFT) Stela from Huilozintla, northern Veracruz. Museo Nacional de Antropología, Mexico City. Ht 4 ft 7.1 in. (1.40 m).

170 (ABOVE) Effigy vessel of black-on-white ceramics with designs resembling the tattoos on three- and two-dimensional renditions of personages. Tanquián, San Luis Potosí. Ht 6.7 in. (17.2 cm).

The Tarascan Kingdom

The Aztecs called the territory of the Tarascans, whom they were never able to conquer, Michoacan, meaning "the place of the masters of fish." This is a fitting name, for much of Tarascan history centers on Lake Pátzcuaro in western Mexico, which abounds in fish. The Tarascans' own name for themselves and for their unique language is Purépecha. While very little field archaeology has yet been carried out in Michoacan, fortunately a long and rich ethnohistoric source has survived: the *Relación de Michoacan*, which is apparently an early Spanish translation of one or more original documents in Tarascan. This gives important details of the Purépecha's past and of their life as it was on the eve of the Spanish Conquest.

In the Late Post-Classic, the Tarascan state was bounded on the south and west by areas under Aztec control, and on the north by the Chichimeca. The people were ethnically mixed, but dominated by the Purépecha, who made up about 10 percent of the population; many of the groups within their territory were in fact Nahuatl-speakers. The *Relación* tells us of migrations of various groups into Michoacan, among whom the most important was the "Chichimec"—probably incipient farmers and speakers of Purépecha, who established themselves on islands in the midst of Lake Pátzcuaro, and who called themselves Wakúsecha. Their first capital was the town of Pátzcuaro, which was established around 1325 CE under their hero-chief Taríakuri; from there they imposed their language and rule on the native and non-native groups.

Eventually, the Purépecha attained statehood and conquered all of present-day Michoacan. They established a series of fortified outposts on their frontiers. Ihuátzio, located on the southeastern arm of the lake, became the capital, to be succeeded by Tzintzúntzan, the royal seat of power when the Spaniards arrived on the scene in 1522.

At the top of the Purépecha hierarchy was the *Kasonsí* (paramount ruler); he acted as war leader and supreme judge of the nation, and had his royal court at Tzintzúntzan. Under him were the rulers of the two other administrative centers, Ihuátzio and Pátzcuaro, and four boundary princes. The *Kasonsí's* court was substantial and attended by a wide variety of officials whose functions give a good idea of the division of labor within the royal household. For instance, there were the heads of such varied occupational groups as the masons, drum-makers, healers, makers of obsidian knives, anglers, silversmiths, and decorators of cups, along with many other functionaries including the king's zookeeper and the head of his war-spies.

The chronicler of the *Relación* spends many pages on the funeral of the *Kasonsí*, which was indeed spectacular, but probably not very different from that of any other Mesoamerican ruler of the time (**figure 171**). He was borne to his final resting place attended by Purépecha and foreign lords, with elaborate rites and music. Accompanying him in death were seven important women from his palace, including his "keeper of the gold and turquoise lip-ornaments," his cook, his wine-bearer, and the "keeper of his urinal." Also sacrificed were forty male attendants, including the healer who had failed to cure him in his last illness! Quite clearly the *Kasonsí's* palace was to be replicated for him in the land of the dead.

Unlike the Aztec (but in the same manner as the late pre-Conquest Maya), the Purépecha priesthood was not celibate. The badge of the priests was the gourd container for tobacco which was strapped to their backs. At the top of the religious organization was the Supreme High Priest, heading a complex hierarchy with many ranks of priests divided as to function.

The Purépecha state religion, which was probably codified within the last 150 years of the pre-Conquest era, seems remarkably un-Mesoamerican. There was no rain deity analogous to Tlaloc, and no Feathered Serpent. Even more remarkable were the absence of both the 260-day count and the use of the calendar for divinatory ends. They did, however, have the approximate solar year of eighteen months of twenty days each, plus the five "extra" days. Ball courts were apparently rare, and none are known for Tzintzúntzan itself.

According to data gathered by anthropologist Helen Perlstein Pollard, the universe was considered to consist of three parts: 1) the sky, associated with eagles, hawks, falcons, and the Wakúsecha elite; 2) the earth, viewed as a goddess with four world-directions; and 3) the Underworld, the place of death and caves, inhabited by such burrowing animals as mice, gophers, moles, and snakes. The sky was the domain of Kurikaweri, the Sun God, the most important deity in the state cult; his worship demanded huge offerings of firewood, which, along with agricultural

171 Funeral ceremonies for the Purépecha *Kasonsí*, from the *Relación de Michoacan.*

172 View of five *yákatas* or rectangular platforms at Tzintzúntzan, Michoacan. Purépecha culture, Late Post-Classic period.

clearances, must have resulted in extensive deforestation of the Michoacan landscape. Kurikaweri was also the patron god of the Wakúsecha and a war god, in whose honor people performed not only human sacrifice but also auto-sacrifice (the shedding of blood from one's own body), and his earthly form was the *Kasonsí* himself.

In the same manner as the divinities on the Greek Mount Olympus, the Purépecha deities were considered to belong to one expansive family. Kurikaweri's consort was Kwerawáperi, the earth-mother, a creator divinity from whom all the other divinities were born; she controlled life, death, and the rains and drought. The most important fruit of the union between the sky and earth deities was Xarátenga, the goddess of the moon and the sea; her domain was in the west (toward the Pacific Coast), and she could take the form of an old woman, a coyote, or an owl. Naturally, there were many local cults, and each of the ethnic groups subdued by the Purépecha had its own tutelary deities, but these were all subsumed in the cosmological kinship system of the official state religion.

There was no formal education for Purépecha boys, who were trained by their fathers for a particular profession or calling, but young women of the Wakúsecha aristocracy were educated in a special communal house; they were considered "wives" of the patron god Kurikaweri, and usually married off to army officers.

The ruins of the final pre-Hispanic capital, Tzintzúntzan, rest on a terraced slope above the northeast arm of Lake Pátzcuaro. An enormous 1,440 ft (440 m) long rectangular platform supports five of the superstructures known as *yákatas*; each *yákata* is a rectangular stepped pyramid joined by a stepped passageway to a round multi-tier "pyramid" (**figure 172**). The *yákatas* were once entirely faced with finely fitted slabs of volcanic stone that recall the perfection of Inca masonry in South America. Those that have been investigated so far contained richly stocked burials, and it is probable that the primary function of these structures was to contain the tombs of deceased *Kasonsís* and their retainers.

What little archaeological evidence we have suggests that the Purépecha were extraordinary craftsmen; many luxury objects in collections that are ascribed to the Mixtecs may well come from Michoacan instead, and it has been suggested that the Purépecha may have taken over some of the northern Toltec trade routes after the downfall of Tula. The most astonishing of their productions were paper-thin obsidian earspools and labrets, faced with sheet gold and turquoise inlay. They were also master workers in gold and silver, and in bimetallic objects using both of these precious substances.

Casas Grandes and the Northern Trade Route

By the Post-Classic, the southwestern region of what is now the United States had been home to complex cultures for several centuries. There is little doubt that the contact with Mesoamerica already noted for the Epiclassic was continued through this period. While certain products may have been traded south to Mesoamerica, we now know that Mesoamerican chocolate made its way to the Southwest by the eleventh century, as witnessed by the discovery of theobromine (a chemical signature of chocolate) in the remains of several ceramic vessels at Pueblo Bonito in Chaco Canyon (northern New Mexico).

Copper bells were also imported in small quantities from west Mexico to the Southwest at the same time or slightly earlier than the appearance of chocolate. It is probably at this time that the people of the Southwest also developed a ritual need for the feathers of tropical birds from Mesoamerica, especially the scarlet macaw.

Central to any interaction with the Southwest during this period would have been Casas Grandes, Chihuahua, not far south of the border with New Mexico. The site, also referred to as Paquimé, may now be dated to around 1200 to 1475. While the population lived in Southwestern-style apartment houses, the Mesoamerican component can be seen in the presence of platform temple mounds, I-shaped ball courts, and the cult of the Feathered Serpent. Charles Di Peso, the excavator of Casas Grandes, found warehouses filled with such rare minerals as turquoise. It is now clear that the regional elite consumed considerable quantities of this precious material. It may well be that Paquimé's turquoise came from the American Southwest, but recent isotopic analysis of Mixtec and Aztec turquoise by Alyson Thibodeau and colleagues clearly indicates that the flow of this material did not continue further south, suggesting that Mesoamerican turquoise did not come from the American Southwest, as has been argued in the past.

Chapter 10

The Aztecs

The Rise of the Aztec State

The beginnings of the Aztec nation, as recorded in Aztec accounts, were so humble and obscure that the group's ascent to supremacy over most of Mexico in the span of a few hundred years seems almost miraculous. It is somehow inconceivable that the remarkable civilization witnessed and destroyed by the Spaniards could have been created by those who, according to their own origin stories, were not many generations removed from foraging bands, yet this is the image they portray in their histories.

But these histories, all of which were written down in Nahuatl (the Aztec language) or in Spanish early in the European colonial period, must be considered in their context, and rigorously evaluated. First, given the nature of central Mexican chronology during the Post-Classic, which was based on the 52-year Calendar Round, it is clear that at least some of the supposedly historical data we are given in the chronicles is cyclical rather than linear: that is, an event that occurs at one point in a given cycle could take place at similar points in other such cycles, both preceding and succeeding. Secondly, given the above, there were ample opportunities for the Aztec royal dynasty to rewrite its own history and the history of the nation as changing times demanded; we are told that this occurred in the reign of the ruler Itzcoatl, and it apparently was done on a far more substantial scale during the sixteenth century to cope with the cataclysm of the Spanish invasion and Conquest. The fully developed Aztec state had a cosmic vision of itself and its place in the universe, which demanded a certain kind of history, and we now realize that even royal genealogies could be tailored to fit this vision.

It is therefore futile to attempt to reconcile the often conflicting native chronicles into a coherent story of Aztec origins and rise to power. The rhetoric of presenting themselves in their accounts as "uncivilized, nomadic foraging newcomers" amid "sedentary, civilized, and autochthonous agriculturalists," and the claim of their place of origin being an island (Aztlan) that is the mirror image of Tenochtitlan, the island capital of the empire, are mythical tropes akin to that of a "promised land." In this way, Aztec histories are political tools of legitimation unrelated to actual historical processes. We suspect that what really took place was a strife between multiethnic city-states in the Basin of Mexico that exacerbated after the collapse of Tula.

To return to the Aztec version, the story begins with events that followed Tula's destruction in the twelfth century. Refugees from this center of Toltec civilization managed to establish themselves in the southern half of the Basin, particularly at the towns of Colhuacan and Xico, both of which became important citadels transmitting the higher culture of their predecessors to the "barbarians" who were then entering the northern half of the Basin in great number. Among the newcomers were the band of Chichimeca under their chief Xolotl, arriving in the Basin by 1244 and settling at Tenayuca; the Acolhua, who founded Coatlinchan around the year 1160; the Otomi, who arrived at Xaltocan by about 1250; and the powerful Tepanecs, who in 1230 took over the town of Atzcapotzalco, which much earlier had been a significant Teotihuacan settlement. There is no question that all of these, with the exception of the Otomi, were speakers of Nahuatl, now the dominant tongue of central Mexico. By the thirteenth century, all over the Basin there had sprung up a group of modestly sized city-states; those in the north were founded by Chichimec opportunists eager to learn from the Toltecs in the south.

According to ethnohistorian Edward Calnek, the accounts imply this was a time of relative peace in the Basin. The Toltec refugees, occupying the rich lands in the south and west, introduced the organization and ideology of rule by the elite (called *pipiltin* in Nahuatl); its guiding principle was that only someone descended from the ancient royal Toltec dynasty could be a ruler or *tlatoani* ("speaker"). Those who lacked such descent could demand—if they were powerful enough—women of royal rank as wives. As time passed, the *pipiltin* came to hold a nearly complete monopoly of the highest offices in each city-state. As for the non-Toltec groups, some adopted the system sooner than others; the Aztecs resisted doing so for the longest.

Into this political milieu stepped the Aztecs themselves, the last "barbaric" tribe to arrive in the Basin of Mexico, the "people whose face nobody knows." The official Aztec histories claimed that they had come from a place called "Aztlan" (meaning "Land of White Herons"), supposedly an island in a lake in the west or northwest of Mexico, and this was why they called themselves the "Azteca." One tradition says that they began their migration toward central Mexico in 1111 CE, led by their tribal deity Huitzilopochtli ("Hummingbird on the Left"), whose physical manifestation was borne on the shoulders of four priests called *teomamaque*. They apparently knew the art of cultivation and wore agave-fiber clothing, but had no political leaders higher than clan and tribal chieftains. It is fitting that Huitzilopochtli was a war god and representative of the sun, for the Aztecs built the image of being extremely adept at military matters, and among the best and fiercest warriors ever seen in Mexico.

Along the route of march, Huitzilopochtli was said to give them a new name, the Mexica, which they were to bear until the Conquest. Many versions of the migration account have them stop at Chicomoztoc ("Seven Caves") from which emerge all of the various ethnic groups who were to make up the nascent Aztec nation. There is a further halt at the sacred Coatepec ("Snake Mountain") where, somewhat miraculously, Huitzilopochtli is born as the Sun God.

Meanwhile, settled groups already occupied all the land in the Basin; they looked with suspicion upon these Aztecs, who were seen as little more than squatters, continually occupying territory that did not belong to them and continually being kicked out. It is a wonder that they were ever tolerated, given that with women being scarce, they took to raiding other groups for their wives. The powerful citizens of Colhuacan finally allowed them to live a degraded existence, working the lands of their masters as serfs, and supplementing their diet with snakes and other vermin. In 1323, however, the Aztecs repaid the kindness of their overlords, who had given their chief a Colhuacan princess as bride, by sacrificing the young lady in the hope that she would become a war goddess. Colhuacan retaliated by expelling the Aztecs, who they now considered to be repulsive savages, from their territory.

We next see the Aztecs following a hand-to-mouth existence in the marshes of the great lake, or "Lake of the Moon." On they wandered, loved by none, until they reached some swampy, unoccupied islands, covered by rushes, near the western shore; it was claimed that there the tribal prophecy was fulfilled: to build a city where an eagle was seen sitting on a cactus, holding a snake in its beak. By 1344 or 1345, the tribe was split in two, one group under their chief, Tenoch, founding the southern capital, Tenochtitlan, and the other settling Tlatelolco in the north. Eventually, as the swamps were drained and brought under cultivation, the islands became one, with two cities and two governments: a state of affairs not to last very long.

The year 1367 marks the turning point of the fortunes of the Aztecs: it was then that they began to serve as mercenaries for the mightiest power on the mainland, the expanding Tepanec kingdom of Atzcapotzalco, ruled by the able Tezozomoc. One after another the city-states of the Basin of Mexico fell to the joint forces of Tezozomoc and his allies; sharing in the resulting loot, the Aztecs were also taken under Tepanec protection.

Up until this time, so claimed the Aztecs, their system of government had essentially been egalitarian, and there were no social classes: the *teomamaque* and the other traditional leaders had remained in control. But in 1375, Tezozomoc gave them their first ruler or *tlatoani*, Acamapichtli ("Bundle of Reeds"), although during his reign there was still a degree of tribal democracy, in that he was not allowed to make or execute important decisions without the consent of the tribal leaders and the assembly. During these years, and in fact probably beginning as far back as their serfdom under Colhuacan, the Aztecs were taking on much of the knowledge that was the heritage of all the nations of the Basin from their Toltec predecessors. Much of this was learned from the mighty Tepanecs themselves, particularly the techniques of statecraft and empire-building so successfully indulged in by Tezozomoc.

Already the small island kingdom of the Aztecs was prepared to exercise its strength on the mainland.

It should go without saying that none of the above is to be taken literally: as is the case with many other Mesoamerican cultures, such as the highland Maya, the Aztecs had myths and accounts describing a migration from an often vague land of origin to a historically known place where they settled, inspired by the prophecy of a deity. Similar legends can be found in the Book of Genesis and among a number of polities in Africa and Polynesia. Their function seems clear: to tell the world that the rule by a particular elite was given by history and supported by divine sanction.

The Consolidation of Aztec Power

The chance came in 1426, when the aged Tezozomoc was succeeded as Tepanec king by his son Maxtlatzin, known to the Aztecs as "Tyrant Maxtla" and an implacable enemy of the growing power of Tenochtitlan. By crude threats and other pressures, Maxtlatzin attempted to rid himself of the "Aztec problem"; and in the middle of the crisis, the third Aztec king died. Itzcoatl, "Obsidian Snake," who assumed the Aztec rulership in 1427, was a man of strong mettle. More importantly, his chief adviser, Tlacaelel, was one of the most remarkable men ever produced by the Mexica. The two of them decided to fight Maxtlatzin, with the result that by the next year the Tepanecs had been entirely crushed and Atzcapotzalco was in ruins. This great battle, forever glorious to the Aztecs, left them the greatest state in Mexico.

In their triumph, and with the demotion of the traditional leaders, the Aztec administration turned to questions of internal polity, especially under Tlacaelel, who remained a kind of grand vizier to the Aztec throne through three reigns, dying in 1475 or 1480. Tlacaelel introduced a series of reforms that completely altered Mexica life. The fundamental reform related to the Aztec conception of themselves and their destiny; for this, it was necessary to rewrite history, and so Tlacaelel did, by having all the manuscripts of conquered civilizations burned since these would have failed to mention Aztec glories. Under his guidance, the Aztecs acquired a mystic-visionary view of themselves as the chosen people, the true heirs of the Toltec tradition, who would fight wars and gain captives so as to keep the fiery sun moving across the sky.

This sun, represented by the fierce god Huitzilopochtli, needed the hearts of enemy warriors; during the reign of Moteuczoma Ilhuicamina, "the Heaven Shooter" (r. 1440–1469), Tlacaelel instituted the "Flowery War," so-called because in Aztec poetry, the battlefield was imagined as a "Field of Flowers." These battles were fought not for conquest and plunder, but to capture enemy warriors who would then be sacrificed to the deities. Under this, Tenochtitlan entered into a Triple Alliance with the old Acolhua state of Texcoco (on the other side of the lake) and the dummy state of Tlacopan in a permanent struggle against the Nahuatl-speaking states of Tlaxcala and Huexotzingo.

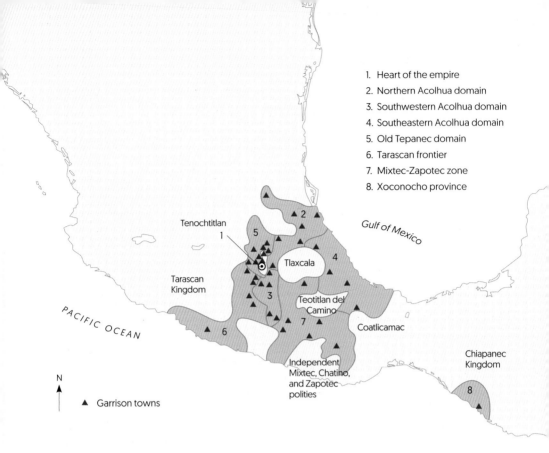

1. Heart of the empire
2. Northern Acolhua domain
3. Southwestern Acolhua domain
4. Southeastern Acolhua domain
5. Old Tepanec domain
6. Tarascan frontier
7. Mixtec-Zapotec zone
8. Xoconocho province

Tenochtitlan
1

Gulf of Mexico

Tlaxcala

Tarascan
Kingdom

Teotitlan del
Camino

Coatlicamac

PACIFIC OCEAN

Chiapanec
Kingdom

Independent
Mixtec, Chatino,
and Zapotec
polities

N

▲ Garrison towns

173 Extent of the Aztec empire in 1519. The provinces into which the Aztec domains were organized are indicated.

Besides inventing the idea of Aztec grandeur through glorification of the Aztec past, other reforms relating to the political-juridical and economic administrations were also carried out under Tlacaelel. The new system was successfully tested during a disastrous two-year famine that occurred under Moteuczoma Ilhuicamina, and from which this extraordinary people emerged more confident than ever in their divine mission.

Given these conditions, it is little surprise that the Aztecs soon embarked with their allies on an ambitious program of conquest. The elder Moteuczoma began the expansion, taking over the Huasteca, much of the land around Mount Orizaba, and rampaging down even into the Mixteca.

Axayacatl (r. 1469–1481) subdued neighboring Tlatelolco on trumped-up charges and substituted a military government for what had once been an independent administration; he was less successful with the Tarascan kingdom of Michoacan, for these powerful people turned the invaders back. Greatest of all the empire-builders was Ahuitzotl (r. 1486–1502), who succeeded the weak and vacillating Tizoc as sixth king. This mighty warrior conquered lands all the way to the Guatemalan border and brought most of central Mexico under Aztec rule (**figure 173**). Probably for the first time since the downfall of Tula, there was in Mexico a single empire as great as, or greater than, that of the Toltecs. Ahuitzotl was a man of great energy; among the projects completed in his reign was a major rebuilding of the Great Temple of Tenochtitlan, completed in 1487, and the construction of an aqueduct to bring water from Coyoacan to the island capital.

Ahuitzotl's successor, Moteuczoma Xocoyotzin ("The Younger") (r. 1502–1520) is surely one of history's most tragic figures, for it was his misfortune to be the Aztec ruler when the Mexica civilization was destroyed. He is described in many accounts, some of them eyewitness, as a very complex person; he was surely not the single-minded militarist that is so well typified by Ahuitzotl. Instead of delighting in war, he was given to meditation in his place of retreat, the "Black House"—in fact, one might be led to believe that he was more of a philosopher-king, along the lines of Marcus Aurelius. As did that Roman emperor, he also maintained a shrine in the capital where all the divinities of captured nations were kept, for he was interested in foreign religions.

In post-Conquest times, this was considered by Spaniards and Native Americans alike to have been the cause of his downfall: according to these later sources, when Cortés arrived in 1519, the Aztec emperor was paralyzed by the realization that this strange, bearded foreigner was Quetzalcoatl himself, returned from the east as the ancient manuscripts had allegedly said he would, to destroy the Mexica. All of his disastrous inaction in the face of the Spanish threat, his willingness to put himself in the hands of Cortés, was claimed to be the result of his dedication to the old Toltec philosophy. The triumphant Spaniards were only too glad to spread the word among their new subjects that this was Moteuczoma's destiny, and that it had been foretold by a series of magical portents that had led to an inevitable outcome.

The Island City

The soldier Bernal Díaz, who was with Hernán Cortés when the Spaniards first approached the island capital of Tenochtitlan on 8 November 1511, recorded his impressions of his first glimpse of the Aztec citadel:

> During the morning, we arrived at a broad causeway and continued our march towards Iztapalapa, and when we saw so many cities and villages built in the water and other great towns on dry land and that straight and level Causeway going towards Mexico, we were amazed and said that it was like the enchantments they tell of in the legend of Amadis, on account of the great towers and temples and buildings rising from the water, and all built of masonry. And some of our soldiers asked whether the things that we saw were not a dream.[7]

The island was connected to the mainland by three principal causeways, described by Cortés as being "each as broad as a horseman's lance," running north to Tepeyac,

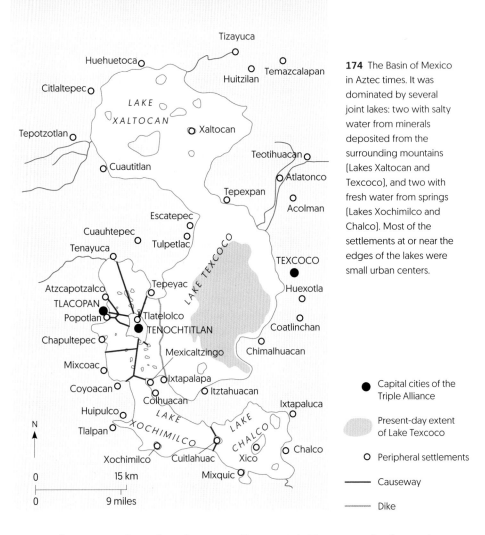

174 The Basin of Mexico in Aztec times. It was dominated by several joint lakes: two with salty water from minerals deposited from the surrounding mountains (Lakes Xaltocan and Texcoco), and two with fresh water from springs (Lakes Xochimilco and Chalco). Most of the settlements at or near the edges of the lakes were small urban centers.

● Capital cities of the Triple Alliance

Present-day extent of Lake Texcoco

○ Peripheral settlements

—— Causeway

----- Dike

west to Tlacopan, and south to Coyoacan (**figure 174**). These were broken at intervals by openings through which canoes could pass, and were spanned by removable bridges, therefore also serving a defensive purpose; moreover, access to the city by the enemy was barred by manned gatehouses. Across the western causeway ran a great masonry aqueduct carrying water to Tenochtitlan from the spring at Chapultepec, the flow being "as thick as a man's body."

The Spanish conquerors called the Aztec capital another Venice, and they should have known, for many of them had actually been to that place. With a total area of about 5 sq. miles (14 sq. km), the city (namely both Tenochtitlan and its satellite, Tlatelolco,) was laid out on a grid, according to a fragmentary sixteenth-century map of one section. Running north and south were long canals thronged with canoe traffic and each bordered by a lane; more sizable canals cut these at angles. Between these watery "streets" were arranged in regular fashion rectangular plots of land with their houses. In effect, this was a *chinampa* city.

The technique of *chinampa* cultivation is well known, for it is still used in the Xochimilco zone to the south of Mexico City, and may have originated with the Teotihuacanos in the Classic (see also p. 124). It belongs to the general category of "raised field cultivation," which is widespread in the tropics of the Western hemisphere, and was in use among the lowland Classic Maya.

The first settlers on the island constructed canals in their marshy habitat by cutting layers of thick water vegetation from the surface and piling them up as if they were mats to make their plots; from the bottom of the canals they spread mud over these green "rafts," which were thoroughly anchored by planting willows all around. On this highly fertile plot all sorts of crops were raised by the most careful and loving hand cultivation. This is why Cortés states that half the houses in the capital were built up "on the lake," and it is how swampy islands became united. Those houses on newly made *chinampas* were necessarily built from light cane and thatch; on drier parts of the island, more substantial dwellings of stone and mortar were possible, some of two stories with flower-filled inner patios and gardens. Communication across the "streets" was by planks laid over the canals.

The greatest problem faced by the inhabitants of the island was the saltiness of the lake, at least in its eastern part. With no outlet, during floods those nitrous waters inundated and ruined the *chinampas*. To prevent this, the Texcocan poet-king Nezahualcoyotl bountifully constructed a 10-mile (16-km) long dike to seal off a spring-fed, freshwater lagoon for Tenochtitlan.

With its willows, green gardens, numerous flowers, and canals bustling with canoes, Tenochtitlan must have been of impressive beauty, as the Nahuatl poem suggests:

> The city is spread out in circles of jade,
> radiating flashes of light like quetzal plumes,
> Beside it the lords are borne in boats:
> over them extends a flowery mist.[8]

It is exceptionally difficult to estimate the population of the capital in 1519. Many early sources say that there were about 60,000 houses, but none say how many persons there were. Basing his calculations on the Aztec tribute lists, Rudolf van Zantwijk estimates that there were enough foodstuffs in the warehouses of Tenochtitlan to support a population of 350,000, even without taking into account local *chinampa* production. The data that we have, however flimsy, suggest that Tenochtitlan (with Tlatelolco) had at least 200,000 to 300,000 inhabitants when Cortés marched in, five times the size of the contemporary London of Henry VIII. Quite a number of other cities of central Mexico, such as Texcoco, also had very substantial populations; all of Mexico between the Isthmus of Tehuantepec and the Chichimec frontier had about 11,000,000 inhabitants, most of whom were under Aztec domination.

The houses of the ordinary class of people, especially those who lived on the *chinampa* plots, were generally of reeds plastered with mud, and roofed with thatch; better-off people had dwellings of adobe bricks with flat roofs; while those of the wealthy were of stone masonry, also with flat roofs, and probably made up house complexes arranged around an inner court, in the same way as those of Tula. The highest

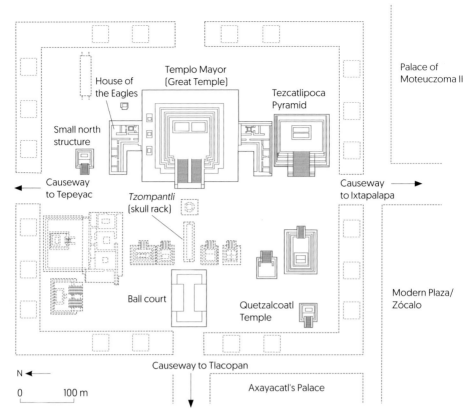

175 The center of Tenochtitlan in 1519. This walled precinct had the most important Aztec ceremonial buildings. Paramount was the Templo Mayor (Great Temple), a pyramidal building with shrines dedicated to the God of War (Huitzilopochtli) and the Rain Deity (Tlaloc). The sculpture at the base of this pyramid recalled the victory of their patron deity. Just to the north is the House of the Eagles, associated with warriors and rulers' self-bleeding sacrifices. To the west of the Templo Mayor were the skull rack and ball court, an important ensemble for the presentation of ball game rites. The northwest corner contained the *calmecac* complex, where elite youngsters were trained in Aztec religious tradition, while outside the precinct to the south and west were the palaces of Aztec rulers.

officials dwelt in great palace complexes, the grandest of which were reserved for the ruler or *Huei Tlatoani* ("Great Speaker") and for the descendants of his predecessors.

The focal point of all the main highways that led in from the mainland was found on the higher ground at the center of Tenochtitlan: the administrative and spiritual heart of the empire, and the conceptual center of the universe (**figure 175**). This was the Sacred Precinct, a paved area surrounded by the Coatepantli ("Snake Wall"), and containing, according to Fray Bernardino de Sahagún—our great authority on all aspects of Aztec life—seventy-eight buildings; approximately forty of these are accounted for in the archaeological record. The Sacred Precinct was dominated by the double Temple of Huitzilopochtli and Tlaloc (the Great Temple), its twin stairways reddened with the blood of sacrificed captives. Other temples were dedicated to the cults of Tezcatlipoca, his adversary Quetzalcoatl, and Xipe Totec, the god of springtime. A reminder of the purpose of the never-ending "Flowery War" was the *tzompantli*, or skull rack, on which were impaled for public exhibition hundreds of human heads. Near it was a very sizable ball court, in which Moteuczoma Xocoy-otzin was said to have played a game with the king of Texcoco challenging the truth of the latter's prediction that the former's kingdom would fall—and lost to him. The magnificent palaces of the Aztec royal line surrounded the Sacred Precinct.

Both in Tenochtitlan and in Tlatelolco proper were great marketplaces, very close to the main temples. The latter market was described by Bernal Díaz in super-lative terms; Cortés says that it was twice the size of the main square of Salamanca, in Spain, and some of the soldiers who had been in Rome and Constantinople claimed that it was larger than any there. Every day over 60,000 people were engaged in buying and selling in the Tlatelolco market, so many that there were market inspectors appointed by the ruler to check the honesty of transactions and to regulate prices. Thieves convicted in the market court were immediately pun-ished by being beaten to death (Aztec law was draconian). As for "money," cacao beans (which sometimes were counterfeited), cotton cloaks, and transparent quills filled with gold dust served that purpose. Befitting its role as the commercial center of an empire, in the Great Market of Tlatelolco one could buy luxury products of gold, silver, jade, turquoise, or feathers; clothing of all sorts; foods both cooked and unprepared; pottery, the most esteemed being elaborately made polychrome dishes and cups from Cholula; chocolate and vanilla; carpenter's tools of copper; cane cig-arettes, tobacco pipes, and aromatic cigars; and slaves, brought in by dealers from the slave center of Atzcapotzalco and exhibited in wooden cages. Merchants had the obligation to furnish war provisions to the state—mainly maize in forms that would not spoil on long marches.

Aztec Society

The fundamental unit of Aztec social organization in the heart of the empire was the *calpolli* (pl. *calpoltin*), a word meaning "big house." Often mistakenly called a "clan"—which would imply real or fictive descent from a common ancestor—the *calpolli* has been defined by Rudolf van Zantwijk as a group of families related by kinship or proximity of residence over a long period of time. Elite members of the group provided its commoner members with arable land and/or non-agricultural occupations, in return for which the commoners would perform various services for their chiefs and render them tribute. In this way the *calpolli* was a localized, land-holding corporation, but it also had ritual functions in that it had its own temple and patron deities, and even an association with a day in the 260-day count. Its principal chief, the *calpollec*, was selected for life by the elite members of the corporate group, and confirmed in office by the ruler. There were more than eighty *calpoltin* in Tenochtitlan, some of which have actually persisted as traditional barrios near the center of modern Mexico City. The *calpoltin* were arranged into the four great quarters into which the Aztec city was divided, separated by imaginary north–south and east–west lines that met at the Sacred Precinct.

The vast bulk of the population in the cities, towns, and villages of the empire consisted of commoners or *macehualtin* (sing. *macehualli*). These worked lands belonging to the *calpoltin*; each family maintained rights over a specific plot as long as it did not lie unused for over two years at a time. Many of these farmers also had a *calmil*, or house garden, which was managed at the household level. The rural *macehualtin* formed the majority of commoners. These people lived in dispersed settlements, constructing small check dams and terrace systems to increase agricultural yield. The modest scale of rural dam and terrace systems suggests that they were organized by the *macehualtin* themselves, unlike the large-scale irrigation systems found throughout the empire that required state-level organization. Whether they had access to state-supported projects or not, all *macehualtin* were required to pay tribute to their overlords, the Aztec nobility.

Near the top of the social ladder were the noblemen or *pipiltin* (sing. *pilli*), who were all the sons of lords: "precious feathers from the wings of past kings," as one source puts it. It was from their rank that the imperial administrators were drawn; these had the use of lands belonging to their office and also owned private lands. Yet the social stratification so apparent in Aztec life was not entirely rigid, for there were also *cuauhpipiltin*, "eagle nobles"—commoners who had distinguished themselves on the field of battle and who were rewarded for their gallantry with noble titles and with private lands.

Above the *pipiltin*, at the apex of the social pyramid, were the *teteuhctin* (sing. *tecuhtli*), the rulers of towns and cities; the emperor himself was a *tecuhtli*. These received the honorific suffix -*tzin* at the ends of their names, and were entitled to wear clothes of the utmost richness. From their palaces they exercised legal powers, and ensured that tribute payments were made to all appropriate levels of the imperial administration. As far as conquered territories were concerned, the Aztecs wisely followed a system of indirect rule, by leaving the indigenous *tecuhtli* and nobles in place, but demoting them to the status of middle- and lower-rank officials.

At the bottom of the social scale were the *mayeque*, bondsmen or serfs who tilled the estates of the noblemen. These, according to Van Zantwijk, comprised about 30 percent of the empire's population, and were often former *macehualtin* who had lost their rights either through conquest or through suppression of rebellion. A study by Edward Hicks shows that the produce from about one third of the land worked by a serf went to his lord, while the rest could be retained by himself and his family (although he was expected to pay tribute from this). Some *mayeque* occasionally became richer and more powerful than the *macehualtin* through the inheritance of tangible property and other rights.

Slaves or *tlacohtin* ("bought ones") were persons who had not been able to meet their obligations, particularly gambling debts. Such individuals could pawn themselves for given lengths of time (including in perpetuity), or they might even be pawned by needy spouses or parents. The institution of slavery was closely defined under Aztec law: for instance, slaves could not be resold without their consent, unless they violated the rules frequently, in which case they might end up in the slave market. They were generally well treated; and often—as among the ancient

Romans—they became domestic servants, farm laborers, and even estate managers. Some achieved considerable prosperity. Comely young female slaves were sometimes taken by rulers as concubines, and were considered as suitable diplomatic gifts (witness the women presented to Cortés).

The empire, on the other hand, was structured at a regional level by groups of small cities and their tributary rural dependencies forming units called *altepetl*. What gave groups of *altepeme* much cohesiveness was that while some of their comprising smaller settlements carried out locally the same administrative functions, more sizable towns and cities had specialized functions at the supra-regional level. There was also intermingling of territories among the units to enhance integration and counteract fragmentation. The intermingling of tributary relations further merged the confederacy of such composite segments. For example, while the Triple Alliance was ultimately comprised of thirty dependent kingdoms, Texcoco, one of the three members, received tribute from some of the *altepeme* affiliated with Mexico-Tenochtitlan and Tlacopan.

The Long-Distance Merchants

Although relatively small in number, the long-distance merchants or *pochteca* constituted a powerful group in Aztec society. These were of far higher status than the ordinary market-vendors, for the emperor treated them as if they were nobility, and if one of them died on an expedition, he went to the paradise of the Sun God in the same way as a fallen warrior. The *pochteca* were directly responsible to the royal palace and the *tlatoani*, for whom they traveled into foreign territories many hundreds of miles from the capital, to obtain such luxury goods as precious quetzal feathers, amber, and the like for the use of the royal house. Allied with the *pochteca* was a more specialized group, the *oztomeca*, who went disguised in the local garb and who spoke the local language; their task was to gather military intelligence as well as exotic goods. In the same way as the businessmen-spies of modern days, the *oztomeca* were often the vanguard for the Aztec takeover of another polity, acting sometimes as agents-provocateurs.

Membership in the *pochteca* was hereditary. There were twelve merchants' organizations or guilds, all located in the heart of the empire, and all under the control of the head merchants in Tenochtitlan-Tlatelolco. The most important commerce of this kind linked the capital with the tropical coasts of southeast Mesoamerica, particularly the Putún Maya port-of-trade at Xicallanco on the Gulf of Mexico; a key nodal point was the Aztec garrison town of Tochtepec, in northern Oaxaca, from which human caravans were sent out to the hot country, and to which they returned. It is apparent from detailed descriptions given by Father Sahagún that the goods exported primarily consisted of cotton mantles and other textiles from the royal warehouses that had been received as tribute, along with cast-gold jewelry fashioned by Tenochtitlan's master craftsmen.

Because the *pochteca* could themselves pay taxes to the palace in luxury goods rather than the produce of their lands, and grew rich and powerful as a consequence, some have seen them as an entrepreneurial middle class in formation. But there were powerful sanctions against them flaunting their wealth: as an example, they had to creep into the city at night after a successful trading expedition, lest they arouse the jealousy of the ruler. There was an additional leveling process operating here, as Rudolf van Zantwijk has stressed. As a merchant rose up the social ladder of the guild, the special ceremony that he was obligated to give on his return from abroad became increasingly costly. One of these was a Song Feast, a lavish banquet for a considerable number of guests; as he achieved even higher office within the *pochteca* organization, the ritual would include not only another and even more grand banquet (at which presents would have to be given out), but the human sacrifice of slaves bought in the market.

While this was a highly honorable enterprise, it was also a highly dangerous one, and many died of disease or injury on the road, or were slain. Because of this, the activities of the *pochteca* were surrounded by ritual dictated by the solar calendar. They even had their own patron deities, in particular Xiuhtecuhtli, the Fire God, and Yacatecuhtli ("Nose Lord"), a deity depicted with a Pinocchio-like nose, a traveler's staff in one hand and a woven fan in the other.

Becoming an Aztec

The enculturation experience—turning an unformed human being into an Aztec—began at birth. After she had cut the umbilical cord, the midwife recited set speeches to the newborn. To an infant girl she would say:

> Oh my dear child, oh my jewel, oh my quetzal feather, you have come to life, you have been born, you have come out upon the earth. Our lord created you, fashioned you, caused you to be born upon the earth, he by whom all live, God. We have awaited you, we who are your mothers, your fathers; and your aunts, your uncles, your relatives have awaited you; they wept, they were sad before you when you came to life, when you were born upon the earth.[9]

A boy was told that the house in which he was born was not a true home, but just a resting place, for he was a warrior: "your mission is to give the sun the blood of enemies to drink, and to feed Tlaltecuhtli, the earth, with their bodies," in contrast to girls, who were admonished to recognize that their place was in the home.

A naming ceremony took place not long after birth, on an auspicious day in the 260-day calendar, with the midwife doing the washing and naming of the child. The gender roles were again emphasized, boys being given a miniature breechclout,

176 Folio 2 of the Codex Mendoza illustrates the mythical founding of Tenochtitlan in 1325, with the eagle perched on the cactus at the center, surrounded by ten early Aztec rulers. Pictured below are the first two conquests of the young Aztec state. Early European colonial period.

a cape, a shield, and four arrows; and girls a little skirt (*cueitl*) and blouse (*huipilli*), along with weaving implements. The early-colonial Codex Mendoza (**figure 176**) shows that a child's subsequent upbringing was spartan and strict. Until the age of fifteen, education took place in the family: a boy at first going out with his father to gather firewood, and later learning how to fish; a girl learning how to spin, and later advancing to weaving, and the grinding of the *nixtamal* for tortillas. Punishments for infractions were drastic: a disobedient boy might be left out naked to the night cold, pricked with maguey spines, or held over burning chile peppers.

In 1519, the Aztecs may have been the only people in the world with universal schooling for both sexes. This began at fifteen for all boys and girls, and lasted until they were of marriageable age (about twenty). There were two kinds of schools, the *calmecac* and the *telpochcalli*. The *calmecac* was a seminary, generally attached to a specific temple, attended by the sons and daughters of the *pipiltin*, but also by some *pochteca* children; in it, the priest-teachers instructed the students in all aspects of Aztec religion, including the calendar, the rituals, the songs that were to be chanted over the sacred manuscripts, and certainly much of the glorious past of the Aztec nation. Having attended a *calmecac* was a prerequisite to holding any kind of high office in the Aztec administration. Those who really wanted to enter the priesthood then passed to a kind of theological graduate school termed the *tlamacazcalli* ("priest's house") for further training.

The *telpochcalli* or "House of Youths" was essentially a military academy, attended by the offspring of *macehualtin* (the commoners) and presided over by Tezcatlipoca, the god of warriors. As in the *calmecac*, the sexes were strictly segregated, and females were here assigned to a *cuicalco*, or "House of Song." Male students were trained in the martial arts, and could even take leave to accompany seasoned warriors as their squires on the field of battle, while girls seem to have concentrated on less violent subjects, including song and dance. Conditions in the male part of the academy seem to have been far less austere than in the *calmecac*, and some sources tell us that sex workers often visited the cadets in their communal quarters.

Marriage

For *macehualtin*, marriage took place at around the age of twenty; one was expected to marry someone within one's own *calpolli*. This union was considered to be a contract between families, not individuals, and was arranged by an elderly woman, who acted as go-between. This was a complicated matter, for consent had to be obtained not only from the prospective bride's family, but also from the young man's masters in the school he had attended. After an auspicious day in the 260-day calendar had been selected for the ceremony, there was an elaborate banquet in the bride's house, when she was arrayed and painted for the event. The actual marriage took place at night. After being dressed and decorated, the bride was placed on the back of the elderly woman and borne in a procession to the groom's house by the light of torches. The young couple were placed on a mat spread before the hearth, they were given presents, and the union was finalized by the tying together of her blouse and his cloak, followed by feasting at which the old people were allowed to get drunk (inebriation being generally prohibited in the Aztec world, for more on which, see p. 227).

There may have been equality of the sexes in the sphere of education, but this did not apply to matrimony. This being a male-oriented society, the new couple always made their home with the bridegroom's family. Moreover, a man could take as many secondary wives or concubines as he could afford: great princes and lords had dozens of such wives, sometimes even hundreds, and Nezahualpilli, the *tlatoani* of Texcoco, was said to have had 2,000 (and 144 children)! On the other hand, women seem to have had equal rights in divorce, which was never easy in any circumstance.

177 Page from the Codex Mendoza, a post-Conquest copy of an Aztec original. This is the tribute list of Moteuczoma Xocoyotzin. Pictured on this sheet is the biannual tribute due from the six towns of Xilotepec, an Otomí-speaking province northwest of the Basin of Mexico. Enumerated are women's skirts and blouses, men's mantles of various sorts, two warrior's costumes with shields, four wooden cribs filled with maize, beans and other foodstuffs, and an eagle.

The Triple Alliance and the Empire

A glance at a map showing the Aztec dominions as they were in 1519 would disclose that while the empire spanned the area between the Gulf of Mexico and the Pacific, it by no means included all of Mesoamerica. Left in place within it were such enemy states as Tlaxcallan (which was to provide tens of thousands of mercenary troops for Cortés), Huexotzingo, and Chollolan (Cholula). Under Axayacatl (r. 1469–1481), the Aztec armies had tried to conquer the Purépecha, and been repelled once and for all, while much of southeastern Veracruz remained free of Aztec control, as did the entire Maya area. Nevertheless, this was a vast empire, with an enormous population held in a mighty system, the main purpose of which was to provide tribute to the Basin of Mexico.

Polities that had fallen to Aztec arms and those of their allies in the Triple Alliance of Tenochtitlan, Texcoco, and Tlacopan were speedily organized as tribute-rendering provinces of the empire. Military governors in Aztec garrisons ensured that such tribute, which was very heavy indeed, was paid promptly and on fixed dates. Most sources state that on arrival in the Basin, tribute was distributed in a 2:2:1 ratio (Tenochtitlan and Texcoco got two-fifths each, and Tlacopan one-fifth). It is fortunate that the tribute list in Moteuczoma's state archives has survived in the form of copies, for the Spaniards were also interested in what they could extract from the old Aztec provinces (**figure 177**). Incredible as it may seem, each year Tenochtitlan received from all parts of the empire 7,000 tons of maize and 4,000 tons each of beans, chia seed, and grain amaranth, and no fewer than 2,000,000 cotton cloaks, as well as war costumes, shields, feather headdresses, and such luxury products as amber, which was unobtainable in the central highlands. Certainly, some of the tribute—especially the cloaks—were farmed out by the royal treasury to the *pochteca* as barter goods to carry to distant ports of trade. But a good deal of the tribute acted as the main financial support of the state edifice, since in an essentially moneyless economy state servants had to be paid in goods and land, and artisans had to receive something for the fine products that they supplied to the palace. Each page of the tribute list covers one province, the various subject towns within it being listed vertically along the edge of the page. The names of these places are written with signs that stand for whole words and/or syllabic spellings, and in the case of the former, often taking advantage of words that sound similar but have different meanings. Therefore, the town called Mapachtepec ("Raccoon Hill") would be expressed by a hand (*ma-itl*) grasping a bunch of Spanish moss (*pach-tli*), over a picture of a hill (*tepe-tl*). Aztec numbers on the list were given in a vigesimal (base twenty) system: one to nineteen by dots or occasionally by fingers, twenty by a flag, 400 by a sign that resembles a feather or fir tree, and 8,000 by a bag or pouch.

Exempt from the payment of tribute were such specialists as painters and singers, along with *pipiltin* who enjoyed the revenues from private lands, and outstanding warriors. *Macehualtin*, no matter where they were, had to pay both with maize ears and with labor, and each was expected to furnish one cotton mantle a year; merchants and ordinary artisans paid in the goods that they produced or that passed through their hands.

As the scholar Fernando Horcasitas once said, the Aztec empire was not so much an empire in the Roman or British sense as an economic empire based on the provision of tribute, paid in full and on a regular basis. Obviously, some of the citizens participating under this arrangement were unwilling partners in the system, and chafed under the Aztec yoke. There was therefore an inherent weakness in the empire, which Cortés was quick to perceive and to exploit.

The Emperor and the Palace

The Aztec emperor was in every sense an absolute ruler, although only in certain domains. His Nahuatl title was *Huei Tlatoani* or "Great Speaker." As the researches of Rudolf van Zantwijk have made clear, his function was the same as that of the "talking chiefs" among North American societies; he was principally to deal with the external side of the Aztec polity: warfare, tribute, and diplomacy. His counterpart handling the internal affairs of Mexico-Tenochtitlan was the man who held the office of *Cihuacoatl* or "Female Snake." Based on an Aztec female deity, the very title celebrates the opposition of male and female principles in the philosophy of dualism so dear to the Aztecs. This man acted as a kind of grand vizier, and was always a close relative of the *Huei Tlatoani*; the most famous *Cihuacoatl* was the great Tlacaelel, who transformed the Aztec realm from a kingdom into an empire.

The *Huei Tlatoani* was elected from the royal lineage by a council composed of the nobles, chief priests, and top war officers; at the same time, the four principal lords who were to act as the *Huei Tlatoani's* executive arm were also chosen. All sources agree on the openness of the process, but while many names were advanced during the convocation, only one was put forth by the council. Scholars are still debating the exact rules of Aztec dynastic succession, but during the last hundred years of the empire, brothers seem to have inherited the office more often than sons.

On the new king's installation, the chief priests took him to pay homage at the temple of the war god, Huitzilopochtli; while he censed the sacred image, the masses of citizens waited expectantly below, in a din caused by the blowing of shell trumpets. The king spent four days in meditation and fasting in the temple, which included prayers and speeches in honor of Tezcatlipoca, the patron deity of the royal house. Before the image of this all-powerful god the new king stood naked, emphasizing his utter unworthiness in such speeches as this:

> O master, O our lord, O lord of the near, of the nigh, O night, O wind... Poor am I. In what manner shall I act for thy city? In what manner shall I act for the governed, for the vassals [*macehualtin*]? For I am blind, I am deaf, I am an imbecile, and in excrement, in filth hath my lifetime been... Perhaps thou mistaketh me for another; perhaps thou seekest another in my stead.[10]

Then the *Huei Tlatoani* was escorted to his palace, which stood adjacent to the Sacred Precinct. To his coronation banquet came even the kings of distant lands, such as the rulers of the Tarascan kingdom, the king of the Totonacs (a puppet prince), and great personages from as far away as Tehuantepec.

The descriptions of the Spaniards make it clear that the *Huei Tlatoani* was a divine embodiment. Even great lords who entered into his presence approached in plain garments, heads bowed, without looking on his face. Everywhere he went, he was borne on the shoulders of noblemen in a litter covered with precious feathers. If he walked, nobles swept the way and covered the ground with cloths so that his feet would not touch the ground. When Moteuczoma ate, he was shielded from onlookers by a gilt screen. No fewer than several hundred dishes were offered by young maidens at each meal for his choosing; during his repast he was entertained by buffoons, dwarfs, jugglers, and tumblers.

Moteuczoma's gardens and pleasure palaces amazed the Spaniards. The royal aviary had ten sizable rooms with pools of salt and fresh water, housing birds of both lake and sea, above which were galleries bordered by hanging gardens for the imperial promenade. Another building was the royal zoo, staffed by trained veterinarians, in which were exhibited in cages animals from all parts of his realm: jaguars from the lowlands, pumas from the mountains, foxes, and so forth, making an unearthly clamor with their roars and howls. Carefully tended by servants, many kinds of people with disfigurements (who would have been considered by Moteuczoma to be curiosities, as was common at that time) inhabited what was essentially a private "sideshow," each with his own room.

Less frivolous activities of the royal household included separate courts of justice for noblemen (and warriors) and for *macehualtin*; the overseeing by stewards of the palace storehouse; the maintenance of the state arsenal, officers' quarters, and the military academy; and the management of the empire-wide tribute system.

Food and Agriculture

All of these state functions, the Aztec war machine, and the Aztec economy itself, ultimately rested on the agricultural basis of the Mexican population—the farming of maize, beans, squash, chile peppers, tomatoes, amaranth, chia, and a host of other cultigens. Thousands of canoes crowded the great lake daily, bearing these products to the capital either as direct tribute or as merchandise to be traded for craft items and other necessities in the marketplaces. A tremendous surplus for the use of the city was extracted from the rich *chinampas* fringing the shallow lake and from fields nearby, while the upper slopes of the surrounding hills were probably primarily given over to the cultivation of maguey, the source of the mildly alcoholic beverage so important to Aztec culture.

Most of the Aztec people, from nobles to serfs, were very well fed, although overindulgent banquets and other excesses were proscribed by the puritanical Aztec ethic. Much of the diet of ordinary citizens consisted of tortillas dipped in a *molli* or sauce made of chiles ground with water; maize could also be taken in the form of steamed *tamales*, to which could be added ground or whole beans, but unlike their modern counterparts, these contained no fat or grease. Sahagún's informants gave him a long list of dishes with their ingredients, and these show that the Aztec cuisine was extremely sophisticated: for example, there were dozens of ways to prepare *tamales*, not just one. Meat and fish dishes were for the elite, or were reserved for feast days, while poorer people ate great quantities of greens instead. Although some of these are not to modern taste, many animal and plant species entered the Aztec cuisine, including the axolotl, a large larval salamander found in *chinampa* canals, which could be stewed in a sauce of yellow chiles, or tadpoles prepared in a variety of styles. Insects, in the form of eggs, larvae, and adults, were widely consumed, as was *tecuilatl*, a scum-like algae gathered from lake margins; the latter was pressed into cakes. A wide variety of fruits, from both the highlands and the tropical lowlands, were available in the markets, and highly appreciated.

Amaranth occupied a special place in the Aztec diet. This eminently nutritious grain crop was imported into the capital in substantial quantities, but it was destined not so much for the kitchens of ordinary folk as for ceremonial use: it was mixed with ground maize, along with honey or maguey sap, formed into idols of the great god Huitzilopochtli, and consumed in this manner on his feast days—to the horror of the Spanish priests, who saw this as a travesty of Holy Communion!

Maize could be consumed not only as tortillas and *tamales*, but also in liquid form, as a maize gruel called *atolli*; another kind of maize drink called *pozolli* was made from slightly fermented maize dough; both could be taken to the fields in gourd containers for the repast of farmers. Chocolate drinks were generally reserved for the elite and the wealthy, for the bean was expensive. Chocolate could be prepared in a variety of ways, with an array of flavors (including chile pepper, vanilla, and other spices); it could even be mixed with *atolli*. As might be expected, given their ethic of moderation and austerity, the Aztecs were ambivalent about *octli* (called by the Spaniards *pulque*), the fermented sap of the maguey plant. One was not supposed to drink more than four cups during a feast, and drunkenness was punished with severity and even death; old people were, however, released from this prohibition and allowed to get thoroughly inebriated whenever they pleased. Nonetheless, *octli* played a major role in Aztec ritual, and there was a whole group of *octli* divinities, as well as a major goddess of the maguey plant, about whom a mythic cycle was created.

War and Human Sacrifice

The Aztec army, as is the case with all armies, traveled on its stomach, and the Aztec military successes that resulted in their empire were in part the outcome of their ability to supply their forces with food—principally dried tortillas—wherever they went. The main goal of the Aztec state was war. Every able-bodied man was expected to bear arms, even the priests and the long-distance merchants; the latter fought in their own units while ostensibly on trading expeditions. To the Aztecs, there was no activity more glorious than to furnish captives or to die for Huitzilopochtli:

> The battlefield is the place:
> where one toasts the divine liquor in war,
> where are stained red the divine eagles,
> where the jaguars howl,
> where all kinds of precious stones rain from ornaments,
> where wave headdresses rich with fine plumes,
> where princes are smashed to bits.[11]

In the rich imagery of Nahuatl songs, the blood-stained battlefield was described as an immense plain covered by flowers, and lucky was he who perished on it:

> There is nothing like death in war,
> nothing like the flowery death
> so precious to Him who gives life:
> far off I see it: my heart yearns for it![12]

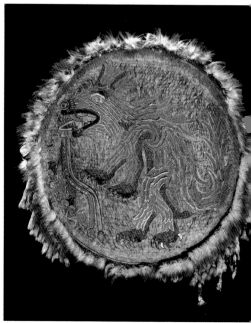

178 This hollow, life-size ceramic figure of an Aztec Eagle Warrior was recovered from the House of the Eagles, in the Great Temple excavations.

179 An Aztec shield of feathers and gold trim. On its face is a feathered coyote emitting the sign "Water-Fire," metaphor for war.

Aztec weapons were the terrible sword-club (*macuahuitl*), with side grooves set with razor-sharp obsidian blades; spears, the heads of which were also set with blades; and barbed and fletched darts hurled from the *atlatl*. Seasoned Aztec warriors were splendidly arrayed in costumes of jaguar skins or suits covered with eagle feathers, symbolizing warrior and other institutional orders (**figure 178**); for defense, Aztec troops were sometimes clad in a quilted cotton tunic and always carried a round shield of wood or reeds covered with hide, often magnificently decorated with colored designs in feathers (**figure 179**). While the battle raged, high-ranking officers could be identified by ensigns worn on the shoulders—towering constructions of reeds, feathers, and the like—which made it all too easy for the soldiers of Cortés to identify and destroy them.

War strategy included the gathering of intelligence and compilation of maps. On the field of battle, generals arranged the ranks of the army. Attacks were spearheaded by an elite corps of veteran warriors, followed by the bulk of the army, to the sound of shell trumpets blown by priests. The idea was not only to destroy the enemy town but also to isolate and capture as many of the enemy as possible for transport to the rear and eventual sacrifice in the capital.

Although the Aztec authority Henry Nicholson has said that among the Aztecs "human sacrifice...was practiced on a scale not even approached by any other ritual system in the history of the world," many scholars are now convinced that this scale was immensely exaggerated by the Spaniards to justify their own violence and aggression against indigenous populations. One of our Spanish sources, for example, reports that over 80,000 victims, all of them war captives, were immolated to celebrate the dedication of the Great Temple in 1487, which is certainly a physical impossibility. Yet it is true, as Nicholson has maintained, that "some type of death sacrifice normally accompanied all important rituals," a custom that surely goes back to the Olmecs; it was practiced in Teotihuacan, as the warrior sacrifices of the Building of the Feathered Serpents so abundantly prove. In all likelihood, many young men lost their lives in the Aztec capital each year, but there is no way to establish an exact figure.

The victims were ideally enemy warriors; when an Aztec took a captive in action, he said to him, "Here is my well-beloved son," and the captive responded "Here is my revered father," establishing the kind of fictive kinship that characterized the warrior-captive relationship in the Americas from the Tupinambá of Brazil to the Iroquois of New York State. All warriors believed that they were destined to die this way, being transformed on death into hummingbirds that went to join the Sun God in his celestial paradise.

After the victim had been ritually bathed, there was an elaborate ceremonial process that included pre-sacrificial, sacrificial, and post-sacrificial rituals. These varied according to the nature of the monthly festivities associated with the solar calendar, and, to some extent, the origin and gender of the victim. Pre-sacrificial rituals included playing a sacred version of the ball game, darting and the ensuing bleeding of the sacrificial victim while tied to a scaffold, brief but repeated exposure to fire, or enacting gladiatorial combat in which the war captive was tethered to a round stone and forced to defend himself against a seasoned warrior using dummy weapons. In addition to a host of symbolic meanings, these preparatory rituals left the sacrificial victims wounded and physically exhausted. The climax of the ritual process was when the body of the victim was stretched over a sacrificial stone at the top of one of the lofty temples, the chest opened with a knife of flint or obsidian, and the heart ripped out; this was then offered to the deities in a *cuauhxicalli*, or "eagle vessel" of carved stone.

Post-sacrificial treatments included the rolling down of the dead body and its dismemberment at the foot of the temple's staircase. Far from an obliteration of the sacrificial offering, the dismemberment of the body enabled its effective dispersal. The decapitated heads, for example, were destined for their public display in skull racks; the severed legs were claimed by the captors who commissioned the fashioning of war trophies from the victims' thigh bones; and other body parts were often buried in front of the temples in order to feed Tlaltecuhtli, the divine dual-gendered Earth.

Perhaps the most elaborate sacrificial sequence took place during "Tlacaxipe-hualiztli," the festivities of the second month. After the gladiatorial combat, the bleeding by darting, the excision of the heart, and the tumbling down of the dead victim, the body was decapitated, and the head and torso separately flayed. Most likely the two-part flayed skin was treated in the same manner as leather before

180a, 180b Front and back views of a stone statue with personification of Xipe Totec, god of spring and fertility, wearing the flayed skin of a sacrificial victim. Carved on the back is the year-date 2 Reed. Tepepan, Xochimilco. Ht 2 ft 6.5 in. (77.5 cm).

being worn by impersonators of Xipe Totec. Stone sculptural representations of these impersonators provide additional details of the ritual process: the tying with a thin rope of an open incision that ran from the apex of the head to the neck; the tying of a second incision that went from the neck to the lower back; the sewing of the chest cut that was made to retrieve the heart; and the still-hanging hands and feet of the sacrificial victim. These sections of the body were not flayed because their multiple skeletal elements would have slowed down the skinning process (**figures 180a, 180b**).

It is incontrovertible that some body parts of these victims ended up being eaten ritually. That said, the sensational hypothesis put forth by Michael Harner, that the Aztec elite practiced cannibalism on an allegedly extensive scale so as to monopolize protein in a protein-poor environment, fails on two grounds: 1) there were abundant sources of protein available to the residents of the Basin of Mexico, not the least of which was *tecuilatl* lake scum; and 2) a close reading of the historical records demonstrates that human flesh was eaten very sparingly and only during tightly controlled rituals—in fact, the practice was more an appropriation of the essences of brave warriors or divine impersonators, as opposed to sheer gluttony. Archaeological evidence for the most substantial instance of cannibalistic rites occurs not in Pre-Columbian times but during the upheavals of the Conquest, where at Tecuaque a Spanish caravan consisting of approximately 500 people was ambushed, sacrificed, and certain body parts of at least some of the victims cooked and eaten over the course of several months. This rather gruesome episode was probably carried out in revenge for the murder of a high-ranking Aztec dignitary.

Aztec Religion

Aztec mythology and religious organization are so extremely complex that they cannot be done justice in the space of this chapter. The data that we have from the early sources, particularly from the pictorial manuscripts and from Fray Bernardino de Sahagún, are more complete in this respect than for any other Meso-american people.

The bewildering multiplicity of divine entities was the embodiment of one cosmic principle of duality: the complementarity of opposites, as personified in the great dual-gendered creator deity, Ometeotl or "Dual Divinity." In Aztec philosophy, this was the only reality, all else being illusion. Ometeotl presided over a layered universe, dwelling in the thirteenth and uppermost heaven, while such various celestial phenomena as the sun, moon, stars, comets, and winds existed in lower heavens. Beneath the surface of the earth were nine stratified underworlds, through which the souls of the dead had to pass in a perilous journey until reaching extinc-tion in the deepest level, Mictlan Opochcalocan, "The Land of the Dead, Where the Streets Are on the Left." This was presided over by another dual divinity, the dread "Lord and Lady of the Land of the Dead," the underworld counterpart of Ometeotl.

Out of the gendered opposition embodied in Ometeotl, the four Tezcatlipocas were born. As was the case with all Mesoamericans and many other Native Amer-ican groups as well, the Aztecs thought of the surface of our world in terms of the four cardinal directions, each of which was assigned a specific color and a specific tree, on the upper branches of which perched a distinctive bird. Where the central axis passed through the earth was the Old Fire God, an avatar of Ometeotl since his epithet was "Mother of the Gods, Father of the Gods." Notable of these four off-spring was the Black Tezcatlipoca ("Smoking Mirror") of the north, the god of war and sorcery, and the patron deity of the royal house, to whom the new emperor prayed on his succession to office. He was everywhere, in all things, and could see into one's heart by means of his magic mirror. This, the "real" Tezcatlipoca, was the giver and taker away of life and riches, and was much feared. The White Tezcat-lipoca of the west was the familiar Quetzalcoatl, the Lord of Life and the patron of the priestly order.

181 Aztec Sun Stone, the most sizable known *cuauhxicalli* (eagle vessel). Originally placed in horizontal position, it served as a platform for human sacrifice. It depicts in its innermost circle the earth-woman/sun-man as devourers of hearts (the sun) and sacrificial victims (the earth), followed by the account of the five ages of creation in Aztec cosmology. It also references the 20-day names of the sacred calendar, the Calendar Round, the sun, the awls of self-penitence, and the offering of blood. The monument names Moteuczoma Xocoyotzin and his patron deity Huitzilopochtli, and in its outermost ring it shows them transformed into their Fire Serpent alter egos. Diameter 11 ft 9.7 in. (3.6 m).

Visually expressed on the famous Sun Stone (the largest known *cuauhxicalli*, **figure 181**) and other Aztec monuments was the belief that the world had gone through four cosmic ages or Suns (similar to the Hindu *kalpas*), each destroyed by a cataclysm; this process of repeated creations and destructions was the result of the titanic struggle between the Black Tezcatlipoca and Quetzalcoatl, in each phase of which one or the other would be triumphant and would dominate the next age. The previous age perished in floods when the sky fell on the earth and all became dark. The current age is that of the Fifth Sun, which was created at Teotihuacan when the deities gathered there to consider what to do to resolve this. After each had declined in turn the honor of sacrificing himself or herself to begin the world anew, the least powerful and most miserable of them, "The Poxy (or Purulent) One," hurled himself into a great fire and rose up to the sky as the new Sun. Another god then repeated this altruistic act, rising as the Moon—but this luminary was casting rays as bright as the Sun, so to dim it the deities hurled a rabbit across the Moon's face, where it can still be seen.

182 Stone statue of a woman named 8 Grass (the glyph is carved on the back of her head) who personifies Coatlicue, the Aztec mother goddess. With a skeletal head, claws in her extremities, and a skirt of intertwined snakes, the piece had inlays of shell as teeth and of other precious materials below the eyes and in the chest. Small perforations around the scalp were meant to keep a wig in place. From Coxcatlan, Puebla. Ht 3 ft 6 in. (1.12 m).

Human beings had existed in the previous world, but they had perished. To re-create them, Quetzalcoatl made a perilous journey into the Underworld, stealing their bones from Mictlantecuhtli/Mictlancihuatl, "Lord and Lady of the Land of the Dead." When he reached the earth's surface, these were ground up in a bowl, and the gods shed blood over them from their perforated members. From this deed, people were born, but they lacked the sustenance that the deities had decreed for them: maize, which had been hidden by the deities inside a primordial mountain. Here again Quetzalcoatl came to the rescue: by turning himself into an ant, he entered the mountain and stole the grains that were to nurture the Aztec people.

Central to the concepts of the Aztec destiny codified by Tlacaelel was the official cult of Huitzilopochtli, the Blue Tezcatlipoca of the south. The result of a miraculous birth from Coatlicue (an aspect of the female side of Ometeotl, **figure 182**), he was the tutelary divinity of the Aztec people; the terrible warrior god of the sun, he needed the hearts and blood of sacrificed human warriors so that he would rise from the east each morning after a nightly trip through the Underworld.

On the east was the Red Tezcatlipoca, Xipe Totec, "Our Lord the Flayed One." He was the god of spring and the renewal of the vegetation, impersonated by priests and those doing penance, wearing the skin of a flayed captive—the new skin symbolizing the "skin" of new vegetation that the earth puts on when the rains come.

183 (LEFT) Late Post-Classic effigy censer, mixing aspects of the Rain Deity Tlaloc and the Maize God.

184 (BELOW) Schematic representation of the *tonalpohualli* or 260-day cycle of the Aztecs. The twenty named days combine with the numbers one to thirteen.

Grass, Reed, Jaguar, Eagle, Vulture, Motion, Flint Knife, Rain, Flower, Crocodile, Wind, House, Lizard, Serpent, Death's Head, Deer, Rabbit, Water, Dog, Monkey

At the end of twenty days the god impersonator could take the skin off, but by this time he "stank like a dead dog," as one source records.

Tlaloc/Chalchiuhtlicue was another dual-gendered divinity, the source of rain and lightning and therefore central to Aztec agricultural rites. Tlaloc could also be quadruple, so that there were black, white, blue, and red Tlalocs, but he was generally depicted as blue, with serpent-like fangs and rings over the eyes (**figure 183**). One of the more dramatic of Aztec practices was the sacrifice of small children on mountain tops to bring rain at the end of the dry season, as an offering to Tlaloc/Chalchiuhtlicue. It was said that the more the children cried, the more the Rain Deity was pleased. His/her cult still survives today among central Mexican peasants, although humans have probably not been sacrificed to this divinity since early European colonial days.

The cults were presided over by a celibate clergy. Every priest had been to a seminary at which he was instructed in the complicated ritual that he was expected to carry out daily. With their soot-painted skin; their long, unkempt hair clotted with blood; and their ears and members shredded from self-mutilations effected with agave thorns and sting-ray spines, smelling of death and putrefaction, such priests must have been awesome spokesmen for the Aztec deities.

The daily life of all Aztecs was bound up with the ceremonies dictated by the combinatory workings of their calendar. The Almanac Year (*tonalpohualli*) of 260 days was the result of the intermeshing of twenty days (given such names as Alligator, Wind, House, Lizard, etc.) with the numbers one to thirteen, which were expressed in their manuscripts by dots only (**figure 184**). To all individuals, each day in the *tonalpohualli* brought good or dreadful tidings in accordance with the prophecies of the priests; but the bad effects could be mitigated; if a child was born on an unfavorable day, his or her naming ceremony could be postponed to a better one. For each of the twenty thirteen-day periods there were special rites and presiding deities; there were also a series of birds ruling over each of the thirteen-day periods, and a constantly repeating series of nine deities who reigned during the night.

The Solar Year of 365 days was made up of eighteen named periods of twenty days each, with an unlucky and highly dangerous period of five extra days before the commencement of the next year. Again, every month had its own special ceremonies in which all the people of the land participated; given this kind of cycle, it is hardly surprising that the months were closely correlated with the agricultural year, but there must have been a constant slippage in this respect since neither the Aztecs nor any other Mesoamericans used Leap Years or any other kind of intercalation to adjust for the fact that the actual length of the year is a quarter-day longer than 365 days. The Solar Years were named after one of the four possible names of the Almanac Year that could fall on the last day of the eighteenth twenty-day period, along with its accompanying numerical coefficient: so in the Aztec calendar, the year names were Reed (13th day), Flint (18th day), House (3rd day), and Rabbit (8th day).

Observations of the sun, moon, planets, and stars were carried out by the Aztec priests, and apparently even by the rulers. After the sun, another important heavenly body to the Aztecs was Venus, particularly in its first appearance, or heliacal rising, as Morning Star in the east, which they calculated took place every 584 days (the true figure is 583.92 days). While the Morning Star was thought to be the apotheosis of Topiltzin Quetzalcoatl, ruler of Tula, its heliacal rising was viewed as fraught with danger and they feared its rays at that time. It is a remarkable fact that every 104 Solar Years, all parts of their calendar coincided: the Almanac Year of 260 days, the Solar Year of 365 days, and the 584-day synodic period of Venus.

It was impressed on the Aztec mind that the close of every 52-year Calendar Round was a point at which the Fifth Sun could be destroyed. On this day, all fires in every temple, palace, and household were extinguished. On the Hill of the Star, just east of Colhuacan in the Basin of Mexico, the Fire Priests anxiously watched to see if the Pleiades (a particular cluster of stars) would cross the meridian at midnight on this date; if they did, then the universe would continue. A fire was kindled on fire-sticks in the newly opened breast of a captive, and the glowing embers were carried by runners to every part of the Aztec realm.

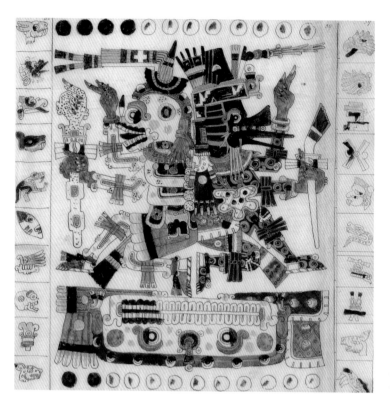

185 Page 56 from Codex Borgia (facsimile). This divination manual might have been painted in Cholula, Puebla. The manuscript is deerskin and is folded in screen fashion; it is 33 ft 9 in. (10.3 m) long and 10.7 in. (27 cm) wide. The scene illustrates Quetzalcoatl and Mictlantecuhtli, patron deities of the twenty thirteen-day cycles (260 days of the Sacred Calendar). The God of Wind presides over the initial days of the even thirteen-day cycles (right), the God of Death over the initial days of the odd thirteen-day cycles (left).

186 Page 55 from Codex Borgia (facsimile). The organization of the day names, of footprints in the two lowermost narrow bands, and the facing direction of the patron deities proceed in boustrophedon from bottom right to top left. The page may have been used to forecast propitious or inauspicious traveling (by journeyers, pilgrims, merchants, warring parties, or ambassadors). The presiding deities are the Sun God (days 1–2), the Goddess of Weaving (days 3, 4, 5), the God of Richness (first for days 6 through 9, then for days 10 through 13, and then for days 14 through 18). The series ends with the God of War (days 19–20). Late Post-Classic period.

All this complex information was recorded in pictorial folding-screen manuscripts of deerskin or bark paper, kept in the temples and seminaries by the priests (**figures 185, 186**). The state archives also included economic accounts, maps, and, possibly, historical works. It is a sad fact that, as a result of the massive book-burnings carried out by the Franciscan friars following the Conquest, no truly Aztec manuscripts from the Basin of Mexico have survived. The Codex Borbonicus, dating from the very early colonial period and preserved in the library of the National Assembly in Paris, probably comes close to how these may have looked.

The ritual round must have provided year-long excitement and meaning to the life of the ordinary citizen of Tenochtitlan, with feasts, decoration of religious images, and dances and songs to the accompaniment of two-toned slit drums, upright drums, conch-shell trumpets, rattles, and flutes. Homage to the deities prescribed individual penances and burning of blood-spattered paper, burning of perfumed copal incense, and immolation of human captives yearly.

As discussed on p. 229, the souls of warriors who had died under the sacrificial knife or on the field of battle went not to the Land of the Dead in the Underworld, but directly to the Paradise of the Sun God (**figure 187**). Curiously, so did the dread spirits of women who died in childbirth (for they also had fought their "warrior" and lost); they rose dutifully from the west each day to greet the sun at noon, conducting it into the nether regions. Others who also avoided extinction in Mictlan were those who had died in some manner connected with the Rain Deity: by lightning, drowning, or sufferers from edema and gout. They went to the Paradise of Tlaloc, where they spent an idyllic afterlife among flowers, butterflies, and other delights.

Most famous among the Aztec sacrifices was that of the handsome young captive annually chosen to impersonate the god Tezcatlipoca. For one year he lived a life of honor, worshipped literally as the embodiment of the deity; toward the end, he was given four beautiful maidens as his mistresses. Finally, he left them sadly, mounted the steps of the temple, smashing one by one the clay flutes that he had played in his brief moment of glory, then was flung on his back so that the flint dagger might be plunged into his breast.

187 Sacrificial knife of flint with mosaic-encrusted handle in the form of a man dressed as an eagle (the avatar of the sun, who fed it with human hearts). Aztec culture, Late Post-Classic period. Length 11.75 in. (30 cm).

188 Colossal statue of Coatlicue. The head and hands appear severed from the body, and snakes rise from the neck and wrists. Those at the top meet to form the face of a serpent. Her necklace is fashioned from human hearts and hands, with a pendant skull. The skirt is a web of writhing snakes. Since the goddess feeds on human corpses, her feet are tipped with claws. Aztec, Late Post-Classic period. Ht 8 ft 2 in. (2.5 m).

189 (OPPOSITE) Statue of Xochipilli, the Aztec "Prince of Flowers," patron god of dances, games, and love, and symbol of summertime. The god sits cross-legged on a throne adorned with a flower, fireflies, and clusters of four dots. He wears the facial flayed skin of a sacrificial victim and as breastplate the skin of an animal, including its eyes and pointed teeth. His body is decorated with flowers of different species. Aztec, Late Post-Classic period. Ht of figure with base 3 ft 11 in. (1.2 m).

Aztec Art and Architecture

The Aztecs were the greatest sculptors seen in Mexico since the demise of the Olmec civilization, capable of turning out masterpieces from tiny works in such semi-precious stones as rock crystal and amethyst, to truly monumental carvings. To some eyes, Aztec sculpture may be repulsive, and there is no doubt that the colossal figures of such deities as Coatlicue may be terrifying, but there is no denying their awesome power (**figure 188**). Power is also reflected in the more "realistic" works, for example the seated stone figure of Xochipilli ("Prince of Flowers," **figure 189**), the god of love and summertime, in which traditions of workmanship perfected by the Toltecs are continued. In the same vein is the remarkable sculptured drum from Malinalco (**figure 190**), which recalls the Nahuatl war song:

The earth shakes: the Mexica begins his song:
He makes the Eagles and Jaguars dance with him!
Come to see the Huexotzinca:
On the dais of the Eagle he shouts out,
Loudly cries the Mexica.[13]

Aztec artisans in Tenochtitlan were arranged in an approximation of guilds and were famous for their fine work in feather mosaics; but they were hardly rivals to the great craftsmen of the Cholula area, who produced a magnificent lacquer-type polychrome pottery. Moteuczoma himself would eat only from cups and plates of Cholula ware, and it is certain that much of the goldwork as well as practically all the

190 (ABOVE) Carved wooden drum (*huehuetl*) from Malinalco, State of Mexico. The drum is carved in relief with scenes representing the "Flowery," or Sacred, War, symbolized by dancing eagles and jaguars carrying the banners of "captives," the sign 4 Motion (the present age of the world), and, as seen here in the upper register, the figure of a man dressed as an eagle. The lower band depicts shields and the "Water-Fire" sign. Aztec, Late Post-Classic period. Ht 3 ft 9 in. (1.15 m).

191 Wooden funerary mask encrusted with turquoise mosaic and shell. This object was certainly one of the many gifts of Mexican workmanship that were shipped by Hernán Cortés to Charles V.

192 Facade of Building I, Malinalco, State of Mexico, a circular structure cut from the living rock. The work was carried out under orders from the Aztec emperors Ahuitzotl and Moteuczoma Xocoyotzin, between 1501 and 1515. The outer wall is now about 9 ft 10 in. (3 m) high. Entrance to the interior was gained through a sizable serpent face. Within, in the center of the floor, can be seen a stone seat in the shape of an eagle, and on the circular banquette at the back of the room, there is a jaguar stone seat in the middle, flanked by an eagle stone seat on either side.

193 Building I at Malinalco as it is today, with its reconstructed thatched roof.

fine masks and other ceremonial paraphernalia of wood encrusted with turquoise mosaic were also manufactured there and in Oaxaca. The stupendous collection of mosaic pieces once in the hands of Charles V and now in the British Museum, in Florence, and in Rome, bears eloquent testimony to late Mexican workmanship in this medium (**figure 191**), although most examples are said to have been stripped and the mosaic pieces recycled for new artworks in the *pietre dure* "laboratories" of Florence in the early nineteenth century.

Aztec architecture was primarily religious, rather than secular in nature. The leveling of the Sacred Precincts of Tenochtitlan and Tlatelolco by the Spaniards for their own administrative buildings, cathedral, and churches destroyed all but the foundations of the major Aztec temples, but some idea can be gained of their magnificence from those that remain elsewhere in the Basin of Mexico, for example, the huge double temple at Tenayuca, or the exceptional rock-carved administrative post at Malinalco, which was circular and probably served as an audience room where a council of four rulers conducted governmental functions (**figures 192, 193**).

It has long been known that the ruins of the Great Temple (or "Templo Mayor") of Tenochtitlan were located a short distance to the northeast of the cathedral, underneath the buildings of colonial and modern-day Mexico City

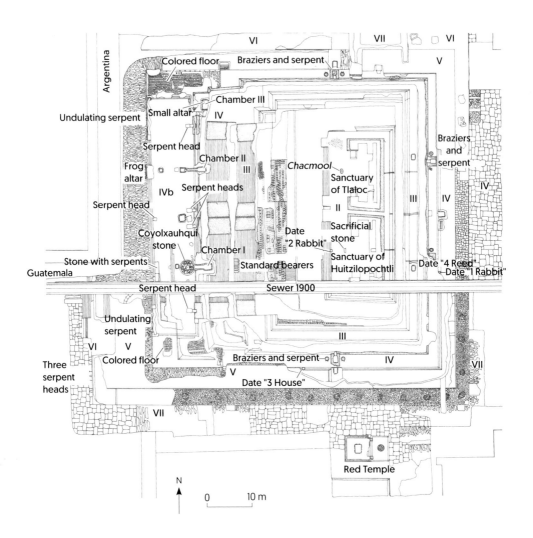

(**figures 194, 195, 196**). The chance discovery in 1978 of a huge oval monument by workers digging a pit for the installation of power transformers led to the rediscovery of the central Aztec temple and the start of the archaeological project that has now uncovered much of the central ceremonial precinct. The workers came first upon the monumental oval sculpture at the base of the Huitzilopochtli side of the temple, directly in front of one of seven successive rebuildings that the temple had undergone since its foundation. It bears on its upper surface a deep relief of the dismembered body of the goddess Coyolxauhqui, the malevolent sister of Huitzilopochtli, and is one of the masterpieces of Aztec sculptural art.

To understand the significance of this monument, we must recount the legend that lies behind it. Huitzilopochtli, the terrible warrior god of the sun, was the miraculous result of the impregnation of his widowed mother, ("She of the Serpent Skirt"), by a ball of feathers as she was sweeping one day on Coatepec ("Serpent Mountain"), near Tula. Angered by what they perceived as her dishonor, her four hundred sons (the stars of the southern sky), egged on by their sister Coyolxauhqui (almost

194 (OPPOSITE) Plan of the excavated foundations of the Great Temple, showing remains of the successive construction stages; the oldest is Stage II. The Coyolxauhqui Stone [**figure 197**, p. 244] is associated with Stage IV. The conquistadores would have seen Stage VI.

195 (RIGHT) Polychrome jars, stone masks, and other offerings found in Chamber III beneath Stage IVb of the Great Temple.

196 (BELOW) Depictions in stone of skulls on a *tzompantli* or skull rack, excavated in the Great Temple precinct.

197 Colossal stone relief of the dismembered goddess
Coyolxauhqui, discovered at the foot of an earlier stage
of the Great Temple of Tenochtitlan. Coyolxauhqui's head
is severed and her cheek is marked with the golden bell
that identifies the goddess. The Nahuatl term Coyolxauhqui
means "the one with jingle bells on her face." Aztec culture,
Late Post-Classic period. Longest dimension 11 ft 2 in. (3.4 m).

198 Excavations in progress at the Great Temple site, looking northeast. The oldest remaining pyramid-platform (Stage II Temple) lies under the protective roof on the right. The Coyolxauhqui Stone can be seen beneath the scaffolding near the center of the picture.

certainly an avatar of the Moon), attempted to kill her. Huitzilopochtli emerged fully armed from Coatlicue's womb, and slew his sister Coyolxauhqui, hurling her body down from the summit of Coatepec, then pursued and defeated his four hundred brothers—surely an astral myth of the defeat by the sun of the moon and the stars (**figure 197**).

The importance of the account, and of its confirmation by the find of the oval monument, is that the Huitzilopochtli side of the Great Temple was known to the Aztecs as "Coatepec." This suggests there was a representation of Coyolxauhqui in front of each successive Huitzilopochtli pyramid, and such seems to have been the case, since two earlier versions of the goddess were found in the right position in older renovations. Coyolxauhqui was only one of a number of particularly powerful female deities represented in monumental sculptures associated with the Great Temple (**figure 198**).

199 (ABOVE) Monumental image of Tlaltecuhtli, the devouring earth goddess of the Aztecs. This colossal stone (*c.* 10 by 13 ft; 3 by 4 m), discovered near the Great Temple, is the most sizable known Aztec stone monument.

200 Reconstruction of original paint color on the Tlaltecuhtli stone, based on extensive paint remnants still adhering to the stone. Reconstruction by Julio Romero and Luz María Muñoz of the Templo Mayor Project.

A spectacular relief of the female version of Tlaltecuhtli was found embedded in the plaza floor just to the west of the Coyolxauhqui monument and on the central axis of the pyramid (**figure 199**). The monument is even larger than the famous Sun Stone or the Coyolxauhqui monument. Because it was covered by yet another plaza floor within twenty years of its creation, it retains significant traces of the ocher, red, and blue paint that once decorated its entire surface. Polychrome sculpture was surely an ancient Mesoamerican tradition, but the preservation of such extensive paint remnants as we see here is rare. Conservators of the Templo Mayor Project were quick to stabilize the pigments, allowing the team to reconstruct a fully colored version (**figure 200**). The top of the monument shows a head framed by claws. The hair is curly—a sign of untidiness for the Aztecs—and has paper banners emerging from the curls in a reference to sacrifice. Blood streams into the mouth from the now destroyed abdomen area. The woven short skirt and the squatting pose at the base of the monument indicate that this is the female version of this voracious deity.

Tlaltecuhtli (Lord and Lady Earth) and related deities were also associated with earthquakes and, as such, the destruction of the current world era—a theme also evident in the Sun Stone (see **figure 181**, p. 232), which was likely set up nearby (and was also once covered in the same reds, ochers, and blues seen in the Tlaltecuhtli stone). Cecilia Klein and Elizabeth Boone have reassessed several monumental female sculptures around the Templo Mayor, including the giant standing "Coatlicue," and found that these are all associated with the *tzitzimime*—the mainly female star demons associated with childbirth, war, and ancestor contact, who were also responsible for devouring the population if the sun should fail. It is interesting to note, as Boone does, that these powerful stellar goddesses were shown decapitated here, perhaps signaling their defeat at the hands of the Aztec patron Huitzilopochtli, just as Coyolxauhqui was defeated and dismembered by that same god.

Immediately underneath the Tlaltecuhtli monument, archaeologist Leonardo López Luján found a stepped depression that led down to a spectacular series of dedicatory offerings. Approximately 15,000 items were buried in these deposits, including small-scale sculptures and many sacrificed animals. Much of the sea life found in this deposit was from the Pacific side of the Aztec empire, where the emperor Ahuitzotl (r. 1486–1502) had his greatest military success. Archaeologists believe that it was Ahuitzotl who commissioned the Tlaltecuhtli monument: the associated offerings served to sacralize the area while pointing to Ahuitzotl's military prowess.

Any discussion of the Great Temple owes a great deal to the remarkable archaeological work done there in the last several decades under Eduardo Matos Moctezuma and Leonardo López Luján. From its earliest stages until the latest, the temple was split between a right-hand or southern half, dedicated to the sun cult of Huitzilopochtli, and a left-hand or northern half devoted to the worship of the Rain Deity, Tlaloc. In the offering caches in the latter were found marvelous, blue-painted Tlaloc vases in both pottery and stone, along with such items as shells and coral imported from the sea, while a sacrificial stone is still in place in the floor of an early stage of the Huitzilopochtli shrine and a *chacmool* in the corresponding

201 Sculpture in the Toltec style of a recumbent *chacmool* in the Sanctuary of Tlaloc, Stage II of the Great Temple. Such figures, common at Tula, indicate the importance that the Toltec cultural heritage had to the nascent Aztec state.

shrine to Tlaloc (**figure 201**). Sculpted serpents emerging from the northern side of the platform were painted with blue highlights, to connect them with the wet fecundity of the Rain Deity, while those on the southern side of the platform were given yellow highlights to emphasize their connection with solar heat (and the warlike solar deity Huitzilopochtli). The Great Temple was the conceptual center of the Aztec universe, so it is no surprise that this immense construction expressed the ancient duality implicit in all Aztec life: the contrast between rain and crop fertility on the one hand, and war and the continued survival of the Fifth Sun on the other.

Aztec Thought and Literature

The amount of surviving literature in the Nahuatl language is truly remarkable; written down in the letters of the European alphabet after the fall of the Aztec nation, these texts have given us a view into native philosophy that has no parallel elsewhere in the Americas. The language used by Aztec poets and thinkers is richly metaphorical, making abundant use of double epithet, in which paired nouns have a third, inner meaning, for example:

Nahuatl	Translation	Meaning
Atl, tepetl	Water, mountain	City
Cuitlapilli, atlapilli	Tail, wing	The commoners
Petlatl, icpalli	Mat, seat	Rulership
Teoatl, tlachinolli	Divine water, blaze	War
Yollotli, eztli	Heart, blood	Cacao
Topco, petlacalco	In a box, in a coffer	Secretly
Teuhtli, tlazolli	Dust, filth	Evil, vice
Mixtitloan, ayautitlan	Out of the clouds, out of the mist	A wonder

References to deities in the prayers and hymns are often shrouded in epithets, the divinity seldom being addressed by his or her true name. This was especially true of the awesome Tezcatlipoca, for whom were reserved such terms as "Lord of the Near, of the Nigh" (an epithet mistakenly applied by the early friars to the Christian God), "Night, Wind," "The Enemy on Both Sides," or "The Mocker." To be able to narrate such discourse, and to understand it, was the mark of an educated person.

The most stylized of these texts were the *Huehuetlatolli*, the "Orations of the Elders": didactic discourses directed to children in the *calmecac* and *telpochcalli*, as well as to adults, which were highly embellished with these literary devices. Book 6 of Sahagún's encyclopedia of Aztec life presents these stock speeches in abundance, including the orations of parents to children, and orations delivered during *pochteca* banquets. From them, one may learn something of the mentality that enabled the Aztec people not only to survive misfortunes, disasters, and privations that would have broken others, but also to create one of the most complex political states ever seen in Mexico. Raised in the sternest fashion in their homes and schools, trained to withstand cold and hunger, Aztec individuals embodied ideals that would have done credit to an "old Roman." Self-restraint and humility were expected even of those whose fortunes soared, including the emperors themselves.

> The mature man:
> a heart as firm as stone,
> a wise countenance,
> the owner of a face, a heart,
> capable of understanding.[14]

Not for them the megalomaniac self-esteem and lust for riches exhibited—to the Aztec disgust—by the Spaniards!

The image of the Aztec people as bloodthirsty savages bent only on rapine and murder—an image carefully fostered by the conquistadores—is belied by the great compendium of Nahuatl poetry preserved to us in the *Cantares Mexicanos*. Poetry was known as *in xochitl, in cuicatl*, "flowers, songs," and was recited in the royal courts to the accompaniment of the *teponaztli*, a log slit-drum played with rubber-tipped drumsticks; the tones and beats of the drum are given in onomatopoeic syllables for some poems, for example, "*totocoto tototo cototo tiquititi titiqui tiquito.*" Although some of the compositions celebrate war and death on the "flowery field" (the battleground), through many of them there runs a singular streak of melancholy and pessimism, a philosophical theme particularly developed by the closely allied Texcocan royal house, known for its learning and cultivation. The transitory nature of life on this earth and the uncertainty of the hereafter appear in a song ascribed to the *tlatoani* Nezahualcoyotl, the poet-king of Texcoco:

> I, Nezahualcoyotl, ask this:
> Is it true one really lives on the earth?
> Not forever on earth,

only a little while here.
Though it be jade it falls apart,
though it be gold it wears away
Not forever on earth,
only a little while here.[15]

To another poet, Tochihuitzin Coyolchiuhqui, life itself is an illusion:

Thus spoke Tochihuitzin,
thus spoke Coyolchiuhqui:
We only rise from sleep,
we only come to dream,
it is not true, it is not true,
that we come on earth to live.
As an herb in springtime,
so is our nature.
Our hearts give birth, make sprout,
the flowers of our flesh.
Some open their corollas,
then they become dry.
Thus spoke Tochihuitzin,
thus spoke Coyolchiuhqui.[16]

Yet finally Nezahualcoyotl came to the realization that "flowers, songs" never perish, and it is only through them that the truly wise man will approach the ultimate reality, the dual creator divinity in whom all things are contained, the Giver of Life. As an artist paints a manuscript, so he has painted us with flowers and songs:

With flowers You paint,
O Giver of life!
With songs You give color,
with songs You shade
those who will live on the earth.
Later You will destroy eagles and jaguars:
we live only in Your painting
here, on the earth.
With black ink You will blot out
all that was friendship,
brotherhood, nobility.
You give shading
to those who will live on the earth.
We live only in Your book of paintings,
here on the earth.[17]

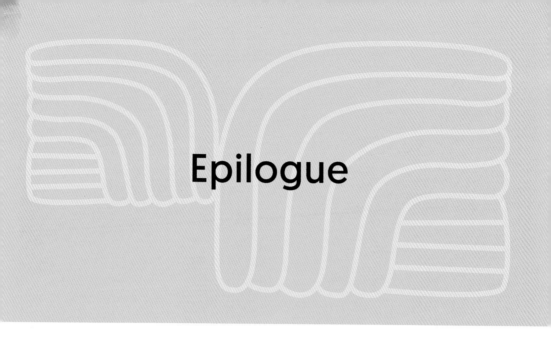

Epilogue

The Spanish Conquest

To the victor go not only the spoils, as the old saw would have it, but also the opportunity to tell the story of a victory without fear of contradiction. The Spaniards and generations of historians, including even the renowned William Prescott, have presented the Conquest of Mexico by a handful of brave and resourceful soldiers as the inevitable consequence of the cultural superiority of European over native cultures. As the Aztec scholar Inga Clendinnen has forcefully put it, "Historians are the camp-followers of the imperialists." Thanks to a closer and more critical reading of the sources, we can now see that there was considerable rewriting and often blatant distortion of the course of events, even with such otherwise reliable figures as Father Sahagún. Particularly untrustworthy are the self-serving letters of Hernán Cortés to his sovereign Charles V, since that wily commander was acting illegally and without royal permission throughout his campaigns on Mexican soil.

In the history partially fabricated by the Spaniards, the Aztecs' terrible destiny had been preordained in the weak and vacillating figure of Moteuczoma Xocoyotzin, held spellbound by a series of sinister omens, and by the myth of the "returning god-ruler": that Topiltzin Quetzalcoatl had come back in the person of Cortés himself. According to these accounts, now held in suspicion by specialists in Aztec culture, strange portents had appeared to the terrified monarch in the final ten years of his reign. The first of these was a great comet "like a tongue of fire, like a flame, as if showering the light of the dawn."[18] Then, in succession, a tower of the Great Temple burned mysteriously; the water of the lake foamed and boiled and flooded the capital; and a woman was heard crying in the night through the streets of Tenochtitlan. Two-headed men were discovered and brought to the ruler, but they vanished as soon as he looked at them. Worst of all, fisherfolk snared a bird similar to a crane, which had a mirror on its forehead; they showed it to

202 Nezahualpilli, *tlatoani* of Texcoco, attired for a dance. From the Codex Ixtlilxochitl, folio 108r.

Moteuczoma in broad daylight, and when he gazed into the mirror, he saw the shining stars. Looking a second time, he saw armed men borne on the backs of deer. He consulted his soothsayers, who could tell him nothing, but Nezahualpilli, King of Texcoco, forecast the destruction of Mexico-Tenochtitlan (**figure 202**).

Inflicting great cruelties on his magicians for their inability to forestall the doom that he saw impending, the Aztec monarch was said to be dumbfounded when an uncouth man arrived one day from the Gulf Coast and demanded to be taken into his presence. "I come," he announced, "to advise you that a great mountain has been seen on the waters, moving from one part to the other, without touching the rocks." Clapping the wretch in jail, he dispatched two trusted messengers to the coast to determine if this was so. When they returned they confirmed the story, adding that strange men with white faces and hands and long beards had set off in a boat from "a house on the water." Secretly convinced that these were Quetzalcoatl and his companions, Moteuczoma had the sacred livery of the god and food of the land offered to them, which they immediately took back to their watery home; this was said to confirm his surmises. The gods had left some of their own foods in the form of sweet-tasting biscuits on the beach; the monarch ordered the holy wafers to be placed in a gilded gourd, covered with rich cloths, and carried by a procession of chanting priests to Tula of the Toltecs, where they were reverently interred in the ruins of Quetzalcoatl's temple.

The "mountain that moved" was in reality the Spanish ship commanded by Juan de Grijalva, which, after skirting the coast of Yucatan, made the first Spanish landing on Mexican soil in the year 1518, near modern Veracruz. This reconnaissance was followed up in 1519 by the armada that embarked from Cuba under the leadership of Hernán Cortés. The people of the Gulf Coast, some of whom were vassals of the Aztec *Huei Tlatoani*, put up little resistance to these strange beings, and Cortés soon learned of their disaffection with the Aztec state and with the heavy tribute that they had been forced to pay. On their way to the Basin of Mexico and the heart of the empire, the conquistadores met with opposition from the Tlaxcallans; after crushing these fierce enemies of the Triple Alliance, Cortés gained them as willing allies (**figure 203**). The Tlaxcallans would come to play a key role in the overthrow of Mexica civilization.

A figure crucial to Cortés's plans was his indigenous interpreter and mistress, known to history as La Malinche. This intelligent woman was of noble birth, and had been presented to Cortés by a merchant prince of coastal Tabasco. Much of his success in dealing with the Aztecs must be attributed to the astuteness and understanding of this remarkable personage. But misunderstandings nevertheless seem to have been the rule in the confrontation and clash of these two cultures. For instance, far from being held in thrall by a view of Cortés as the returned Quetzalcoatl, in actuality Moteuczoma appears to have dealt with him as what he said he was: an ambassador from a distant and unknown ruler. As such, Cortés had to be treated with respect and hospitality. Welcomed into the great capital and even into the royal palace, Cortés chose to take his host captive, to the chagrin and disgust of the *Huei Tlatoani*'s subjects.

The dénouement of this tragic story is well known. Learning that a rival military expedition under Pánfilo de Narváez had been sent to Veracruz by his enemy, the governor of Cuba, with orders for his arrest, Cortés moved down to the coast and defeated the interlopers. On his return to Tenochtitlan, he found the capital in full

203 Cortés and nobles of the Tlaxcallan state, 1519 CE. The alliance between the conquistadores and Tlaxcallans was significant in contributing to the overthrow of the Aztec empire. From the *Lienzo de Tlaxcala*.

revolt. During the uprising, Moteuczoma was killed—the Spaniards being possible perpetrators—and the booty-laden conquistadores were forced to flee the city by night, with great loss of life.

This ended the first phase of the Conquest. Withdrawing to the friendly sanctuary of Tlaxcallan, the invaders recovered their strength while Cortés made new plans. Eventually, both armies met in a pitched battle on the plains near Otumba, a confrontation in which Spanish arms triumphed. Then, joined by his allies from Tlaxcallan, Cortés once again marched against Tenochtitlan, building an invasion fleet along the shores of the Great Lake. The siege of Tenochtitlan began in May 1521, and ended after a heroic defense led by Cuauhtemoc, the last of the Aztec emperors, on 13 August of that year. There then ensued a bloodbath at the hands of the revengeful Tlaxcallans that sickened even the most battle-hardened conquistadores. Although Cortés received Cuauhtemoc with honor, he had him hanged, drawn, and quartered three years later. The Fifth Sun had indeed perished.

How was it that a tiny force of about 400 men had been able to overthrow a powerful empire of at least 11 million people? First of all, the Spaniards fought side by side with many indigenous allies. The role played by thousands upon thousands of seasoned Tlaxcallan warriors—the deadliest enemies of the Triple Alliance—can hardly be overlooked. Not only were they vital to the defeat of the Aztec empire, but they continued to serve as an auxiliary army in the conquest of the rest of Mesoamerica, even participating in the takeover of the highland Maya states.

A second factor was the different rules of engagement. The Spaniards fought by rules other than those that had prevailed for millennia in Mesoamerica. To the Aztecs, as Inga Clendinnen has noted, "battle was ideally a sacred duel between matched warriors"; in fact, before the Aztecs waged war on a town or province, they would often send them arms to make sure that the contenders were so matched. The "level playing field" meant nothing to the Spaniards, whom the Aztecs perceived as cowards—they shot their weapons at a distance, avoided hand-to-hand combat with native warriors, and took refuge behind their cannons; the Spaniards' horses were held in far higher estimation! Equally incomprehensible and, therefore, devastating to the Aztecs' defense was the Spanish policy of wholesale terror, so well exemplified by the act of Cortés in cutting off the hands of over fifty Tlaxcallan emissaries admitted in peace into the Spanish camp, or the massacre of vast numbers of unarmed warriors at the order of the terrible Pedro de Alvarado, while they were dancing at a feast.

Thirdly, there is the difference in warfare technology. The weaponry of these men of the Renaissance was a mismatch to the lithic and wood armament and the thick cotton-padded body protection of the Aztecs. Thundering cannon, steel swords wielded by mounted horsemen, steel armor, crossbows, and mastiff-like war dogs previously trained in the Antilles to savor the flesh of humans: all contributed to the Aztec downfall.

But most significant of all was that invisible and deadly ally brought by the invaders from Europe: infectious disease, to which the native population of Mesoamerica had absolutely no resistance. Smallpox was apparently introduced by a sailor who arrived with the Narváez expedition of 1520, and ravaged Mexico; it had decimated central Mexico even before Cortés began his siege. Along with measles, whooping cough, and malaria (and perhaps yellow fever as well), it led to a terrible mortality that must have enormously reduced the size and effectiveness of Aztec field forces and led to a general feeling of despair and hopelessness among the population. Given these four factors, it is a wonder that Aztec resistance lasted as long as it did. The completeness of the Aztec defeat is poignantly defined in an Aztec lament:

> Broken spears lie in the roads;
> we have torn our hair in our grief.
> The houses are roofless now, and their walls
> are red with blood.
> Worms are swarming in the streets and plazas,
> and the walls are splattered with gore.
> The water has turned red, as if it were dyed,
> and when we drink it,
> it has the taste of brine.
> We have pounded our hands in despair
> against the adobe walls,
> for our inheritance, our city, is lost and dead.
> The shields of our warriors were its defense,
> but they could not save it.[19]

New Spain and the Colonial World

Within the space of about three years following the fall of Tenochtitlan, most of Mexico between the Isthmus of Tehuantepec and the Chichimec frontier had fallen to the Spaniards and their Tlaxcallan allies. During this period, there were a number of indigenous revolts (such as occurred among the Tarascans), but these were quickly suppressed. This vast territory became organized as New Spain, with a viceroy responsible to the Spanish king through the Council of the Indies.

The conquistadores had not been ordinary soldiers, but adventurers expecting riches. To placate them, the Crown granted them *encomiendas*, in which each *encomendero* would receive tribute payments from vast numbers of Native Americans; in return, the *encomendero* would ensure that their souls would be saved through conversion to Christianity. In time, this led to incredible abuses against the indigenous population, and in 1549 a new system, *repartimiento*, was substituted, in which they were supposed to get fair wages for their labor. Through the cupidity of their Spanish overlords and bureaucratic abuse, however, *repartimiento* swiftly turned into a system of forced labor.

Almost immediately following the Conquest, Mexico's social, economic, and religious life was transformed; even the landscape suffered immense changes. The fate of the elite class that had ruled the old pre-Spanish cities was twofold: many of them lost their economic and political clout, and with them the elite culture that they had created, while others—perhaps more pliant—were given titles by the new regime and used as tribute and labor gatherers; it was these latter who were significant agents of acculturation, as they were converted to the new religion and learned the Castilian language.

The great cities and towns of pre-Spanish Mexico were leveled, along with thousands of temples perceived by the Spaniards as "pagan," to be replaced by urban settlements laid out on the grid pattern favored by the authorities in urban New Spain. The old *calpoltin* became wards, and the *calpolli* temples parish churches.

The economic transformation of Mexico began with the introduction of chickens, pigs, and the herd animals so important to life in Europe, cattle, horses, sheep, and goats (the two latter contributing to the destruction of the landscape through overgrazing); iron tools and the plow; European fruit trees; and such crops as wheat and chickpeas (the Spaniards initially spurned native foods such as maize and beans). The *repartimiento* system led to the growth of vast haciendas, at first dependent upon forced labor; after abolition in later centuries, this was transformed into debt bondage, a state of affairs that was to last until the Mexican Revolution. New Spain proved to be the Spanish empire's richest source of silver, and hundreds of thousands of indigenous people were put to work in the silver mines under the most terrible conditions.

In line with the doctrine promulgated by the papacy—that the people of the Western hemisphere had souls and, therefore, must not be enslaved but converted to the True Faith—the conquistadores were truly serious about conversion. This task was placed in the hands of the mendicant orders, and twelve Franciscan friars duly arrived in the newly founded Mexico City (built on the ruins of Mexico-Tenochtitlan); as they walked unshod and in patched robes through the city's streets, the native population was truly awestruck by their poverty and sincerity. The Franciscans viewed indigenous people with paternalistic kindliness, and saw them as raw material on which to fashion a new Utopian world, free from the sins that were so apparent in the Spanish settlers. They quickly learned Nahuatl and other native languages, and began early to instruct the sons of the indigenous nobility in Christian values and learning. Naturally, they came into frequent conflict with the *encomenderos*. Other orders soon followed: Augustinians, Dominicans, and eventually the Jesuits.

Conversion, though, was often only skin deep and, later on in the sixteenth century, the secular and religious clergy came to recognize this. The basic similarity between many aspects of the Aztec religion and Spanish Catholicism has led to a syncretism between the two that persists today in many parts of Mexico: there truly were (and often are) "idols behind altars." The Church's attempts to stamp out "paganism," however, were hampered by the exemption that indigenous groups had from the investigations of the Inquisition, and many old beliefs and practices flourished, particularly in the field of medicine.

Away from the mines and the great haciendas, many indigenous communities preserved their self-sufficiency, and had their own lands. These were known as "*Repúblicas de Indios*," and were organized on the Spanish *cabildo* system of town administration. On top was an elected governor, in early years often an indigenous noble. Below him were *alcaldes* (judges for minor crimes or civil suits) and *regidores* (councilors who legislated laws for local matters). At first, all electors were from the nobility, but as this dwindled, the commoners or *macehualtin* took over. Under the friars' tutelage, indigenous communities had adopted the religious confraternities so important to Spanish life, and these became intertwined with the *cabildo* system: one advanced in this civil religious hierarchy through a series of cargos, or burdensome offices (for example peace officer, tax collector, or scribe), and as they achieved ever higher rank and honor, they were expected to give increasing amounts of time to their ritual duties, and to hold ever more costly public feasts. One can see such a hierarchy in many indigenous communities today.

The "Ladinoization" of Mexico

As historian Woodrow Borah has demonstrated, after 1600, New Spain entered a profound "Century of Depression," when supplies of both food and labor suffered an enormous drop. That this was a direct result of a crash in the indigenous population is shown by the following figures: in 1519, on the eve of the Conquest, there were an estimated eleven million people in central Mexico; by the close of the sixteenth century, there were only about two-and-a-half million people left, and by 1650 no more than one-and-a-half million, just 13.6 percent of the pre-Conquest total. While the Spanish clergy was prone to ascribe this demographic disaster to the allegedly drunken habits of their charges, it is clear that the major cause was a series of great epidemics, beginning in 1520 but especially drastic in 1545–46 and 1576–79. Intolerable working conditions in the silver mines and on the great estates certainly added to the toll.

At the same time as this collapse of the indigenous demographic, the white and mestizo (mixed) population was steadily increasing. When the great sugarcane haciendas were established in the Gulf Coast lowlands, such landowners as Cortés had imported African slaves, and these certainly contributed to the biological mixture in those areas. But it was the people of mixed indigenous-white ancestry, or *ladinos* as they are known, who came to represent the majority of the Mexican people, at least toward the end of the European colonial era. Peninsular Spanish notions of purity of race and superiority of the Catholic religion were transformed during the centuries to a system of values in which hispanicized people of light skin, wearing European clothing and living in or near the center of a community, who had Spanish surnames, and were able to read and write, were considered inherently superior to the darker skinned, "superstitious," frequently illiterate indigenous people. Accordingly, the *ladinos* came to occupy the middle rank of the political and economic hierarchy, while indigenous people occupied the lowest. This is the situation that still prevails in many parts of Mexico. If there had been no demographic catastrophe among the native population, their political and cultural status would have been very different indeed.

Aftermath

This state of affairs became further entrenched through the centuries. Eventually, myriad sociopolitical developments (including, but certainly not limited to, the Napoleonic invasion of Spain in 1808, the French Revolution and American Revolution, an economic crisis in New Spain, and growing dissatisfaction among the *ladino* population), led to Mexico achieving independence from Spain by 1821. This did little, however, to ameliorate the oppression of its indigenous people; in fact, the Spanish Crown and the Church had been the principal protectors of indigenous rights throughout Spanish colonial history, against the abuses of the settlers. For much of the nineteenth century, Mexico was in the throes of continuous wars, a situation only brought to an end with the dictatorial regime of Porfirio Díaz, himself a primarily Zapotec *ladino* from Oaxaca.

The Mexican Revolution, which began in 1910, brought sweeping changes to the Mexican countryside, and therefore to the indigenous population, who were mainly poor, rural peasants. The old haciendas were broken up and the land distributed to farming communities in the form of *ejidos*, communal land-holding groups supposedly based (according to Revolutionary ideology) on Aztec institutions. Debt slavery was abolished.

Especially under the radical presidency (1934–40) of Lázaro Cárdenas, the rights of indigenous people to economic well-being were at last recognized by the Mexican government. With the establishment of a National Indigenous Institute, rural schools and economic assistance centers were set up in indigenous communities. But the goal of these government programs remained the incorporation of these communities into "national life," in other words "ladinoization" in modern dress. Every effort was made to wean people away from their language and from their traditional culture, a process that was accelerated in some areas where massive hydroelectric projects have uprooted many thousands of people from their traditional lands.

As is also the case with "Fourth World" populations elsewhere in the "Third World," where rapid economic development is the national goal, the right of Mexico's original inhabitants to their own cultures and their own languages is under constant threat. Yet, even though a world of change may be upon them, the resilience of indigenous groups, together with their struggle to maintain their cultural integrity, remains a guiding force.

The Principal Domestic Plants
of Pre-Spanish Mesoamerica

Common name	Latin name	Comments
* Avocado	*Persea americana*	
Agave (century plant)	*Agave* spp.	Fiber from leaves, pulque from base of flower stalk
Amaranth	*Amaranthus hybridus*	Pot herb, grain
* Annatto	*Bixa orellana*	Flavoring, food coloring
* Arrowroot	*Maranta arundinacea*	Root crop
Black nightshade	*Solanum nigrum*	Pot herb
Black sapote	*Diosbyros ebenaster*	Fruit tree
Bottle gourd	*Lagenaria siceraria*	Container
* Cacao	*Theobroma cacao*	Beans, the source of chocolate, used for money
* Calabash tree	*Crescentia cujete*	Rind of fruit used as container
* Cashew	*Anacardium occidentale*	Fruit tree
Chayote	*Sechium edule*	Squash-like fruit
Chia	*Salvia hispanica*	Seeds used for beverage, oil
Chile pepper	*Capsicum frutescens, C. annuum*	
Common bean	*Phaseolus vulgaris*	
Copal	*Protium copal*	Resin used as incense
Cotton	*Gossypium hirsutum*	
Dahlia	*Dahlia* spp.	Flower
Goosefoot	*Chenopodium* spp.	Pot herb
* Guava	*Psidium guajava*	Fruit tree
* Hog plum	*Spondias mombin*	Fruit tree
Husk tomato or tomatillo	*Physalis ixocarpa*	Vegetable
Indigo	*Indigofera suffruticosa*	Dye
Jack bean	*Canavalia ensiformis*	
Jícama	*Pachyrhizus erosus*	
Maize	*Zea mays*	
* Manioc	*Manihot esculenta*	Root crop
Marigold	*Tagetes erecta*	Flower, medicine
* Papaya	*Carica papaya*	Fruit tree
Peanut	*Arachis hypogaea*	Of Andean origin
* Pitahaya	*Hylocereus undatus*	Fruit of epiphytic cactus
Prickly pear	*Opuntia* spp.	Fruit and cactus pods eaten
Pumpkin	*Cucurbita pepo*	
* Rubber	*Castilla elastica*	Trunk tapped for latex
* Sapota	*Pouteria mammosa*	Fruit tree
Scarlet runner-bean	*Phaseolus coccineus*	
* Soursop	*Annona muricata*	Fruit tree
* Star-apple	*Chrysophyllum cainito*	Fruit tree
Sweet potato	*Ipomoea batatas*	
Tepary bean	*Phaseolus acutifolius*	
Tobacco	*Nicotiana tabacum*	
Tomato	*Lysopersicon esculentum*	
* Vanilla	*Vanilla planifolia*	An epiphytic orchid
Walnut squash	*Cucurbita mixta*	
Warty (crookneck) squash	*Cucurbita moschata*	
White sapota	*Casimiroa edulis*	Fruit tree
* Yam bean	*Pachyrhizus erosus*	Has edible tuber
Yucca	*Yucca elephantipes*	Hedges; flowers edible

* grown mainly in the lowlands

Chronological Table

Dates (cal.)	Periods	Central Highlands	North and Central Gulf	Southern Gulf Coast	Oaxaca	Significant Developments
1521					Chila	Spanish Conquest, fall of Tenochtitlan
	Late Post-Classic	Aztec Empire	Isla de Sacrificios	Independent states	Mitla, City-states	Aztec Triple Alliance formed
1200		City-states				Aztecs claim to have reached the Basin of Mexico
	Early Post-Classic	Tollan			Liobaa	Toltec State
900		Mazapan				
				Villa Alta		
	Epiclassic		El Tajín		Xoo	Competing regional capitals
650		Coyotlatelco				Destruction of Teotihuacan
		Metepec	Late Remojadas		Peche	
	Classic	Xolalpan-Tlamimilolpa (Teotihuacan III)	Classic Veracruz	Cerro de las Mesas Late Tres Zapotes	Pitao	Height of Teotihuacan influence
		Miccaotli (Teotihuacan II)			Tani	
150				La Mojarra		Isthmian script
CE / BCE		Tzacualli (Teotihuacan I)	Early Remojadas		Nisa	Building of Pyramid of the Sun, city planning at Teotihuacan Invention of Long Count calendar
	Late Formative			Early Tres Zapotes		
		Chupícuaro Cuicuilco			Pe	
400		Ticomán				
		Zacatenco			Danibaan	Construction of Monte Albán First writing at San José Mogote
	Middle Formative			La Venta	Rosario	Spread of La Venta Olmec influence
		Chalcatzingo				
		El Arbolillo		Nacaste	Guadalupe	
1200				San Lorenzo B		
		Tlatilco { Manantial, Ayotla	El Trapiche	San Lorenzo A	San José	Spread of San Lorenzo Olmec influence Early Olmec civilization at San Lorenzo
	Early Formative			Chicharras Bajío Ojochi	Tierras Largas	
		Nevada-Tlalpan				Origins of village life, pottery, figurines
1800		Purrón?			Gheo-Shih, Oaxaca Archaic	
	Archaic	Abejas				Early agriculture; hunting, fishing, gathering

Reigning Monarchs of the Aztec State

Acamapichtli (1375–1395)
Huitzilihuitl (1396–1417)
Chimalpopoca (1417–1426)
Itzcoatl (1427–1440)
Moteuczoma Ilhuicamina (1440–1469)
Axayacatl (1469–1481)
Tizoc (1481–1486)
Ahuitzotl (1486–1502)
Moteuczoma Xocoyotzin (1502–1520)
Cuitlahuac (1520)
Cuauhtemoc (1520–1525)

Text References

References 1–5, 8, and 11–14 were translated by Michael D. Coe from Spanish versions of the original Nahuatl texts. Other translations are as follows: 7, A. P. Maudslay; 9, Louise Burkhart (unpublished translation); 10, Charles E. Dibble and Arthur J. O. Anderson; 15–17, 19, Miguel Léon-Portilla; 18, Anthony Pagden.

1. M. Léon-Portilla, *Los Antiguos Mexicanos a través de sus Crónicas y Cantares*, (Mexico City: Fondo de Cultura Económica, 1961), 1–2.
2. Ibid., 23.
3. Ibid., 26–7.
4. A. M. Garibay, *Historia de Literatura Nahuatl*, (Mexico City: Porrúa, 1953–4), 316.
5. M. Léon-Portilla, *Los Antiguos Mexicanos*, 33.
6. P. Bíró and E. Pérez de Heredia. "El Disco de El Caracol de Chichén Itzá (929-932 CE). Algunas Consideraciones de Epigrafía e Iconografía." *Estudios de Cultura Maya*, no. 48 (2016): 129–62.
7. B. Díaz del Castillo, *The Discovery and Conquest of Mexico*, (London: Routledge and Kegan Paul, 1938). By permission.
8. M. Léon-Portilla, *Los Antiguos Mexicanos*, 63.
9. B. de Sahagún, *General History of the Things of New Spain*, Book 6, (Santa Fe, NM: School of American Research, 1969). By permission.
10. Ibid. 42. By permission.
11. A. M. Garibay, *Historia de Literatura Nahuatl*, 76.
12. Ibid., 215.
13. A. M. Garibay, *Poesia Nahuatl*, vol. 3, (Mexico City: Universidad Nacional Autónoma de México, Instituto de Investigaciones Históricas, 1968), 20.
14. M. Léon-Portilla, *Los Antiguos Mexicanos*, 147.
15. M. Léon-Portilla, *Fifteen Poets of the Aztec World*, (Norman, OK: University of Oklahoma Press, 1992), 80.
16. Ibid., 153.
17. Ibid., 83.
18. H. Cortés, *Letters from Mexico*, trans. and ed. A. Pagden, (New Haven and London: Yale University Press, 1986).
19. M. Léon-Portilla, *The Broken Spears: Aztec Accounts of the Conquest of Mexico*, (Boston, MA: Beacon Press, 1966), 137–8.

Further Reading

This is by no means an exhaustive coverage of Mexican archaeology; rather, the below is a list of works used to prepare this and previous editions, which might be profitably consulted for further information.

Several ongoing journals contain up-to-date articles on the subject; especially recommended are *Ancient Mesoamerica*, *Estudios de Cultura Nahuatl*, *Mexicon*, and *Arqueología Mexicana*. The various volumes resulting from the Dumbarton Oaks Conferences also present significant advances in the field. Extremely useful are the comprehensive encyclopedias by Nichols and Pool (2012), Evans and Webster (2001), and Carrasco (2001).

Significant internet sources include Mesoweb (www.mesoweb.com) and the indispensable Bibliografía Mesoamericana (research.famsi.org/mesobib.html).

Aramoni Burghete, María Elena. *El Mundo Prehispánico de Guanajuato. Plazuelas: Lugar de la Serpiente de Fuego*. Mexico City: Instituto Nacional de Antropología e Historia, 2014. (Report of some of the most salient discoveries at the Epiclassic site of Plazuelas.)

Aveleyra Arroyo de Anda, Luis. "The Primitive Hunters." In *Handbook of Middle American Indians* 1, ed. Robert Wauchope and Robert C. West, 384–412. Austin, TX: University of Texas Press, 1964. (Excellent treatment of the Early Hunters stage in Mesoamerica.)

Aveni, Anthony. *Skywatchers: A Revised and Updated Version of Skywatchers of Ancient Mexico*. Austin, TX: University of Texas Press, 2001. (Clearly written presentation of Mesoamerican astronomy.)

Barlow, R. H. "The Extent of the Empire of the Culhua Mexica." *Ibero-Americana* 28 (1949). (Classic study defining the Aztec empire on the basis of tribute lists.)

Beekman, Christopher S. "Recent Research in Western Mexican Archaeology." *Journal of Archaeological Research* 18 (2009): 41–109. (Important synthesis of Teuchitlan and related cultures.)

Benson, Elizabeth P. (ed.). *Dumbarton Oaks Conference on the Olmec*. Washington, DC: Dumbarton Oaks Research Library and Collection, Trustees for Harvard University, 1968. (First conference on Olmec problems since the California project at La Venta, and the Yale excavations at San Lorenzo.)

──── and Michael D. Coe (eds.). *The Olmec and Their Neighbors: Essays in Memory of Matthew W. Stirling.* Washington, DC: Dumbarton Oaks Research Library and Collection, Trustees for Harvard University, 1981. (For its time, a comprehensive treatment of Olmec archaeology and civilization.)

──── and Beatriz de la Fuente. *Olmec Art of Ancient Mexico.* Washington, DC: National Gallery of Art, 1996. (Catalog of an important show with descriptions of work at all major Olmec sites.)

Berdan, Frances F. et al. *Aztec Imperial Strategies.* Washington, DC: Dumbarton Oaks Research Library and Collection, 1996. (Detailed look at the empire through documents and artifacts.)

Berlo, Janet Catherine (ed.). *Art, Ideology and the City of Teotihuacan.* Washington, DC: Dumbarton Oaks Research Library and Collection, 1992. (Essays on Classic Teotihuacan civilization.)

──── and Richard A. Diehl (eds.). *Mesoamerica after the Decline of Teotihuacan.* Washington, DC: Dumbarton Oaks Research Library and Collection, 1989. (Results of a conference on Epi- and Post-Classic Mesoamerica.)

Berrin, Kathleen and Virginia M. Fields. *Olmec: Colossal Masterworks of Ancient Mexico.* Los Angeles: Los Angeles County Museum of Art, and San Francisco: Fine Arts Museums of San Francisco, 2011. (Splendidly illustrated catalog of a major exhibition; essays by leading scholars.)

──── and Esther Pasztory (eds.). *Teotihuacan: Art from the City of the Gods.* San Francisco: Fine Arts Museums of San Francisco, New York and London: Thames & Hudson, 1993. (Important essays and an extensive catalog of objects from the metropolis.)

Blanton, Richard E. et al. *Ancient Oaxaca: The Monte Albán State.* Cambridge: Cambridge University Press, 1999. (Summary of settlement pattern, urban, and political studies.)

Blomster, Jeffrey P. *Etlatongo: Social Complexity, Interaction, and Village Life in the Mixteca Alta of Oaxaca.* Belmont, CA: Thomson-Wadsworth, 2006. (Olmec influence on a Formative site in the highlands.)

Boone, Elizabeth Hill (ed.). *The Aztec Templo Mayor.* Washington, DC: Dumbarton Oaks Research Library and Collection, 1987. (Essays from a conference dealing with the discoveries in the Great Temple.)

──── *Stories in Red and Black: Pictorial Histories of the Aztec and Mixtec.* Austin, TX: University of Texas Press, 2000. (The richest introduction to the codices.)

Borah, Woodrow. "New Spain's Century of Depression." *Ibero-Americana* 35 (1951). (Analysis of the economic and demographic collapse in seventeenth-century Mexico.)

Braswell, Geoffrey (ed.). *The Maya and Teotihuacan: Reinterpreting Early Classic Interaction.* Austin, TX: University of Texas Press, 2004. (Essays on a critical case of highland-lowland interaction.)

Brittenham, Claudia. *The Murals of Cacaxtla: The Power of Painting in Ancient Central Mexico.* Austin, TX: University of Texas Press, 2015. (Comparative study of the murals by a leading art historian.)

Buchand, Bruce R. and Lynneth S. Lowe. "Chiapa de Corzo's Mound 11 Tombs and the Middle Formative Olmec." Paper presented at the conference *Arqueología de Chiapas: Avances e Interpretaciones*, 2011. (Report on the most spectacular Olmec tomb found outside the "heartland.")

Burkhart, Louise M. *The Slippery Earth: Nahua-Christian Moral Dialogue in Sixteenth-Century Mexico.* Tucson, AZ: University of Arizona Press, 1989. (Perceptive study of early understandings and misunderstandings between two cultures and religions.)

Byers, Douglas S. and Richard S. MacNeish (gen. eds.). *The Prehistory of the Tehuacan Valley.* 5 vols. Austin, TX: University of Texas Press, 1967–77. (Comprehensive final report on MacNeish's Tehuacan project, especially important for its information on agricultural origins.)

Cabrera Castro, Ruben, Saburo Sugiyama, and George L. Cowgill. "The Templo de Quetzalcoatl Project at Teotihuacan." *Ancient Mesoamerica* 2 (1991): 77–92. (Spectacular discovery of warrior sacrifices in a major Teotihuacan structure.)

Carrasco, David (ed.). *To Change Place: Aztec Ceremonial Landscapes.* Boulder, CO: University Press of Colorado, 1991. (Examines how the Aztec calendar and ceremonialism are related to sacred landscapes in the Basin of Mexico.)

────, Lindsay Jones, and Scott Sessions (eds.). *Mesoamerica's Classic Heritage: from Teotihuacan to the Aztecs.* Boulder, CO: University Press of Colorado, 2000. (Important essays on Teotihuacan's place in Mexican and Maya history.)

──── *The Oxford Encyclopedia of Mesoamerican Cultures.* 3 vols. Oxford and New York: Oxford University Press, 2001.

Carrasco, Pedro. *The Tenochca Empire of Ancient Mexico.* Norman, OK: University of Oklahoma Press, 1999. (Treatment of the Aztec empire that supersedes the work by Barlow.)

Caso, Alfonso. "Calendario y Escritura de las Antiguas Culturas de Monte Albán." In *Obras Completas*, 6 vols., i, Miguel Othón de Mendizabal, 113–45. Mexico City: 1946–47. (Pioneering study of the Zapotec script of early Monte Albán.)

──── *The Aztecs: People of the Sun.* Norman, OK: University of Oklahoma Press: 1958. (Clearly written general treatment of Aztec religion.)

──── "Mixtec Writing and Calendar." In *Handbook of Middle American Indians*, vol. 3, pt. 2, ed. Robert Wauchope, 948–61. Austin, TX: University of Texas Press, 1965. (Clear introduction to Late Post-Classic Mixtec writing and calendrics from the pioneering scholar of that system.)

──── *Calendarios Prehispánicos.* Mexico City: Universidad Nacional Autónoma de México, 1967. (Indispensable collection of essays on non-Maya calendars of Mesoamerica.)

──── *El Tesoro de Monte Albán. Memorias del Instituto Nacional de Antropología e Historia* 3. Mexico City: Instituto Nacional de Antropología e Historia, 1969. (Final report on the great Late Post-Classic tomb of Monte Albán.)

──── and Ignacio Bernal. *Urnas de Oaxaca.* Mexico City: Instituto Nacional de Antropología e Historia, 1952. (Study of the iconography of Zapotec funerary urns.)

Cheetham, David. "The Americas' First Colony." *Archaeology* 59 (1) (2006): 42–45. (Evidence for an Olmec outpost in the Soconusco region of Chiapas.)

Clark, John E. (ed.). *Los Olmecas en Mesoamerica.* Mexico City: El Equilibrista, 1994. (Treatments of early pottery, Teopantecuanitlan, and the objects found at El Manatí, among other contributions.)

──── and Michael Blake. "The Power of Prestige: Competitive Generosity and the Emergence of Rank Societies in Lowland Mesoamerica." In *Factional Competition in the New World*, ed. Elizabeth M. Brumfiel and John W. Fox, 17–30. Cambridge: Cambridge University Press, 1994. (Insightful model to account for the origins of social inequality in Mesoamerica.)

Clendinnen, Inga. *Aztecs: An Interpretation.* Cambridge and New York: Cambridge University Press, 1991.

(Eloquent, authoritative account, generally from the Aztecs' point of view.)

Coe, Michael D. and Richard A. Diehl. *In the Land of the Olmec.* 2 vols. Austin, TX: University of Texas Press, 1980. (The final report on archaeological and ecological investigations at San Lorenzo Tenochtitlan.)

———— et al. *The Olmec World: Ritual and Rulership.* Princeton, NJ: The Art Museum, Princeton University, in association with Harry N. Abrams, 1995. (Key iconographic studies with a beautifully illustrated catalog.)

Cortés, Hernán. *Letters from Mexico.* Trans. and ed. Anthony Pagden. New Haven and London: Yale University Press, 1986. (Fascinating but devious and unreliable reports, written by Cortés to justify his actions to the Hapsburg court.)

Cowgill, George. "Discussion." *Ancient Mesoamerica* 7 (1996): 325–31. (Discussion of some changes in Teotihuacan and Aztec chronologies.)

———— "State and Society at Teotihuacan." *Annual Review of Anthropology* 26 (1997): 129–61. (Thoughtful, fundamental synthesis of Teotihuacan history.)

Cyphers, Ann. *Escultura Olmeca de San Lorenzo Tenochtitlán.* Mexico City: Universidad Nacional Autónoma de México, 2004. (Catalog of all known sculpture of the site, including monuments discovered since the 1960s.)

Díaz del Castillo, Bernal. *The True History of the Conquest of New Spain.* Trans. A. P. Maudslay. London: 1908–16, and New York: 1958. (Gripping, eyewitness account, written by a conquistador in his old age.)

Diehl, Richard A. *Tula: The Toltec Capital of Ancient Mexico.* London and New York: Thames & Hudson, 1983. (Semi-popular account of Tula and the University of Missouri archaeological project.)

———— *The Olmecs: America's First Civilization.* London and New York: Thames & Hudson, 2004. (The most complete and up-to-date coverage of the subject.)

Drucker, Philip. "The Cerro de las Mesas Offering of Jade and Other Materials." *Bureau of American Ethnology,* Bulletin 157 (1955): 25–68. (An Early Classic cache with heirloom materials.)

————, Robert F. Heizer and Robert J. Squier. "Excavations at La Venta, Tabasco, 1955." *Bureau of American Ethnology,* Bulletin 170 (1959). (Final report on the University of California excavations at a key Olmec site.)

Durán, Fr. Diego. *The History of the Indies of New Spain.* Trans. and annotated Doris Heyden. Norman, OK: University of Oklahoma Press, 1993. (After Sahagún, the most important early source on Aztec life and history.)

Evans, Susan T. *Ancient Mexico and Central America: Archaeology and Culture History,* 3rd ed. London and New York: Thames & Hudson, 2013. (Complete coverage of all of Mesoamerica in one volume.)

———— and David L. Webster. *Archaeology of Ancient Mexico and Central America: An Encyclopedia.* New York: Garland, 2001. (Short treatments of a great number of archaeological sites in addition to regional syntheses.)

————, Joanne Pillsbury, and Jeffrey Quilter (eds.). *Ancient Mexican Art at Dumbarton Oaks: Central Highlands, Southwestern Highlands, Gulf Lowlands.* Washington, DC: Dumbarton Oaks Research Library and Collection, 2010. (Well-researched catalog of a premier collection.)

Fash, William Leonard and Leonardo López Luján (eds.). *The Art of Urbanism: How Mesoamerican Kingdoms Represented Themselves in Architecture and Imagery.* Washington, DC: Dumbarton Oaks Research Library and Collection, 2009. (Mesoamerican city planning and symbolism, including sections on some of the most important ancient Mesoamerican capitals.)

Flannery, Kent V. (ed.). *The Early Mesoamerican Village.* New York: Academic Press, 1976. (Highly influential volume on the Formative, with important data on early Oaxaca.)

———— and Joyce Marcus (eds.). *The Cloud People: Divergent Evolution of the Zapotec and Mixtec Civilizations.* New York: Percheron Press, 1983. (A major collection of essays on all aspects of pre-Conquest Oaxaca.)

————, ————, and Stephen A. Kowalewski. "The Preceramic and Formative of the Valley of Oaxaca." In *Supplement to the Handbook of Middle American Indians 1: Archaeology,* 48–93. Austin, TX: University of Texas Press, 1981. (Extended synthesis of early Oaxacan archaeology.)

Fuente, Beatriz de la (ed.). *La Pintura Mural Prehispánica en México I: Teotihuacan.* 2 vols. Mexico City: Universidad Nacional Autónoma de México, 1995. (Complete catalog of the murals along with substantial essays.)

Fuente, Beatriz de la, and Ma. Teresa Uriarte (eds.). *La Pintura Mural Prehispánica en México III: Oaxaca.* 4 vols. Mexico City: Universidad Nacional Autónoma de México, 2008. (Complete catalog of the murals along with substantial essays.)

Furst, Peter T. "House of Darkness and House of Light." In *Death and the Afterlife in Pre-Columbian America,* ed. Elizabeth P. Benson, 33–68. Washington, DC: Dumbarton Oaks Research Library and Collection, 1975. (Application of ethnological data to the understanding of West Mexican tomb sculpture.)

Garibay, Angel María. *Historia de la Literatura Nahuatl.* 3 vols. Mexico City: Porrúa, 1953–54. (Classic study of Aztec poetry and prose.)

Gerhard, Peter. *A Guide to the Historical Geography of New Spain.* Cambridge: Cambridge University Press, 1972. (Basic work on the civil and ecclesiastical organization of colonial Mexico, and to the documentary sources.)

Gillespie, Susan. *The Aztec Kings.* Tucson, AZ: University of Arizona Press, 1989. (Iconoclastic study of Aztec dynastic succession and Toltec "history," based on a structural analysis of data.)

Grove, David C. "The Olmec paintings of Oxtotitlan, Guerrero, Mexico." In *Dumbarton Oaks Studies in Pre-Columbian Art and Archaeology,* no. 6. Washington, DC: Dumbarton Oaks, Trustees for Harvard University, 1970. (Early report of Formative cave painting.)

———— *Chalcatzingo: Excavations on the Olmec Frontier.* London and New York: Thames & Hudson, 1984. (General account of the most important highland Olmec site, famed for its relief carvings.)

———— (ed.). *Ancient Chalcatzingo.* Austin, TX: University of Texas Press, 1987. (Final report on the University of Illinois project.)

Harbottle, Garman and Phil C. Weigand. "Turquoise in Pre-Columbian America." *Scientific American* (1992): 78–85. (Archaeological data and neutron-activation analysis of the turquoise trade between the American Southwest and Mesoamerica.)

Hassig, Ross. *Aztec Warfare.* Norman, OK: University of Oklahoma Press, 1988. (The definitive study.)

Healan, Dan M. (ed.). *Tula of the Toltecs.* Iowa City, IA: University of Iowa Press, 1989. (Final report on the University of Missouri project.)

Heyden, Doris. "Caves, Gods and Myths: World-View and Planning in Teotihuacan." In *Mesoamerican Sites and World Views,* ed. Elizabeth P. Benson, 1–39. Washington, DC: Dumbarton Oaks Research Library and Collection, 1981. (Implications of the discovery of a cave beneath the Pyramid of the Sun.)

Hirth, Kenneth G. *Archaeological Research at Xochicalco.* 2 vols. Salt Lake City, UT: University of Utah Press, 2000. (Extensive report of archaeology and iconography in the Epiclassic capital.)

Irwin-Williams, Cynthia. "Summary of Archaeological Evidence from the Valsequillo Region, Puebla, Mexico." In *Cultural Continuity in Mesoamerica*, ed. David Broman, 7–22. The Hague: Mouton, 1978. (Report on a key site of the Early Hunters stage in Mexico.)

Jansen, Maarten. "The Ancient Mexican Books of Time: Interpretative Developments and Prospects." *Analecta Praehistorica Leidensia* 43/44, ed. Corrie Bakels and Hans Kamermans (2012): 77–94. (Outlines the most up-to-date framework to interpret the mantic pre-Hispanic manuscripts).

Jiménez Moreno, Wigberto. "Tula y los Toltecas Segun las Fuentes Históricas." *Revista Mexicana de Estudios Antropológicos* 5 (1941): 79–83. (The article that established Tula, Hidalgo, as the Toltec capital.)

Joralemon, Peter David. "A Study of Olmec Iconography," *Dumbarton Oaks Studies in Pre-Columbian Art and Iconography*, no. 7. Washington, DC: Dumbarton Oaks, Trustees for Harvard University, 1971. (This and the following are the key works on Olmec religion and iconography.)

–––– "The Olmec Dragon: A Study in Pre-Columbian Iconography." In *Origins of Religious Art and Iconography in Preclassic Mesoamerica*, ed. H. B. Nicholson, 27–71. Los Angeles: UCLA Latin American Center Publications, 1976.

Joyce, Arthur. *Mixtecs, Zapotecs, and Chatinos: The Ancient Peoples of Southern Mexico.* Malden, MA: Wiley-Blackwell, 2010. (Major synthesis of the archaeology in three regions of Oaxaca, including the Central Valleys of Oaxaca, the Mixtec Highlands, and the Pacific Littoral.)

Kirchhoff, Paul. "Meso-America." In *Heritage of Conquest*, ed. Sol Tax, 17–30. Glencoe, IL: Free Press, 1952. (The first definition of "Mesoamerica.")

Koontz, Rex. *Lightning Gods and Feathered Serpents: The Public Sculpture of El Tajín.* Austin, TX: University of Texas Press, 2009. (Analysis of the public sculpture in a key Epiclassic capital.)

Kowalski, Jeff K. and Cynthia Kristan-Graham (eds.). *Twin Tollans: Chichén Itzá, Tula, and the Epiclassic to Early Postclassic Mesoamerican World.* Washington, DC: Dumbarton Oaks Research Library and Collection, 2007. (Several views on the symbolism and archaeology of Chich'en Itza and Tula, with related questions on the Early Post-Classic period.)

Kubler, George. "Chichén Itzá y Tula." *Estudios de Cultura Maya* 1 (1961): 47–79. (Argues that it was Chich'en Itza that influenced Tula, and not the reverse.)

León-Portilla, Miguel. *Aztec Thought and Culture.* Norman, OK: University of Oklahoma Press, 1963. (A profound study of Aztec philosophy and religion.)

–––– *The Broken Spears: Aztec Accounts of the Conquest of Mexico.* Boston, MA: Beacon Press, 1966. (A deeply affecting antidote to the self-glorifying accounts of the victors in the great struggle for Mexico.)

–––– (ed. and trans.). *Coloquios y Doctrina Cristiana.* Mexico City: Universidad Nacional Autónoma de México, 1986. (An extraordinary dialogue conducted in Nahuatl during a 1524 meeting between the Franciscan friars and Aztec intellectuals.)

–––– *Fifteen Poets of the Aztec World.* Norman, OK: University of Oklahoma Press, 1992.

Lind, Michael, and Javier Urcid. *The Lords of Lambityeco: Political Evolution in the Valley of Oaxaca during the Xoo Phase.* Boulder, CO: University Press of Colorado, 2010. (Detailed account of the excavations of elite houses at Lambityeco, a secondary center during the apogee of Classic-period Monte Albán.)

López Austin, Alfredo. *The Human Body and Ideology: Concepts of the Ancient Nahuas.* Salt Lake City, UT: University of Utah, 1988. (Innovative, detailed account of indigenous concepts of the body.)

López Luján, Leonardo. *The Offerings of the Templo Mayor of Tenochtitlan.* Albuquerque, NM: University of New Mexico Press, 2005. (Comprehensive analysis of the nearly 200 offerings of the Main Temple of the Aztecs.)

–––– and Giacomo Chiari. "Color in Monumental Mexica Sculpture." *Res: Anthropology and Aesthetics* 61/62: 330–42. (Report on the original colors in key Aztec stone monuments.)

––––, R. H. Cobean T., and A. Guadalupe Mastache F. *Xochicalco y Tula.* Milan: Jaca Book, 1995. (Summary of what is known along with recent excavations, all gloriously illustrated.)

–––– and Linda Manzanilla, eds. *Historia Antigua de México.* 3rd ed. Mexico City: Universidad Nacional Autónoma de México. Instituto de Investigaciones Antropológicas, 2014. (Collection of synthetic articles by top Mexican archaeologists covering all aspects of Mesoamerican culture and history.)

–––– and Eduardo Matos Moctezuma. *Monumental Mexica Sculpture.* Mexico City: Fundación Conmemoraciones, 2010. (Outstanding account of the biography and meaning of some of the most important Aztec stone monuments.)

–––– et al. "The Destruction of Images in Teotihuacan: Anthropomorphic Sculpture, Elite Cults, and the End of a Civilization." *Res: Anthropology and Aesthetics* 49/50 (2006): 14–39. (Report on a key Teotihuacan palace and its demise.)

MacNeish, Richard S. "Preliminary Archaeological Investigations in the Sierra de Tamaulipas, Mexico." *Transactions of the American Philosophical Society* 48, pt. 6 (1958). (Early Hunters and Archaic occupation in northeasternmost Mexico.)

Mangelsdorf, Paul C. *Corn: Its Origin, Evolution and Improvement.* Cambridge, MA: Harvard University Press, 1974. (Gives Mangelsdorf's side of the controversy over the origin of corn.)

Marcus, Joyce and Kent V. Flannery. *Zapotec Civilization: How Urban Society Evolved in Mexico's Oaxaca Valley.* London and New York: Thames & Hudson, 1996. (Major synthetic work spanning all aspects of pre-Columbian Zapotec history.)

Marquina, Ignacio. *Arquitectura Prehispánica.* Mexico City: Instituto Nacional de Antropología e Historia, 1951. (In spite of its age, still useful for plans and drawings of major sites and buildings.)

–––– (coordinator). *Proyecto Cholula.* Mexico City: Instituto Nacional de Antropología e Historia, 1970. (Various reports on the Mexican 1960s investigations at this major site.)

Martínez Donjuan, Guadalupe. "Los Olmecas en el Estado de Guerrero." In *Los Olmecas en Mesoamérica*, ed. John E. Clark, 143–63. Mexico City: El Equilibrista, 1994. (A synthesis of work at Teopantecuanitlan.)

Mastache, Alba Guadalupe, Robert H. Cobean, and Dan M. Healan. *Ancient Tollan: Tula and the Toltec Heartland.* Boulder, CO: University Press of Colorado, 2002. (Final report on long-term investigations in the Toltec capital.)

Matos Moctezuma, Eduardo. *The Great Temple of the Aztecs.* London and New York: Thames & Hudson, 1988. (Semi-popular account of the excavations at the remains of the most important structure in the Aztec empire.)

––––– and Leonardo López Luján. *Escultura Monumental Mexica*. Mexico City: Fondo de Cultura Económica, 2012. (Comprehensive treatment and detailed commentaries of major Aztec stone monuments, richly illustrated.)

Miller, Mary Ellen. *The Art of Mesoamerica: From Olmec to Aztec*, 5th ed. London and New York: Thames & Hudson, 2012. (A concise and well-illustrated introduction to all of Mesoamerica.)

––––– and Karl Taube. *An Illustrated Dictionary of the Gods and Symbols of Ancient Mexico and the Maya*. London and New York: Thames & Hudson, 1997. (Immensely useful dictionary and guide to Aztec and pre-Aztec religion and iconography.)

Millon, René. *Urbanization at Teotihuacan, Mexico*, vol. 1, pts 1 and 2. Austin, TX: University of Texas Press, 1973. (Excellent summary of Teotihuacan culture, along with detailed maps of the entire city.)

––––– "Teotihuacan: City, State, and Civilization." In *Supplement to the Handbook of Middle American Indians, vol. 1: Archaeology*, 198–243. Austin, TX: University of Texas Press, 1981. (Important update of the earlier essay.)

Nelson, Ben A. "Chronology and Stratigraphy at La Quemada, Zacatecas, Mexico." *Journal of Field Archaeology* 24, no. 1 (1997): 85–110. (Synthesis of work on Mesoamerica's northern frontier.)

Nichols, Deborah L. and Christopher A. Pool (eds.). *The Oxford Handbook of Mesoamerican Archaeology*. Oxford and New York: Oxford University Press, 2012. (Broad and most updated survey of research in Mesoamerica.)

Nicholson, Henry B. "Religion in Pre-Hispanic Central Mexico." In *Handbook of Middle American Indians* 10, ed. Robert Wauchope, Gordon Ekholm, and Ignacio Bernal, 395–446. Austin, TX: University of Texas Press, 1971. (The essential work concerning Aztec religion.)

Niederberger Betton, Christine. *Paléopaysages et Archéologie Pré-urbaine du Bassin de Mexico*, 2 vols. Mexico City: Collection Études Mesoaméricaines, 1987. 1–11. (Late Archaic and Formative occupation in the Tlapacoya region, Basin of Mexico.)

Offner, Jerome. *Law and Politics in Aztec Texcoco*. Cambridge: Cambridge University Press, 1988. (Definitive work on the unique legal system of the Aztecs.)

Ortiz de Montellano, Bernard R. "Aztec Cannibalism: An Ecological Necessity?" *Science* 200 (1978): 611–17 (Careful refutation of the Harner thesis.)

Paddock, John (ed.). *Ancient Oaxaca*. Stanford, CA: Stanford University Press, 1966. (Excellent background material on Zapotec and Mixtec archaeology and ethnohistory.)

Paradis, L.-I., C. Bélanger, D. Raby, and B. Ross. "Le Style Mezcala Découvert en Contexte au Guerrero (Mexique)." *Journal de la Société des Américanistes* 76 (1990): 199–213. (Archaeological dating of objects in the Mezcala style.)

Pasztory, Esther. *Aztec Art*. New York: H. N. Abrams, 1983. (The most complete treatment of the subject.)

––––– *Teotihuacan: An Experiment in Living*. Norman, OK: University of Oklahoma Press, 1997. (Synthesis of Teotihuacan iconography and aesthetics.)

Piperno, Dolores R. "The Origins of Plant Cultivation and Domestication in the New World Tropics." *Current Anthropology* 52, no. 4 (2011): 453–70. (Contains the latest data on maize origins by a leading authority on the subject.)

Plunket, Patricia and Gabriela Uruñuela. "Preclassic Household Patterns Preserved under Volcanic Ash at Tetimpa, Puebla, Mexico." *Latin American Antiquity*, 9 (4) (1998): 287–309. (Excavation of a Formative village with preserved house groups.)

––––– and ––––– *Cholula*. Mexico City: Fondo de Cultura Económica, 2018. (Comprehensive diachronic discussion of Cholula and its regional context.)

Pohl, John M. D. and Bruce Byland. "Mixtec Landscape Perception and Archaeological Settlement Patterns." *Ancient Mesoamerica* 1, no. 1 (1990): 113–31. (Identifies a host of toponyms found in the codices.)

––––– and ––––– *In the Realm of 8 Deer: The Archaeology of the Mixtec Codices*. Norman, OK: University of Oklahoma Press, 1994. (The most important addition to Caso's original readings.)

––––– and Angus McBride. *Aztec, Mixtec and Zapotec Armies*. London: Osprey, 1991. (Strikingly illustrated popular work on indigenous Mexican warfare.)

Pollard, Helen Perlstein. "The Construction of Ideology in the Emergence of the Prehispanic Tarascan State." *Ancient Mesoamerica* 2 (1991): 167–69. (Perceptive study of the origin and nature of the Tarascan kingdom, based on the re-analysis of ethnohistoric sources.)

––––– *Tariacuri's Legacy: The Pre-Hispanic Tarascan State*. Norman, OK: University of Oklahoma Press, 1993. (Synthetic study of the Tarascan kingdom.)

Pool, Christopher A. *Olmec Archaeology and Early Mesoamerica*. Cambridge and New York: Cambridge University Press, 2007.

Pope, Kevin O. et al. "Origin and Environmental Setting of Ancient Agriculture in the Lowlands of Mesoamerica." *Science* 292 (2001): 1370–73. (Early maize near La Venta, Tabasco.)

Porter, Muriel N. *Tlatilco and the Pre-Classic Cultures of the New World*. New York: Wenner-Gren Foundation for Anthropological Research, 1953. (Diffusionist explanation of Tlatilco, but still the best treatment of this important Formative site.)

Proskouriakoff, Tatiana. "Varieties of Classic Central Veracruz Sculpture." *Carnegie Institution of Washington, Contributions to American Anthropology and History* 58 (1954). (Pioneering definition of Central Veracruz style.)

Relación de Michoacan (1541). Transcription, prologue, introduction, and notes by José Tudela. Madrid: Aguilar, 1956. (The primary ethnohistoric source on Tarascan culture.)

Robb, Matthew, ed. *Teotihuacan: City of Water, City of Fire*. San Francisco: Fine Arts Museums of San Francisco and University of California Press, 2017. (Well-illustrated catalog of exhibition with accounts of recent finds.)

Sahagún, Fray Bernadino de. *General History of the Things of New Spain*. Trans. from the Nahuatl by Arthur J. O. Anderson and Charles F. Dibble. 12 vols. Santa Fe, NM: School of American Research, 1950–69. (A massive scholarly encyclopedia of almost all aspects of Aztec life by its greatest student. Book 12 presents an absorbingly interesting account of the Conquest from the indigenous point of view; Sahagún would later refute this in a pro-Spanish work.)

Sanders, William T., Jeffrey R. Parsons, and Robert S. Santley. *The Basin of Mexico: Ecological Processes in the Evolution of a Civilization*. New York: Academic Press, 1979. (Results of a massive survey of settlement patterns in the entire Basin of Mexico from earliest times through the Conquest.)

Sandstrom, Alan. *Corn is Our Blood: Culture and Ethnic Identity in a Contemporary Aztec Village*. Norman, OK: University of Oklahoma Press, 1991. (Sensitive rendering of contemporary Nahua world view.)

Smith, Mary Elizabeth. *Picture Writing from Southern Mexico: Mixtec Place Signs and Maps*. Norman, OK: University of Oklahoma Press, 1973. (Analysis of the

Mixtec writing system, from a linguistic and art-historical perspective.)

Smith, Michael E. and Frances F. Berdan. *The Postclassic Mesoamerican World*. Salt Lake City, UT: University of Utah Press, 2004. (Essays on Post-Classic Mesoamerica as a world system.)

Soustelle, Jacques. *The Daily Life of the Aztecs*. New York: Macmillan, 1962. (A very readable introduction to many aspects of Aztec life and culture.)

Spores, Ronald. *The Mixtecs in Ancient and Colonial Times*. Norman, OK: University of Oklahoma Press, 1984. (An update of the preceding.)

Stark, Barbara L. and Philip J. Arnold (eds.). *From Olmec to Aztec: Settlement Patterns in the Ancient Gulf Lowlands*. Tucson, AZ: University of Arizona Press, 1997. (Synthesis of data on human occupation throughout Veracruz.)

Stirling, Matthew W. "Stone Monuments of Southern Mexico." *Bureau of American Ethnology*, Bulletin 138 (1943). (Early report on Olmec and post-Olmec sculptures and sites.)

Storey, Rebecca. *Life and Death in the Ancient City of Teotihuacan: A Modern Paleodemographic Synthesis*. Tuscaloosa, AL: University of Alabama Press, 1992. (Life and health in the Classic metropolis as seen through the human skeletal remains.)

Stuart, George E. "Mural Masterpieces of Ancient Cacaxtla." *National Geographic* 182, no. 3 (1992): 120–36. (Splendid photographs of these hybrid Maya-Mexican murals.)

Taube, Karl A. "The Teotihuacan Spider Woman." *Journal of Latin American Lore* 9 (2) (1983): 107–89. (Identification of the "Great Goddess" of the ancient city.)

———— "The Iconography of Mirrors at Teotihuacan." In *Art, Ideology, and the City of Teotihuacan*, ed. Janet C. Berlo, 169–204. Washington, DC: Dumbarton Oaks Research Library and Collection, 1992. (Mirrors as military paraphernalia in early Mexico.)

———— "The Temple of Quetzalcoatl and the Cult of Sacred War." *Res* 21: (1992): 53–87. (Crucial account of Teotihuacan war iconography in the light of the spectacular dedicatory offerings.)

———— *Olmec Art at Dumbarton Oaks*. Washington, DC: Dumbarton Oaks Research Library and Collection, 2004. (Extremely important update of Joralemon 1971.)

———— "Teotihuacan and the Development of Writing in Early Classic Central Mexico." In *Their Way of Writing: Scripts, Signs, and Pictographies in Pre-Columbian America*, ed. Elizabeth Hill Boone and Gary Urton, 77–109. Washington, DC: Dumbarton Oaks Research Library and Collection, 2011. (Argues for the existence of an imperial writing system in Classic Mesoamerica's most powerful city-state.)

Tolstoy, Paul and Louise I. Paradis. "Early and Middle Preclassic culture in the Basin of Mexico." *Science* 167 (1970): 344–52. (Should be read together with Niederberger Betton, loc. cit., for a comprehensive view of the first Formative cultures in the Basin of Mexico.)

Townsend, Richard F. *Ancient West Mexico: Art and Archaeology of the Unknown Past*, rev. ed. London and New York: Thames & Hudson, 2000. (Important account of archaeological discoveries and revised history of the region.)

———— *The Aztecs*, 3rd ed. London and New York: Thames & Hudson, 2009. (A succinct account of Aztec history and life by a leading art historian.)

Urcid Serrano, Javier. *Zapotec Hieroglyphic Writing*. Washington, DC: Dumbarton Oaks Research Library and Collection, 2001. (Definitive summary and analysis of the Zapotec script and calendar.)

Uriarte, María Teresa and Rebecca B. González Lauck (eds.). *Olmeca: Balance y Perspectivas*. 2 vols. and CDs. Mexico City: Universidad Nacional Autónoma de México, 2008. (Essays presented at a round table on the Olmec culture.)

———— and Fernanda Salazar (eds.). *La Pintura Mural Prehispánica en México V: Cacaxtla*. 2 vols. Mexico City: Universidad Nacional Autónoma de México, 2013. (Varied interpretative essays on the murals.)

Vaillant, George C. "Excavations at Zacatenco." *Anthropological Papers of the American Museum of Natural History* 32, pt. 1 (1930). (With the following, reports pioneer excavations in Formative occupations of the Basin of Mexico, in the pre-radiocarbon era.)

———— "Excavations at El Arbolillo." *Anthropological Papers of the American Museum of Natural History* 35, pt. 2 (1935).

Von Winning, Hasso. *La Iconografía de Teotihuacan*. 2 vols. Mexico City: Universidad Nacional Autónoma de México, 1987. (Detailed study of important symbols in use in the Classic city.)

———— and Nelly Gutiérrez Solano. *La Iconografía de la Cerámica de Río Blanco, Veracruz*. Mexico City: Universidad Nacional Autónoma de México, 1996. (In-depth study of one aspect of Classic Veracruz ceramics.)

Wauchope, Robert (ed.). *Handbook of Middle American Indians*. 16 vols. Austin, TX: University of Texas Press, 1964–92. (A multi-volume series covering all aspects of life in Mesoamerica.)

Wendt, Carl J. "Excavations at El Remolino: Household Archaeology in the San Lorenzo Olmec Region." *Journal of Field Archaeology* 30 (2) (2005): 163–80. (Village site on San Lorenzo's periphery.)

White, Christine et al. "Geographic Identities of the Sacrificial Victims from the Feathered Serpent Pyramid, Teotihuacan: Implications for the Nature of State Power." *Latin American Antiquity* 13 (2) (2002): 217–36. (Locates the home regions of the sacrificial victims.)

————, T. Douglas Price, and Fred J. Longstaffe. "Residential Histories of the Human Sacrifices at the Moon Pyramid, Teotihuacan." *Ancient Mesoamerica* 18 (1) (2007): 159–72. (More information on the origins and residential histories of sacrificial victims and burials.)

Whitecotton, Joseph W. *The Zapotecs: Princes, Priests, and Peasants*. Norman, OK: University of Oklahoma Press, 1977. (History and anthropology of the Zapotecs, from earliest times to the present.)

Whittington, E. Michael (ed.). *The Sport of Life and Death: The Mesoamerican Ballgame*. New York and London: Thames & Hudson, 2001.

Wilkerson, S. Jeffrey K. *El Tajín: A Guide for Visitors*. Xalapa, Veracruz: Universidad Veracruzana, 1987. (Beautifully illustrated handbook to the ruins.)

Winfield Capitaine, Fernando. "La Estela 1 de La Mojarra, Veracruz, Mexico." *Research Reports on Ancient Maya Writing* 16 (1988). (Reports on the discovery of Mesoamerica's longest hieroglyphic text, in the early Isthmian script.)

Winter, Marcus. *Oaxaca: The Archaeological Record*. Mexico City: Minutiae Mexicana, 1989. (A broad coverage of the archaeology of Southwestern Mesoamerica.)

Wolf, Eric (ed.). *The Valley of Mexico: Studies in Pre-Hispanic Ecology and Society*. Albuquerque, NM: 1976. (Papers presented at a School of American Research Conference; the subject matter is heavily ecological.)

Zantwijk, Rudolf A. van. *The Aztec Arrangement*. Norman, OK: University of Oklahoma Press, 1985. (Organization of the Aztec capital, state, and empire by a structural anthropologist and expert in Aztec ethnohistory.)

Sources of Illustrations

Drawings are by Dr Patrick Gallagher, unless otherwise indicated.

Frontispiece British Museum, London; **1** ML Design; **2** Emmanuel Flores/AFP/Getty Images; **3** courtesy Michael D. Coe; **4** Peter Bull after Dr Patrick Gallagher; **5** ML Design; **6** Guadalupe Sánchez; **8** Instituto Nacional de Antropología e Historia, Mexico City; **9** From Richard S. MacNeish, *Second Annual Report of the Tehuacan Archaeological-Botanical Project*; **10** Robert S. Peabody Foundation for Archaeology, Phillips Academy, Andover, MA; **13, 14** courtesy Michael D. Coe; **15** Peter Bull after drawing in Christine Niederberger, "Early Sedentary Economy in the Basin of Mexico" in *Science* 12 Jan 1979: vol. 203, issue 4376 [131–42]; **16** Peter Bull after Dr Patrick Gallagher; **17** Based on K. Dixon, *Ceramics from Two Pre-Classic Periods*; **18** courtesy Michael D. Coe; **19** Compiled from M. N. Porter, *Tlatilco and the Pre-Classic Cultures of the New World*; **20, 21** Photo Bruce M. White/Trustees of Princeton University; **22** Compiled from M. N. Porter, *Tlatilco and the Pre-Classic Cultures of the New World*, and from R. Piña Chan, *Tlatilco*; **23** courtesy J. J. Klejman; **24** Peabody Museum of Natural History, Yale University, New Haven, CT. Photo R. House, 2016; **25** Interfoto/Alamy Stock Photo; **26** Barbier-Müller Museum, Geneva; **27** Metropolitan Museum of Art, New York. Bequest of Arthur M. Bullowa, 1993 (1994.35.659); **28** Collection of Alan and Marianne Schwartz, Bloomfield Hills, MI; **29** Los Angeles County Museum of Art. The Proctor Stafford Collection, purchased with funds provided by Mr. and Mrs. Allan C. Balch (M.86.296.154); **30** Map Jean Blackburn/Instituto Nacional de Antropología e Historia, Mexico City; **31** American Museum of Natural History, New York; **32** Metropolitan Museum of Art, New York. The Michael C. Rockefeller Memorial Collection, Bequest of Nelson A. Rockefeller, 1979 (1979.206.702); **33** Peter Bull after Dr Patrick Gallagher; **34** American Museum of Natural History, New York; **35** Museo de Antropología, Xalapa, Mexico; **36, 37** courtesy Michael D. Coe; **38** After figs. 37 and 38 in Paul Westheim et al., *Cuarenta Siglos de Plástica Mexicana* (Mexico: 1969); **39** Metropolitan Museum of Art, New York. The Michael C. Rockefeller Memorial Collection, Bequest of Nelson A. Rockefeller, 1979 (1979.206.940); **40** American Museum of Natural History, New York. Photo akg-images/Interfoto; **41** Elbis Domínguez; **42** Drawing Felipe Davalos/National Geographic Image Collection; **43** courtesy Colin McEwan; **44** courtesy Matthew W. Stirling and the National Geographic Society; **45** courtesy Michael D. Coe; **46** Photo DEA/G. Dagli Orti/De Agostini/Getty Images; **47** courtesy Kent Reilly; **48** courtesy Michael D. Coe; **49** courtesy John E. Clark; **51** Museo de la Venta, Villahermosa, Mexico City. Photo akg-images/Album/Oronoz; **52** courtesy Jorge Pérez de Lara; **53** courtesy Michael D. Coe; **54** courtesy Jorge Pérez de Lara; **55** courtesy Robert F. Heizer and the National Geographic Society; **56** courtesy Matthew W. Stirling and the National Geographic Society; **57** courtesy Michael D. Coe/drawing Stephen Houston; **58a** National Museum of Natural History, Department of Anthropology (A222579). Photo Donald E. Hurlbert. Smithsonian Institution, Washington, D.C.; **58b** From W. H. Holmes, "On a nephrite statuette from San Andres Tuxtla, Vera Cruz, Mexico"; **59** courtesy Antonio Attini/Archivio White Star; **60** courtesy Jorge Pérez de Lara; **61** From Michael D. Coe, *The Jaguar's Children: Pre-Classic Central Mexico*; **62, 63** courtesy Michael D. Coe; **64** Joyce Marcus and Kent V. Flannery; **65, 66** courtesy Michael D. Coe; **67, 68** courtesy Javier Urcid and Elbis Domínguez; **69** Photo Phil Clarke Hill/In Pictures via Getty Images; **70, 71** courtesy Javier Urcid and Elbis Domínguez; **72** Elbis Domínguez after Marcus and Flannery, 1996: 187; **73** Metropolitan Museum, New York. The Michael C. Rockefeller Memorial Collection, Bequest of Nelson A. Rockefeller, 1979 (1979.206.947); **74** Photo Jeff Brzezinski; **75a** courtesy Sarah Barber and Arthur Joyce; **75b** Elbis Domínguez; **76** courtesy Matthew W. Stirling and the National Geographic Society; **77** Drawing courtesy George Stuart; **78** Peter Bull after Dr Patrick Gallagher; **79** Photo from René Millon, *Urbanization at Teotihuacán, Mexico*. © René Millon; **80** Drazen Tromic, drawing after René Millon, "Teotihuacán" in *Scientific American* (1967), 5; **81** Photo Adina Tovy/Robert Harding; **82** courtesy Antonio Attini/Archivio White Star; **83** Saburo Sugiyama; **84** Zona de Monumentos Arquelógicos de Teotihuacán; **85** Drawing Oralia Cabrera, modified from Plan 104 of the Proyecto Arqueologico de Teotihuacán 1980–82; **86** Photo Sergio Gómez Chàvez; **87** Drazen Tomic; **88** Photo DeAgostini/Getty Images; **89** Instituto Nacional de Antropología e Historia, Mexico City; **90** From H. von Winning, "Representations of temple buildings as decorative patterns on Teotihuacan pottery and figurines" (fig. i); **91** courtesy Michael D. Coe; **92** Museo Nacional de Antropología, Mexico City; **93, 94** courtesy Michael D. Coe; **95** Based on A. Villagra, "Teotihuacan, sus pinturas murales" (fig. 1); **96** Dumbarton Oaks Research Library and Collection, Washington, D.C.; **97** Compiled from S. Linné, *Archaeological Researches in Mexican Highland Cultures*; **98** Redrawn and modified after Jesper, Nielsen, and Christophe Helmke, "Reinterpreting the Plaza De Los Glifos, La Ventilla, Teotihuacan," *Ancient Mesoamerica* 22 (02) (2011), 323–43, fig. 6, detail; **99** Museo Nacional de Antropología, Mexico City; **100** imageBroker/Alamy Stock Photo; **101** courtesy Javier Urcid; **102** Museo Antropologico, Xalapa, Veracruz, Mexico/Jean-Pierre Courau/Bridgeman Images; **103** Yale University Art Gallery, New Haven, CT; **104** Metropolitan Museum of Art, New York. The Michael C. Rockefeller Memorial Collection, Gift of Nelson A. Rockefeller, 1963 (1978.412.15); **105** Metropolitan Museum of Art, New York. The Michael C. Rockefeller Memorial Collection, Bequest of Nelson A. Rockefeller, 1979 (1979.206.425); **106** American Museum of Natural History, New York; **107** Drawing Daniela Koontz; **108** Elbis Domínguez; **109, 110** courtesy Javier Urcid; **111** courtesy Javier Urcid and Elbis Domínguez; **112** Photo Michel Zabé, Archivo Fotográfico "Manuel Toussaint", Instituto de Investigaciones Estéticas, UNAM; **113** Elbis Domínguez; **114** courtesy Jorge Pérez de Lara; **115** Drawing Drazen Tomic after William H. Bond in Stuart 1992, 122–23; **116, 117, 118** courtesy Javier Urcid and Elbis Domínguez; **119** courtesy Michael D. Coe; **120** Drawing courtesy Rex Koontz; **121** Photo courtesy Rex Koontz; **122** courtesy Javier Urcid and Elbis Domínguez; **123** Museo de las Culturas, Oaxaca; **124** Photo Marco Antonio Pacheco/Raíces; **125** Photo courtesy Rex Koontz; **126** Photo Uwe Dürr; **127** Cleveland Museum of Art, OH. Purchase from the J. H. Wade Fund (1973.3)/Bridgeman Images; **128** courtesy Michael D. Coe; **129** Museo de Antropología, Xalapa, Mexico; **130** Photo akg-images/Veintimilla; **131** courtesy Michael D. Coe/Drawing Michael Kampen, courtesy of University of Florida Press; **132** Dallas Museum of Art (1970.5); **133** American Museum of Natural History, New York; **134** Metropolitan Museum of Art, New York. The Michael C. Rockefeller Memorial Collection, Bequest of Nelson A. Rockefeller, 1979 (1979.206.561); **135** Museo de Antropología, Xalapa, Mexico; **136, 137** Museo de Antropología, Xalapa/Universidad Veracruzana/Catálogo digital; **138** courtesy Sanchez Scott, 2001; **139** courtesy Javier Urcid and Elbis Domínguez; **140, 141** courtesy Javier Urcid; **142** Los Angeles County Museum of Art. Shinji Shumeikai Acquisition Fund (M.2000.54.2); **143** Plazuelas Archaeological Site, San Juan el Alto, Municipality of Penjamo, Guanajuato, Mexico; **144** Instituto Nacional de Antropología e Historia, Mexico City; **145** Photo John Elk III/Alamy Stock Photo; **146** Peter Bull after Dr Patrick Gallagher; **147** Peabody Museum of Natural History, Yale University, New Haven, CT; **149** Martin Schneiter/Dreamstime.com; **150, 151, 152, 153** courtesy Michael D. Coe; **154** Museo Nacional de Antropología, Mexico City; **155** Drawn from E. Seler, *Gesammelte Abhandlungen*; **156** Drawn from S. Linné, *Archaeological Researches* (figs. 62, 73, 112); **157** Drawing courtesy Richard A. Diehl; **158, 159, 160** courtesy Michael D. Coe; **161** British Museum, London; **162** Photo DeAgostini/Getty Images; **163** Museo de las Culturas, Oaxaca; **164** *Historia del Arte de Oaxaca*, Instituto Oaxaqueño de las Culturas: 1997, photo Jesus Sanchez Uribe; **165** Middle American Research Institute, Tulane University, New Orleans, LA; **166** Elbis Domínguez; **167** Museo Nacional de Antropología, Mexico City; **168** courtesy Javier Urcid and Elbis Domínguez; **169** Museo Nacional de Antropología, Mexico City. Photo Scala, Florence; **170** Elbis Domínguez after C. Seler, 1916; **171** Real Biblioteca de San Lorenzo de El Escorial, España (Ms.c.IV.5, f. 29v); **172** age fotostock/Alamy Stock Photo; **173** Peter Bull after R. H. Barlow, *Extent of the Empire of the Culhua Mexica*; **174** Peter Bull after Dr Patrick Gallagher and ML Design; **175** ML Design; **176** courtesy Michael D. Coe; **177** Bodleian Library, Oxford. Medieval and Renaissance Manuscripts (MS. Arch. Selden. A. 1, f. 031r); **178** Salvador Guilliem, courtesy the Great Temple Project; **179** courtesy Museum für Volkerkunde, Vienna; **180a, 180b** National Museum of the American Indian, Smithsonian Institution, Washington, D.C. (16/3621). Photo NMAI Photo Service; **181** Museo Nacional de Antropología, Mexico City; **182** courtesy Jorge Pérez de Lara; **183** courtesy Yale University Art Gallery and the Olsen Collection, New Haven, CT; **185, 186, 187** British Museum, London; **188** Instituto Nacional de Antropología e Historia, Mexico City; **189** Instituto Nacional de Antropología e Historia, Mexico City. Photo Jorge Pérez de Lara; **190** Instituto Nacional de Antropología e Historia, Mexico City; **191** British Museum, London; **192** Instituto Nacional de Antropología e Historia, Mexico City; **193** Heritage Image Partnership Ltd/Alamy Stock Photo; **194** Drawing courtesy the Great Temple Project; **195** Salvador Guilliem, courtesy the Great Temple Project; **196** Photo Werner Forman/Universal Images Group/Getty Images; **197** Museo del Templo Mayor, Mexico City, Mexico/Bildarchiv Steffens/Henri Stierlin/Bridgeman Images; **198** Salvador Guilliem, courtesy the Great Temple Project; **199** Photo Michael Calderwood; **200** Matos Moctezuma, Eduardo, and Leonardo López Luján, *Escultura Monumental Mexicana*. México, D.F.: Fondo de Cultura Económica, 2012, p. 413; **201** Salvador Guilliem, courtesy the Great Temple Project; **202** Bibliothèque Nationale de France, Paris.

Index